T0351117

# Applications of Optimization and Machine Learning in Image Processing and IoT

This book presents state-of-the-art optimization algorithms followed by Internet of Things (IoT) fundamentals. The applications of machine learning and IoT are explored, with topics including optimization, algorithms and machine learning in image processing and IoT.

*Applications of Optimization and Machine Learning in Image Processing and IoT* is a complete reference source, providing the latest research findings and solutions for optimization and machine learning algorithms. The chapters examine and discuss the fields of machine learning, IoT and image processing.

## KEY FEATURES:

- Includes fundamental concepts towards advanced applications in machine learning and IoT

- Discusses potential and challenges of machine learning for IoT and optimization

- Reviews recent advancements in diverse researches on computer vision, networking and optimization field.

- Presents latest technologies such as machine learning in image processing and IoT

This book has been written for readers in academia, engineering, IT specialists, researchers, industrial professionals and students, and is a great reference for those just starting out in the field as well as those at an advanced level.

# Applications of Optimization and Machine Learning in Image Processing and IoT

Edited by
Dr. Nidhi Gupta

CRC Press
Taylor & Francis Group
Boca Raton London New York

CRC Press is an imprint of the
Taylor & Francis Group, an **informa** business

A CHAPMAN & HALL BOOK

Designed cover image: © Shutterstock

First edition published 2024
by CRC Press
2385 NW Executive Center Drive, Suite 320, Boca Raton FL 33431

and by CRC Press
4 Park Square, Milton Park, Abingdon, Oxon, OX14 4RN

*CRC Press is an imprint of Taylor & Francis Group, LLC*

ISBN: 978-1-032-42909-0 (hbk)
ISBN: 978-1-032-42660-0 (pbk)
ISBN: 978-1-003-36485-6 (ebk)

DOI: 10.1201/9781003364856

Typeset in Minion Pro
by Apex CoVantage, LLC

*Dedicated to the strongest and most beautiful person
I know, my respected late Mother . . .
whom I miss every day . . .
and my sweet little niece, Shubhi*

# Contents

CHAPTER 10 ■ CNN-Based Fire Prediction Using Fractional Order Optical Flow and Smoke Features    156

MUZAMMIL KHAN, PUSHPENDRA KUMAR
AND NITISH KUMAR MAHALA

CHAPTER 11 ■ Early Prediction of Cardiac Diseases Using Ensemble Learning Techniques: A Machine Learning Technique to Deal with Heart Disease Problems    181

RIMA SEN AND A. MANIMARAN

# Preface

THE INTERPLAY BETWEEN MACHINE learning and optimization is one of the most significant developments in the emerging domain of research. Machine learning, however, is not simply a consumer of optimization technology but a rapidly evolving field that is itself generating new optimization ideas. Optimization formulations and techniques perform vital role in the developing algorithms to extract essential information from big data. In addition, rapid developments in the field, like hardware, software and communication technologies, have facilitated the emergence of Internet-connected sensory devices to provide observations and data measurements from the real world. The number of such Internet-connected and -based devices are increasing day by day. With these developments, the need for security, maintenance and research have also increased. The increased volume of data need to be maintained safely and securely in the cloud. Such requirements extend the connectivity and interactions between the physical and cyber worlds. In addition to this increased volume of data, the need for optimization has emerged. Furthermore, the images play an important role in any field, such as automation, security, medicine and other real-life applications. Various artificial-intelligence-based techniques work on images to achieve specific objectives. Among such tools, optimization is another standard method to facilitate researchers. The application of image processing occurs in all areas from automated systems and smart healthcare devices to agricultural tools and security.

This book covers the state-of-the-art techniques from fundamentals of optimization and machine learning to advanced-level applications. The book enables researchers understand the different means of optimization. Many of these techniques draw inspiration from different subfields. Within this book's chapters, various methods of optimization related to IoT and image processing provide a deep analysis. Intelligent processing is the key to developing smart IoT optimized applications. This book provides detailed knowledge of various applications of IoT in different fields, such as making smart cities, verification schemes in networking, waste management, as well as optimized clustering. Also presented are machine learning methods to deal with the challenges presented by IoT data, as in considering smart cities. Machine learning in the field of image processing has taken on vital role in research. Such applications include the identification of herbal drugs, fire prediction, and cardiac prediction in medical imaging. The potential and challenges of machine learning for IoT data and cloud-based optimization is also discussed.

This book, comprising 11 chapters, is organized as follows. Chapter 1 gives state-of-the-art of optimization approaches for damage detection in steel bridges. The next chapter details IoT structure and its advancements in various fields. Chapters 3 to 7 provide applications of IoT in multiple areas like clusters, smart cities, smart healthcare, waste management, and networking for verification schemes. Chapter 8 to Chapter 11 consist of artificial intelligence and computer vision applications in real-time problems, like in agriculture, fire prediction, identification using herbal images, and disease prediction using medical images.

The book enriches the overall concept behind the applications of machine learning and optimization in IoT and image processing.

# Acknowledgments

I T IS MY PROUD privilege to express my deep sense of gratitude to all the contributors in this book, who put together their efforts and have presented their recent research in the trending field of optimization, machine learning, Internet of Things and image processing. I am extremely grateful to all the authors for showing support, patience and faith in me throughout the journey. This publication has been at the core of my heart since I started my research journey in the area of machine learning, optimization, IoT and image processing. With time, I gained knowledge in the field of Internet of Things as well. In order to explore these fields, beginners can look for the fundamental theories underlying the advanced stages of applications. Readers will find this book helpful regarding conceptual clarification. Without the contributions of the supportive authors, this journey could never have been completed.

Further, I personally thank the publishers and their remarkable efforts to furnish this book in a readable and presentable form for its bright and enthusiastic readers and researchers. The consistent efforts of the whole publication team made it possible to publish this book.

The chain of my gratitude would be definitely incomplete if I forgot to thank Almighty God for His blessings, care and love. Because of whom, I have successfully enjoyed the journey and have published this book.

I hope readers will find the content engaging and enjoyable. Happy reading!

# About the Editor

**Dr. Nidhi Gupta** is currently working as Assistant Professor in the department of Computer Applications at the National Institute of Technology Kurukshetra, Haryana. Prior to this, she served as Assistant Professor in the department of Mathematics and Scientific Computing at the National Institute of Technology Hamirpur, Himachal Pradesh. She received the President's International Fellowship Initiative from the Chinese Government to pursue postdoc from the National Laboratory of Pattern Recognition, Institute of Automation, Chinese Academy of Sciences, Beijing, China, in 2018. She is currently working as Co-PI with Isnartech Pvt Ltd. for multiple projects based on artificial intelligence. She received her MTech and PhD degrees from PDPM Indian Institute of Information Technology, Design and Manufacturing, Jabalpur, India, in 2013 and 2018, respectively. She received a BSc degree in Computer Science from the Central University of Allahabad (AU), India, in 2008 and a MSc degree in Computer Science from the JK Institute of Applied Physics and Technology, AU, in 2010. She has qualified with the national-level eligibility tests, UGC NET and GATE, in computer science and applications. She is an outstanding reviewer of various Scopus indexed national and international conferences and journals of repute. She has chaired technical sessions, delivered talks and conducted workshops in India. She has been a member of the technical society of IEEE since 2022. She has published more than 15 papers in several journals of repute and national/international conferences along with two book chapters. She has explored various countries during her academic visits. Her research interests include computer vision, machine learning, artificial intelligence, image Processing, pattern recognition, medical imaging, document imaging and CAD systems.

# Contributors

**Ashish Baldi**
Maharaja Ranjit Singh Punjab
 Technical University
Bathinda, Punjab, India

**Urvashi Bansal**
Dr. B. R. Ambedkar National
 Institute of Technology
 Jalandhar
Jalandhar, Punjab, India

**Chinu**
Dr. B. R. Ambedkar National
 Institute of Technology Jalandhar
Jalandhar, Punjab, India

**Nisha Devi**
Maharaja Agrasen University
Baddi, HP, India

**Jayesh Dwivedi**
Pacific Academy of Higher
 Education and Research
 University
Udaipur, Rajasthan, India

**Satish Kumar Injeti**
Kakatiya Institute of Technology
 and Science

Warangal, Telangana, India
National Institute of Technology
Warangal, Telangana, India

**Abhishek Kesharwani**
ABES Engineering College
Ghaziabad, Uttar Pradesh,
 India

**Muzammil Khan**
Maulana Azad National Institute
 of Technology
Bhopal, India

**Neha Kishore**
Maharaja Agrasen University
Baddi, HP, India

**Sowjanya Kotte**
Kakatiya Institute of Technology
 and Science
Warangal, Telangana, India
National Institute of Technology
Warangal, Telangana, India

**Pushpendra Kumar**
Maulana Azad National Institute
 of Technology
Bhopal, India

**Nitish Kumar Mahala**
Maulana Azad National Institute
    of Technology
Bhopal, India

**Sumit Kumar Mahana**
Maharishi Markandeshwar
    (deemed-to-be-university)
Mullana-Ambala, Haryana, India

**A. Manimaran**
VIT-AP University
Andhra Pradesh, India

**Subh Naman**
Maharaja Ranjit Singh Punjab
    Technical University
Bathinda, Punjab, India
CT University
Ludhiana, Punjab, India

**Roop Pahuja**
Dr. B. R. Ambedkar National
    Institute of Technology
Jalandhar, Punjab, India

**Sakshi Patni**
Research Professor
Gachon University, South Korea

**Anubhav Kumar Prasad**
United Institute of Technology
Naini, Prayagraj, Uttar Pradesh,
    India

**Chitranjan Kumar Rai**
Dr. B. R. Ambedkar National
    Institute of Technology
Jalandhar, Punjab, India

**Rima Sen**
VIT-AP University
Andhra Pradesh, India

**Anshul Sharma**
National Institute of Technology
Hamirpur, Himachal Pradesh, India

**Bharti Sharma**
Maharishi Markandeshwar
    (deemed-to-be-university)
Mullana-Ambala, Haryana, India
Panipat Institute of Engineering &
    Technology
Samalkha, Haryana, India

**Sanyam Sharma**
Maharaja Ranjit Singh Punjab
    Technical University
Bathinda, Punjab, India
Pacific Academy of Higher Education
    and Research University
Udaipur, Rajasthan, India

**Kamalesh Kumar Singh**
Banaras Hindu University
Varanasi, Uttar Pradesh, India

**Dharm Raj Singh**
Jagatpur Post Graduate College
Varanasi, Uttar Pradesh, India

**Smriti Snehil**
Banaras Hindu University
Varanasi, Uttar Pradesh, India

**Ojaswi Vindhyachalam**
Banaras Hindu University
    Varanasi, Uttar Pradesh, India

# State-of-the-Art on Evolved Optimization Approaches for Damage Detection in Steel Bridges

Anshul Sharma

*Department of Civil Engineering, National Institute of Technology, Hamirpur, Himachal Pradesh, India*

## 1.1 INTRODUCTION

Steel bridge health monitoring deals with damage location identification and the extent determination inside the steel members utilizing collected vibration responses containing dynamic modal information of the steel bridge under analysis. The sensors used to collect the data present the challenge of data contamination due to unwanted noise from operational conditions and can be effectively eradicated by determining optimum sensor placing positions. The multi-objective optimization techniques utilize $N$ Pareto optimum solutions to investigate and achieve more realistic results for real-world problems of damage determination in steel bridges. Steel-bridges-related problems such as damage identification, operational research, retrofitting decisions, service life forecasting etc., are solved using multi-objective optimization techniques available since the 1990s. The accurate and robust outcomes of optimization techniques enabled researchers to apply these techniques in various domains [1, 2].

DOI: 10.1201/9781003364856-1

Optimization is applied to achieve the perfect, efficient solution (minimum or maximum) for the desired problem (system design, decision making) under the influence of the given circumstances [3]. The selected parameters are used to classify the optimization techniques with multiple objectives. The computer programs utilizing optimization techniques are employed to obtain optimum solutions for the complex geometry problems of steel truss bridges.

This chapter is chronologically organized. The first section includes an introduction to the health monitoring of steel bridges using optimization techniques. The second section briefly describes the significance of the optimization model. The third section involves detail about different phases involved in optimization models. Lastly, The fourth section includes the conclusions drawn and future scope for the improved application of optimization approaches while solving steel bridge problems.

## 1.2 OPTIMIZATION MODEL

The optimization model includes four phases, which are applied independently to achieve optimum outcomes, as shown in Figure 1.1. Phase 1 comprises the collection of reliable data on which the computational accuracy of optimization model directly depends [4–6]. Phase 2 includes the development of a problem using the identification of decision variables, forming model objective function and model boundary conditions constraints formulation. Some steps are intended to be attentive to the consideration of important elements in problem, a number of known and unknown variables utilized to form mathematical equations used to describe the system, model complexity and the degree of accuracy to be achieved from the model. Phase 3 includes the estimation of selected parameters and the development of mathematical description of the model [7, 8]. Model validation and performance are evaluated using statistical tools such as $R^2$ and root mean square values. The inputs for the chosen model parameters are analyzed using sensitivity analysis. The data used for model formulation is different from that used for model validation. Phase 4 involves the assortment of a suitable optimization algorithm based on the specific nature of the problem. The iterations are performed in Phases 3 and 4 and may lead to a repeat Phase 2 for achieving the required results.

The optimization model must have validity (the degree to which the real system matches the model's inferences) and tractability (the practical

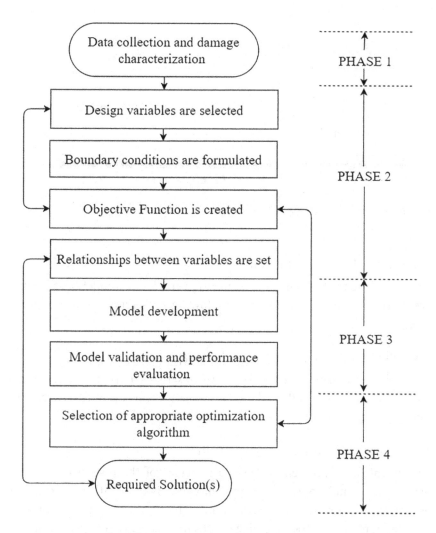

FIGURE 1.1   Flowchart showing procedure followed during optimization process.

nature of the convenience analysis) as shown in Figure 1.2. The model should be adequate; otherwise it leads to faulty calculations.

Optimization deals with certain difficulties that involve the high costs of evaluation of a certain function and the contamination of objective as well as constraint functions with undesired noise. The occurrence of discontinuities in the objective functions poses another obstacle in the application of established standard methods.

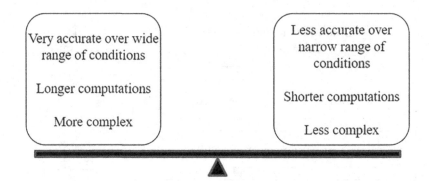

FIGURE 1.2    Validity vs. tractability.

## 1.3  OPTIMIZATION PHASES

The subdivided phases in the optimization model for model-based damage detection are elaborated in the following subsections, and the literature is studied.

### 1.3.1  Phase 1: Data Collection and Damage Characterization

Data collection taken for analysis is done by sensors optimally mounted on a steel bridge [4]. The collected data is wirelessly transmitted and archived into files, either onsite or offsite, using computer systems.

### 1.3.2  Phase 2: Formulation of Problem

An optimization problem is framed in terms of the objective function depicting the main objective of model, which is to be either maximized or minimized through the set of known or unknown variables controlling the outcomes of the objective function within a set of constraints, as shown in Figure 1.3.

### 1.3.3  Phase 3: Development of Objective Features and Functions

The objective features of a steel bridge are the extracted values from raw time domain data using methods such as mean values, maximum values, variances, frequency response functions, spectral densities, frequencies, mode shapes, etc. Based on the residual between measured responses from the steel bridge, numerical analysis is used to form an objective function to optimize the objective features. The inability to determine every instance of damage in different steel bridges in any particular domain is

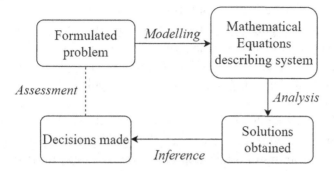

FIGURE 1.3    Working framework of the optimization problem.

the major limitation of prevailing methods; hence more in-depth study in this domain is required to find suitable solutions for this problem.

The time domain methods utilize the features of peak accelerations, temporal moments, root mean square (rms), mean, median, etc. to indicate the presence of damage in any constituent member of a structure. Askan et al. estimated the parameters by using the sensitivity-based approach with the direct input of time-history-based responses in model-based techniques [9]. Masri et al. proposed the use of time response data in the training and testing of neural networks for damage detection [10]. Lu and Liu used a model updating method based on sensitivity approach using time history responses of either bridge or vehicle acceleration [11].

The frequency domain methods incorporate features based on observing the changes in amplitudes due to the shift in resonance or antiresonance of signal responses. The frequency response functions contain meaningful information related to natural frequencies of a structure [12, 13]. The structural responses gathered are the only measurements required for the transmissibility functions and preclude the need for measuring excitation input. Various studies have shown their remarkable damage sensitivity work. Zhou et al. and Kumar et al. studies show various damage indicators extracted from the frequency response functions of a structure such as transmissibility, frequency response function curvature, strain energy etc. [14, 15].

The modal domain features provide direct and physically meaningful information about the structure that is easier to interpret than other domain features. The features showing damage sensitivity include natural eigenfrequencies, a modal assurance criterion based on mode shapes and their derivatives [16], modal strain, modal strain energy [17], residual force vector, damping [18], dynamic flexibility matrix and combinations of these such as modal damping and strain energy computed distribution [19]. Modal curvatures are found to be useful when applied with response-based methods but fail to give meaningful results with a model-based approach.

Time domain analysis gives suitable results with nonlinear responses of a structure and minimizes the data reduction that is the main reason for the loss of meaningful information from the data. Its limitation includes the time and effort required for computing time responses. Frequency domain analysis provides accurate damage information in a particular range of frequencies. Modal domain analysis requires only responses collected from the structure during its operational conditions without any need for excitation input measurement.

### 1.3.4 Phase 4: Model Development, Validation and Performance Evaluation

The model development phase in optimization procedure includes a mathematical description of the problem and objective function, the estimation of various input/output parameters, input variables and software development. This phase is iterative in nature, and unsatisfactory outcomes may result in returning to the optimization model definition and formulation phase. The model validation and performance evaluation are concerned with the checking of the optimization model as a whole. The selected parameters, opted assumptions for the functioning of the model, are validated in this phase. The fitting of measured data with respect to regression the line is checked by $R^2$ value and root mean square error values. The optimized model performance is determined through mean square error values. The testing of parameters taken as inputs is done through sensitivity analysis. The iteration occurs in this phase too, and unsatisfactory results are sent back to the model definition and formulation phase.

A sensitivity study is helpful in minimizing parameter space and in the selection of appropriate objective features from its property of determining the effect of input parameters on the output features of the considered structure. The sensitivity analysis can be performed locally or globally. A sensitivity analysis done locally deals with the introduction of model output to small input perturbations, whereas sensitivity analysis done globally deals with the study of variation of the global range of inputs. Global sensitivity analysis overcome the limitations of local sensitivity analysis such as local variations, normality and linearity assumptions [20, 21]. A review of various global sensitivity analysis covering a wide range one at a time is based on sensitivity measures, differential sensitivity analysis and regression coefficients to the application of statistical tests. The effect of a change in the input variable on the model variance is determined using screening methods. The parameter spaces are used for designing experimental methods; if the parameter nonlinearity is increased, stochastic sampling strategies are preferred [22]. Errors in the optimization model can be evaluated by any standard method such as $R^2$ value or root mean square error methods.

### 1.3.5 Phase 5: Selection of Optimization Algorithms

This is a machine learning technique that executes a study by comparing various solutions available in order to find the best alternative solution under the known constraints. The different optimization problems require different modeling approaches to obtain the desired optimum solutions, as shown in Figure 1.4. An optimization problem can be a single objective (e.g., finding an electrical car with minimum cost) or multi-objective (finding an electrical car with minimum cost and maximum comfort) oriented.

#### 1.3.5.1 Mathematical Programming Optimization Approaches

Steel bridge optimization problems having a complex nature can be easily solved using mathematical programming, which involves going through its mathematical structure in order to determine appropriate optimization technique. The optimization with mathematical tools includes calculus, linear programming, calculus of variations, nonlinear programming, quadratic programming, geometric programming and dynamic integer programming. Masoumi and Akgul selected linear programming as the optimization method with probability and cost matrices as inputs to determine damaged steel bridges on the basis of priority in cost minimization [23]. Albayrak and Albayrak developed a mathematical model to justify the use of considered cross sections of steel members in a steel bridge with optimum minimum cost expenditure [24]. Togan and Daloglu compared the genetic algorithm results with mathematical models such as sequential quadratic programming, sequential convex programming and evolution strategy to determine the minimum weight of a steel truss bridge under a moving load [25]. Assimi et al. studied a spatial steel truss structure using genetic programming to obtain optimal cross section and

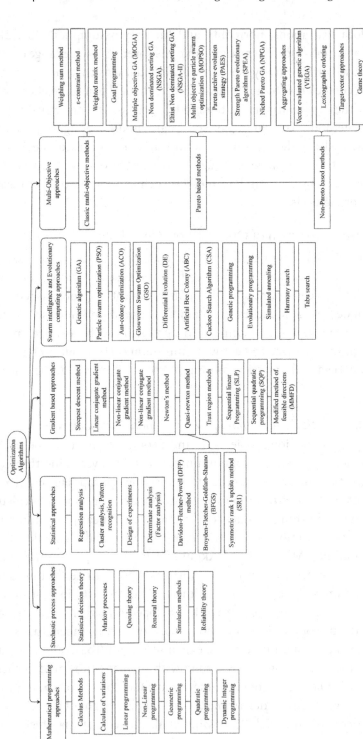

FIGURE 1.4  Flowchart of some major types of optimization algorithms.

joint connectivity within steel members to achieve the minimum weight of steel truss [26].

Mathematical programming methods are flexible and simply structured, and they can easily solve complex, nonlinear real-world problems associated with steel bridges. It improves the final decision making accuracy of the individual. The uncertainty of mathematical models is always a concern as they are computed by empirical formulas and are a representation of multiple processes. The poor calibration of input parameters with output parameters with limited constraints affects the accuracy of mathematical models.

### 1.3.5.2 Scalarization-Based Optimization Approaches

Multi-objective optimization works within constraints and helps in obtaining an optimum solution for one or more objectives conflicting simultaneously. While finding a single solution for real-life problems, variation in an objective may tend to degrade other objective(s); to encounter such problems, multi-objective optimization approaches are utilized to obtain optimum solutions. A large number of multi-objective optimization approaches existing nowadays includes the weighting-based approach, goal-programing-based approach, ε-constraint-based approach, Pareto- and non-Pareto-based approach. The further subdivision of Pareto-based approach gives Pareto-based elitist and non-elitist approach. The elitist approach is formed of Pareto archived evolutionary strategy, strength Pareto evolutionary algorithm, elitist non-dominated sorting genetic algorithm and Pareto-envelope-based selection algorithm. The non-elitist approaches involve a multi-objective niched and non-dominated sorting genetic algorithm.

The population-based non-Pareto approaches based on population consist of lexicographic ordering, vector-evaluated genetic algorithm, contact theorem, game theory, non-generational genetic algorithm. Kim and Weck discussed the use of the adaptive changing weighted sum method rather than selecting prior weights for determining Pareto optimal solutions for bi-objective optimization [27]. Ok et al. studied the application of stochastic of Pareto optimal solutions to successfully assess the damage locations in a two-span steel continuous laboratory bridge. The countering of sensor noise is done by collecting large data sets under appropriate loading cases [28]. Liang et al. evaluated and compared the performance of a non-dominated sorting genetic algorithm II, a multi-objective particle swarm optimizer and a group search optimizer, in determining the optimal weight of a planar steel truss structure [29]. Li et al. determined the optimal position of sensors on a composite plate by analyzing the measured impact responses through principal components, wavelet decomposition, and a non-dominated sorting genetic algorithm [30].

The multi-objective optimization approaches work in both complex as well as non-complex spaces and help in finding points on the Pareto optimal front. The weighted method is suitable for convex issues, but the ε-constrained method can work for both convex or non-convex issues. Goal programming requires selection of a definite set of aspirational goals and finding the minimum distance up to them. Its limitation includes that it requires selection of appropriate constraint values.

### 1.3.5.3 Stochastic Process Optimization Approaches

Stochastic optimization approaches are a valuable asset in analyzing, designing and operating today's modern systems sorting along with the difficulties of percolating system noise, the high non-linear behavior of system or analysis concerned with high dimensions. Stochastic optimization approaches are used to analyze engineering problems defined using random variables having known probabilities [31]. Stochastic approaches include Markov processes, reliability theory, statistical decision theory, renewal theory, queuing theory and simulation methods. Huang et al. used stochastic modeling to observe the fatigue crack growth in steel members and optimized the cost-effective maintenance repairs required during the remaining life span of the bridge [32]. Frangopol et al. proposed the stochastic dynamic-programming-based optimization for planning steel bridge maintenance and also determined the most suitable combination available for a steel bridge network [33].

Stochastic process optimization approaches combine both linear programs and simulation, which helps in minimizing uncertainties and in achieving accurate meaningful results. The best solution is obtained after repetitive refining and development of alternate solutions. These models create error in optimization function as they become corrupted due to unwanted noise.

### 1.3.5.4 Statistical Optimization Approaches

The empirical models are developed to analyze experimental data by statistical approaches to find a more precise and accurate representation of real-world physical situations. Statistical optimization approaches use the response data set to construct mathematical models in order to extract meaningful knowledge about location, severity of damage in a bridge structure. Various methods, such as pattern recognition, factor analysis, regression analysis, design of experiments, and cluster analysis, are included in statistical optimization approaches. Farreras–Alcove et al. developed a statistical technique for analyzing a monitored steel bridge's welded joints for any irregularity under variable temperature and traffic-induced strain conditions [34]. Seo et al. determined the load rating for a steel bridge through multi-regression models. The role of axle weight and axle width in vehicles running over a bridge has significant effect on load rating [35]. Kim et al. utilized the stress spectra-based fatigue prediction model to determine cracks developed in various members of steel bridge [36]. Yang and Nagarajaiah studied damage detection in a steel frame using a sparse regression application on a dictionary of various possible damage probability scenarios and deducted the specific damage scenario that is best suited for the provided test signal. Cluster analysis analyzes the inherent pattern and internal framework of the collected data without making use of data labels in the damage detection of a particular structure [37]. Park et al. experimented with a steel beam to get impedance data, which is processed by a clustering algorithm applied over principal component projections [38]. Cao et al. studied the fuzzy clustering algorithm to know the location and extent of damage in a railway steel truss arch bridge [39]. Yadollahi et al. applied fuzzy factor analysis over selected factors influencing the sustainable maintenance and rehabilitation of a steel bridge [40]. Factor analysis (FA) is a data minimization technique that is needed in capturing variance among variables in the smaller data set. The steps of FA include factor extraction, determination of a number of factors, interpretation and rotation of factors. Widaman presented the differences among the factor analysis and principal component analysis techniques with respect to selected model parameters [41].

Regression handles problems with multiple dimensions with ease and better interpretability. Regression models are affected when the collected data suffers from sparsity, overfitting or loss of meaningful data sets. The clustering approaches are successful in forming groups of parameters satisfying a single objective. The clustering algorithms are limited in application with real-life structures due to multiple influencing objective functions, leading to low convergence rate, centroid selection and local optima determination. The factor analysis helps in explaining correlation among multiple outcomes using selected factors. The selection of factors for study is a tedious task and requires skills to interpret the pattern among them. The primary difference between factor and principal component analyses is that the former is a measurement model of the latent variable, whereas the latter is stated as a linear combination of variables.

### 1.3.5.5 Gradient-Based Optimization Approaches

Gradient-based mathematical optimization approaches determine the best convergence behavior using gradient information. The gradient-based methods can be subdivided as the quasi-Newton method, steepest descent method, trust region methods, conjugate gradient method, Newton's method, and non-linear conjugate gradient method. The Davidon–Fletcher–Powell method, symmetric rank 1 update method, and Broyden–Fletcher–Goldfarb–Shanno method are included in the quasi-Newton method. Similarly, the sequential quadratic/linear programming and modified method of feasible directions are the algorithms that encounter the non-linear constrained optimization problems. Due to the better convergence property and robust results for solving differentiable nonlinear programs, sequential quadratic programming algorithm is a commonly used approach. Lin and Gea discussed the gradient-based transformation method application in the design of complex problems such as steel beam anchor, steel frame or steel bridge [42]. Raju et al. estimated the optimized self-weight of steel members using the reduced gradient method [43]. Hare et al. presented a literature survey on non-gradient optimization techniques applied in structural engineering [44]. Gradient-based optimization approaches require minimal information and are a simple iterative process. Large-scale problems can be evaluated but with less accuracy.

### 1.3.5.6 Swarm and Evolutionary Optimization Approaches

Optimization inspired by both natural processes and living creatures is applied to real-world complex problems by developing mathematical models by various researchers. Darwin evolution, social group behavior, foraging process, etc. are some of the natural processes behind the generation of nature-inspired optimization algorithms. Swarm intelligence and evolutionary computing methods are two distinguished optimization methods having their own separate features used to handle optimization and intractable search problems [45–47]. The hybrid algorithms formed of these two methods reinforce one another's efficiency, accuracy and performance, which provide fruitful results when applied to complex problems. Swarm intelligence is defined by intelligent behavior shown by the collective response of decentralized, self-organized and natural or artificial systems. The organic frameworks associated with nature are the basic causes of the development of swarm intelligence, whereas evolutionary optimization begins with an evaluation of a random population with the iteration of selection in fit individuals to develop offspring individuals, followed by future mutation, survival selection and termination. The swarm intelligence and evolutionary approaches include genetic algorithm, glowworm swarm optimization, differential evolution particle swarm optimization, ant colony optimization, genetic programming, artificial bee colony, evolutionary programming, cuckoo search algorithm, simulated annealing, tabu search, harmony search, etc. Wang et al. applied multiple-layer genetic algorithm for determining damage in a steel truss bridge. The comparison among the outcomes of a multiple-layer genetic algorithm and conventional genetic algorithm was also performed [48]. Shabbir and Omenzetter updated cable-stayed steel footbridge finite element model using particle swarm optimization to obtain physically meaningful results [49].

Cao et al. computed the efficiency of an enhanced particle swarm optimization algorithm in determining the optimum shape and size of members of steel truss structures [50]. Mohan and Baskaran presented a literature survey for the application of ant colony optimization in various problems associated with the engineering domain [51]. Camp and Bichon performed a comparative study among ant colony optimization, genetic algorithm and classical optimization techniques while optimally designing weight, cost parameters keeping in the mid-performance of steel space trusses [52]. Kaipa and Ghose presented a study about the working principal and the evolution and application of glowworm swarm optimization in the engineering domain [53]. Yang and Peng studied the artificial bee colony optimization in achieving a quicker convergence rate and better sensor placement on a railway steel bridge for improved global search ability [54]. Jayanthi et al. proposed a cuckoo search algorithm to provide improved steel truss design results as a comparison to genetic algorithm, the ant colony optimization algorithm [55]. Hasancebi investigated the evolution strategies application in steel trusses to optimally determine geometric design variables allied with steel truss [56]. Hasancebi applied a simulated annealing algorithm in obtaining the optimal design of steel frame structure [57]. Yoo et al. provided an overview of the application of the harmony search algorithm with respect to civil engineering problems [58]. Mishra et al. applied the ant lion optimizer to detect damage with better convergence in obtaining local optima in a steel bridge [59]. Perera et al. optimized a steel truss with inverse problems having modeling errors using both genetic and particle swarm optimization approaches [60].

The swarm and evolutionary optimization approaches are flexible and are applied according to problem requirements. The complexity of the swarm methods leads to time-consuming analysis and unpredictable results, which is a serious limitation. It is based on observing nature and then mimicking nature in computer programs. Thus the systems are easily adaptable to new situations. The gradient information is not needed for applying evolutionarily based optimization techniques to achieve the optimum solution.

## 1.4 CONCLUSIONS

This study examined the literature of the past few decades keeping the focus of different optimization algorithms applied to steel bridge problems. A detailed overview of optimization model—types of optimization model; different phases involved in the optimization model; theoretical and application-related overview about mathematical programming; stochastically, statistically, gradient-, swarm-and-evolution-, multi-objective-based optimization approaches applied in steel bridges—is provided in the study. The underlying conclusions are discussed based on different optimization models applied to different problems in previous studies.

- The optimum placement of sensors using optimization algorithms reduces data contamination due to unwanted noise and also reduces the total number of sensors required for damage determination.

- The steel bridge designing can be optimally done, which is helpful in reducing the overall weight of structure and the minimization of cost expenses.

- The multi-optimization algorithms are capable to deliver multiple optimization solutions for various input variables simultaneously.

- The efficiency and optimum configuration of the truss with a large number of joints is improved by deploying an evolutionary algorithm with only two variables in design, i.e., number of panels and depth of truss.

- Sensitivity analysis is useful in assessing the small variations in input variables; also, modern developed software is used to arrive at the optimum section.

- The quantity of construction materials can be optimized through optimization algorithms to enhance the fatigue life of a steel bridge.

- Some possible reasons for lowered opting of optimization techniques for complex structures includes:

  - The idea of using weight minimization through the optimization process doesn't necessarily reflect minimum cost, especially when composite materials are used in construction such as reinforced concrete construction.

  - The accuracy in optimization of cost is limited to only simpler, small problems such as optimization of small structural members when compared with weight optimization.

  - The optimization process does not include the aesthetic appeal in its consideration, which influences the design process of the structure.

  - The outcomes of multi-optimization algorithms widely depend on the accuracy in the formulation of the optimization model. Hence, a great deal of time and resources must be utilized to develop a reliable optimization model for particular problem.

**Future Scope**

The ideas provided here can be added in the future scope for development in optimization approaches:

- Various soft computing tools can be hybridized like neuro-genetic, fuzzy-genetic, neuro-fuzzy-genetic, etc., which may prove helpful in analyzing steel bridges.

- The optimization of steel bridge materials, which can be used in high-temperature elevation conditions due to fire without losing their stiffness or strength.

- The application of genetic algorithm operators such as duplication, inversion dominance segregation, etc. can be used in steel bridge optimization.

- The non-linear response of various joints, which includes rotational stiffness etc., can be included in future studies.

- Guidelines for simulating different types of connections are to be provided.

- Unit width and spacing in girders are to be included in an optimization study for exterior girders.

- Available resources are to be considered for their impact on cost and the surrounding environment of the structure.

**Declaration of Interest Statement**

The authors state that in the publication of this chapter, there is no conflict of interests.

## REFERENCES

[1] Cho, J.H., Wang, Y., Chen, R., Chan, K.S., Swami, A.: A survey on modeling and optimizing multi-objective systems. *IEEE Communications Surveys & Tutorials* 19(3), 1867–1901 (2017).

[2] Nabavi, S., Gholampour, S., Haji, M.S.: Damage detection in frame elements using Grasshopper Optimization Algorithm (GOA) and time-domain responses of the structure. *Evolving Systems* 13(2), 307–318 (2022).

[3] Sarma, K.C., Adeli, H.: Life-cycle cost optimization of steel structures. *International Journal for Numerical Methods in Engineering* 55(12), 1451–1462 (2002).

[4] Sony, S., Laventure, S., Sadhu, A.: A literature review of next-generation smart sensing technology in structural health monitoring. *Structural Control and Health Monitoring* 26(3), 1–22 (2019).

[5] Sharma, A., Kumar, P., Vinayak, H.K., Walia, S.K.: Identification of joint discrepancy in steel truss bridge using Hilbert transform with root-MUSIC and ESPRIT techniques. *International Journal of Civil Engineering* 19, 653–668 (2021).

[6] Sharma, A., Kumar, P., Vinayak, H.K., Patel, R.K., Walia, S.K.: Steel truss bridge vibration-based condition monitoring using Savitzky-Golay filter, Hilbert transform, MUSIC and ESPRIT. *Journal of Engineering, Design and Technology* 20(5), 1297–1319 (2022).

[7] Arora, J.S.: Formulating design problems as optimization problems. *Encyclopedia of aerospace engineering* (2010). https://onlinelibrary.wiley.com/doi/abs/10.1002/9780470686652.eae494, 19/08/2021.

[8] Zakian, P., Kaveh, A.: Seismic design optimization of engineering structures: A comprehensive review. *Acta Mechanica* 234(4), 1305–1330 (2023).

[9] Askan, A., Akcelik, V., Bielak, J., Ghattas, O.: Parameter sensitivity analysis of a nonlinear least-squares optimization-based anelastic full waveform inversion method. *Comptes Rendus Mécanique* 338(7–8), 364–376 (2010).

[10] Masri, S.F., Nakamura, M., Chassiakos, A.G., Caughey, T.K.: Neural network approach to detection of changes in structural parameters. *Journal of Engineering Mechanics* 122(4), 350–360 (1996).

[11] Lu, Z.R., Liu, J.K.: Identification of both structural damages in bridge deck and vehicular parameters using measured dynamic responses. *Computers & Structures* 89(13–14), 1397–1405 (2011).

[12] Kim, Y.S., Eun, H.C.: Comparison of damage detection methods depending on FRFs within specified frequency ranges. *Advances in Materials Science and Engineering* 2017(8), 1–9 (2017).

[13] Garcia-Palencia, A., Santini-Bell, E., Gul, M., Catbas, N.: A FRF-based algorithm for damage detection using experimentally collected data. *Structural Monitoring and Maintenance* 2(4), 399–418 (2015).

[14] Zhou, Y.L., Qian, X., Cao, H., Magd, A.W.: Damage detection in structures using frequency response functions ensemble with extended cosine based indicator. *Journal of Physics: Conference Series* 843(1), 1–7 (2017).

[15] Kumar, K.A., Reddy, D.M.: Application of frequency response curvature method for damage detection in beam and plate like structures. *IOP Conference Series: Materials Science and Engineering* 149(1), 1–12 (2016).

[16] Simoncelli, M., Aloisio, A., Zucca, M., Venturi, G., Alaggio, R.: Intensity and location of corrosion on the reliability of a steel bridge. *Journal of Constructional Steel Research* 206, 107937 (2023).

[17] Tan, Z.X., Thambiratnam, D.P., Chan, T.H., Razak, H.A.: Detecting damage in steel beams using modal strain energy based damage index and artificial neural network. *Engineering Failure Analysis* 79(9), 253–262 (2017).

[18] Yang, D.S., Wang, C.M.: Modal properties identification of damped bridge using improved vehicle scanning method. *Engineering Structures* 256, 114060 (2022).

[19] Dammika, A.J., Kawarai, K., Yamaguchi, H., Matsumoto, Y., Yoshioka, T.: Analytical damping evaluation complementary to experimental structural health monitoring of bridges. *Journal of Bridge Engineering* 20(7), 1–12 (2014).

[20] Iooss, B., Lemaître, P.: A review on global sensitivity analysis methods. *Uncertainty management in simulation-optimization of complex systems.* Springer, Boston, MA (2015).

[21] Svendsen, B.T., Petersen, Ø.W., Frøseth, G.T., Rønnquist, A.: Improved finite element model updating of a full-scale steel bridge using sensitivity analysis. *Structure and Infrastructure Engineering* 19(3), 315–331 (2022).

[22] Liu, D., Bao, Y., Li, H.: Machine learning-based stochastic subspace identification method for structural modal parameters. *Engineering Structures* 274, 115178 (2023).

[23] Masoumi, F., Akgül, F.: A damage-based maintenance and repair optimization method using linear programming for bridges. *International Journal of Engineering and Technology* 4(5), 668–671 (2012).

[24] Albayrak, G., Albayrak, U.: Approach of non-linear programming for cost optimization of plane truss system. *International Journal of Engineering and Technology* 10(2), 167–170 (2018).

[25] Toğan, V., Daloğlu, A.T.: Bridge truss optimization under moving load using continuous and discrete design variables in optimization methods. *Indian Journal of Engineering and Materials Sciences* 16(8), 245–258 (2009).

[26] Assimi, H., Jamali, A., Zadeh, N.N.: Sizing and topology optimization of spatial truss structures using hybrid algorithm of genetic programing and Nelder-Mead. *Modares Mechanical Engineering* 17(6), 32–40 (2017).

[27] Kim, I.Y., Weck, O.L.: Adaptive weighted-sum method for bi-objective optimization: Pareto front generation. *Structural and Multidisciplinary Optimization* 29(2), 149–158 (2005).

[28] Ok, S.Y., Jung, S., Song, J.: Multiobjective optimization approach for robust bridge damage identification against sensor noise. *Shock and Vibration* 2018(8), 1–13 (2018).

[29] Liang, J.C., Li, L.J., He, J.N.: Performance-based multi-objective optimum design for steel structures with intelligence algorithms. *International Journal of Optimization in Civil Engineering* 5(1), 79–101 (2015).

[30] Li, P., Huang, L., Peng, J.: Sensor distribution optimization for structural impact monitoring based on NSGA-II and wavelet decomposition. *Sensors* 18(12), 1–15 (2018).

[31] Sharma, A., Kumar, P., Vinayak, H.K., Patel, R.K., Walia, S.K.: A review of modeling and data mining techniques applied for analyzing steel bridges. *International Journal of Software Computing and Testing* 7(1), 1–15 (2021).

[32] Huang, T.L., Zhou, H., Chen, H.P., Ren, W.X.: Stochastic modelling and optimum inspection and maintenance strategy for fatigue affected steel bridge members. *Smart Structures and Systems* 18(3), 569–584 (2016).

[33] Frangopol, D.M., Liu, M.: Bridge network maintenance optimization using stochastic dynamic programming. *Journal of Structural Engineering* 133(12), 1772–1782 (2007).

[34] Farreras-Alcover, I., Chryssanthopoulos, M.K., Andersen, J.E.: Regression models for structural health monitoring of welded bridge joints based on temperature, traffic and strain measurements. *Structural Health Monitoring* 14(6), 648–662 (2015).

[35] Seo, J., Czaplewski, T.M., Kimn, J.H., Hatfield, G.: Integrated structural health monitoring system and multi-regression models for determining load ratings for complex steel bridges. *Measurement* 75(11), 308–319 (2015).

[36] Kim, J.H., Jeong, M.C., Lee, T.H., Lee, W.W., Kong, J.S.: Development of fatigue prediction model for steel bridges based on characteristics of variable stress spectra. *International Journal of Damage Mechanics* 26(7), 951–967 (2017).

[37] Yang, Y., Nagarajaiah, S.: Structural damage identification via a combination of blind feature extraction and sparse representation classification. *Mechanical Systems and Signal Processing* 45(1), 1–23 (2014).

[38] Park, S., Lee, J.J., Yun, C.B., Inman, D.J.: Electro-mechanical impedance-based wireless structural health monitoring using PCA-data compression and k-means clustering algorithms. *Journal of Intelligent Material Systems and Structures* 19(4), 509–520 (2008).

[39] Cao, B., Ding, Y., Zhao, H., Song, Y.: Damage identification for high-speed railway truss arch bridge using fuzzy clustering analysis. *Structural Monitoring and Maintenance* 3(4), 315–333 (2016).

[40] Yadollahi, M., Nazari, R., Spanos, N.J., Minner, N.: An application of fuzzy factor analysis for sustainable bridge maintenance and retrofit projects.

*International Journal of Management Science and Engineering Management* 12(4), 225–236 (2017).

[41] Widaman, K.F.: Common factor analysis versus principal component analysis: Differential bias in representing model parameters. *Multivariate Behavioral Research* 28(3), 263–311 (1993).

[42] Lin, P.T., Gea, H.C.: A gradient-based transformation method in multidisciplinary design optimization. *Structural and Multidisciplinary Optimization* 47(5), 715–733 (2013).

[43] Raju, P.M., Rao, G.R., Kumari, G.H., Gowthami, E.: Mathematical model for estimation of self weight of flexural steel members. *International Journal of Optimization in Civil Engineering* 7(2), 241–255 (2017).

[44] Hare, W., Nutini, J., Tesfamariam, S.: A survey of non-gradient optimization methods in structural engineering. *Advances in Engineering Software* 59(5), 19–28 (2013).

[45] Ab Wahab, M.N., Nefti-Meziani, S., Atyabi, A.: A comprehensive review of swarm optimization algorithms. *PLoS One* 10(5), 1–36 (2015).

[46] Zhou, A., Qu, B.Y., Li, H., Zhao, S.Z., Suganthan, P.N., Zhang, Q.: Multi-objective evolutionary algorithms: A survey of the state of the art. *Swarm and Evolutionary Computation* 1(1), 32–49 (2011).

[47] Sarjamei, S., Massoudi, M.S., Sarafraz, M.E.: Damage detection of truss structures via gold rush optimization algorithm. *International Journal of Optimization in Civil Engineering* 12(1), 69–89 (2022).

[48] Wang, F.L., Chan, T.H., Thambiratnam, D.P., Tan, A.C.: Damage diagnosis for complex steel truss bridges using multi-layer genetic algorithm. *Journal of Civil Structural Health Monitoring* 3(2), 117–127 (2013).

[49] Shabbir, F., Omenzetter, P.: *Model updating of a full-scale bridge structure using particle swarm optimization*. 22nd Australasian Conference on the Mechanics of Structures and Materials, 26th Nov, 959–964 (2012).

[50] Cao, H., Qian, X., Chen, Z., Zhu, H.: Enhanced particle swarm optimization for size and shape optimization of truss structures. *Engineering Optimization* 49(11), 1939–1956 (2017).

[51] Mohan, B.C., Baskaran, R.: A survey: Ant colony optimization based recent research and implementation on several engineering domain. *Expert Systems with Applications* 39(4), 4618–4627 (2012).

[52] Camp, C.V., Bichon, B.J.: Design of space trusses using ant colony optimization. *Journal of Structural Engineering* 130(5), 741–751 (2004).

[53] Kaipa, K.N., Ghose, D.: *Glowworm swarm optimization: Theory, algorithms, and applications*. Springer Nature, Gewerbestrasse, Switzerland (2017).

[54] Yang, J., Peng, Z.: Improved ABC algorithm optimizing the bridge sensor placement. *Sensors* 18(7), 1–18 (2018).

[55] Jayanthi, V., Manigandan, M., Velrajkumar, G., Saravanan, M.: Optimization of truss structures using cuckoo search algorithm. *International Journal of Advanced Structures and Geotechnical Engineering* 3(2), 1–4 (2014).

[56] Hasançebi, O.: Optimization of truss bridges within a specified design domain using evolution strategies. *Engineering Optimization* 39(6), 737–756 (2007).

[57] Hasançebi, O., Çarbaş, S., Saka, M.P.: Improving the performance of simulated annealing in structural optimization. *Structural and Multidisciplinary Optimization* 41(2), 189–203 (2010).

[58] Yoo, D.G., Kim, J.H., Geem, Z.W.: Overview of harmony search algorithm and its applications in civil engineering. *Evolutionary Intelligence* 7(1), 3–16 (2014).

[59] Mishra, M., Barman, S.K., Maity, D., Maiti, D.K.: Ant lion optimisation algorithm for structural damage detection using vibration data. *Journal of Civil Structural Health Monitoring* 9(1), 117–136 (2019).

[60] Perera, R., Fang, S.E., Ruiz, A.: Application of particle swarm optimization and genetic algorithms to multiobjective damage identification inverse problems with modelling errors. *Meccanica* 45(5), 723–734 (2010).

# CHAPTER 2

# IoT and Its Advancement

Anubhav Kumar Prasad,[1] Dharm Raj Singh[2] and Abhishek Kesharwani[3]

1 United Institute of Technology, Naini, Prayagraj, U.P., India

2 Jagatpur Post Graduate College, Varanasi, U.P., India

3 ABES Engineering College, Ghaziabad, U.P., India

## 2.1 INTRODUCTION

The growing need for devices to assist human comfort and to help humans in different ways ranging from household activities like handling a bulb to monitoring health and security led to a new field of technology known as IoT (Internet of Things) [1, 2]. The concept of IoT is pretty simple—to make communication possible among machines themselves and with humans. This communication occurs through the Internet and hence is known as the Internet of Things. Here, things are meant for physical objects and can be further categorized into two categories: smart objects [3–5] and non-smart objects [6–8], in other words, objects with intelligence and those without intelligence. We will now move to components or contributors of the IoT ecosystem.

### 2.1.1 Components of IoT

The components of IoT are devices/things, storage or cloud, data analytics part, and the user interface. Figure 2.1 shows the IoT components.

DOI: 10.1201/9781003364856-2

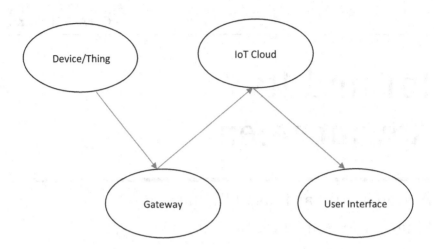

FIGURE 2.1 Components of IoT.

### 2.1.1.1 Device/Thing

This can be termed as a tracking device having sensors that can be used for tracking body temperature to proximity detection. Depending on the need, the sensor can be of different types, like pressure sensor, humidity sensor, light detection sensor, RFID tags, etc. These devices or objects can be broadly divided into two categories: smart and non-smart objects.

2.1.1.1.1 Smart Objects    The basic idea of smart objects is to provide processing and calculating powers apart from storing and networking capabilities. This is in the context of minimizing human interaction in any framework, and this can be done using smart objects. That is why they are termed the "building blocks" of IoT. For instance, a smartwatch capable of measuring heart rate can check heart rate readings from time to time and process the data on its own to make the wearer alert to any issue regarding heart rate. Here, human intervention is not required as the smartwatch is collecting and calculating the data on its own, producing the required output.

The following are the features of the smart objects:

1. **Physical Shape:** The object must have a physical shape to fit it into the appropriate place. For example, a smartwatch must have a physical shape compact enough to fit on a person's wrist.

2. **Unique Identifier:** The unique physical identity can be used by humans to distinguish it from other devices. For example, a TV remote and a keypad mobile can be differentiated based on their unique identification.

3. **Communication:** The smart object must be able to send and receive data over the Internet as the communicating medium.

4. **Unique Name and Address:** The identity of the smart object over the network infrastructure must be unique so that it is easily identifiable with other devices over the same medium. This is about the non-physical identifier of the same object.

5. **Processing Power:** Being a smart object, it must be able to do the processing as per the environment.

6. **Sensing Capabilities:** The reason for having sensing capabilities is to gather data from the environment in order to process it. For instance, the object responsible for handling room temperature must be able to sense the temperature of its surroundings.

2.1.1.1.2 Non-Smart Objects    There is a need for devices/objects that are meant to collect and transmit the data only. Sensors and actuators are examples of such objects.

1. **Sensors:** It can be simply considered as a subpart of the smart object that is meant to gather the data or, in other words, sense the environment. Its role is to send the data to the specified object of the IoT system for processing.

2. **Actuators:** The role of the actuator is to perform a physical action as instructed by the controller. The data required by the control system or controller is provided by the sensor. For instance, the sensor in a refrigerator sends the temperature data to the control system, and the control system, based on its algorithm, instructs the actuator to either increase or decrease the temperature. Thus, in simple terms, an actuator is a mover which does some physical activity based on the electronic signal that it receives from the control system.

### 2.1.1.2 IoT Cloud

The term "cloud" specifically relates to data storage on the server. The use of the cloud can be extended to data processing or other types of services.

Cloud computing [9] is discussed in detail in a later section. The IoT cloud is responsible for data collection from the object, as well as its processing, management, and archiving. In other words, the data gathered by the object is stored and converted to information in the IoT cloud using various algorithms of AI/ML like a support vector machine, k-Nearest Neighbor, etc.

### 2.1.1.3 User Interface

A user interface is software designed to monitor and manipulate processed data. The user interface must be designed to provide maximum interaction with the least complexity.

2.1.1.3.1 Architecture of IoT    The architecture of the IoT depends upon the implementational role and the sector where it is needed [10]. Based on these, the following four architectures are available:

1. **Sensing Layer:** This layer contains the objects related to the collection of data. The sensors and actuators are part of this layer. This layer may or may not process the data depending on the smart or non-smart object configuration type. It is just like the end-point devices needed for interfacing between the physical and the digital worlds.

2. **Network Layer:** This bridges the connection between the sensing layer with other servers, communicating devices and network devices. This layer is responsible for the movement of the data collected by the sensors and the actuators of the sensing layer. There are two main components of this system: DAS (data acquiring system) and the network/Internet gateway. The main responsibility of the DAS is to convert the analog signal to the digital signal, i.e., to the data aggregation and conversion part.

3. **Processing Layer:** The digital signal received from the network layer is eventually sent to the data center, where the software application will access the data. So it is the responsibility of this layer (processing layer) to do the pre-processing. Here Edge IT or edge analytics [11] comes into the picture.

4. **Application Layer:** The user interaction is done in this layer. It is simply an application that a user can operate to monitor the data and

to control the working of the IoT device. For instance, a user might change the color of a smart bulb just by selecting the desired color provided in the application interface.

### 2.1.1.4 Advancement of IoT

The advancement of the history of IoT can be described in terms of smart and non-smart objects. The control loop is a message that triggers certain actions based on the data it receives. This trigger of action may or may not be a decision-based action. For instance, reading a bar code and validating the data is a non-smart object task.

On the other hand, switching on a bulb when someone enters the room may be a smart object task as it should switch on the bulb when it is dark. Decisions made in the control loop must meet application latency requirements, which are often referred to as the length of the control loop. If the data is sent to the server each time for the calculation, this may slow down the work for which the data was intended. For instance, a half-minute delay in opening a gate for a yard may reduce the number of vehicles that can enter the yard. This indicates that, as needs grow, IoT devices start becoming smart with the use of AI. The very first example of IoT comes from the 1980s when a group of university students modified a Coca-Cola vending machine for tracking its contents. However, the technology was bulky and was not up to the mark and had limited efficiency. This technology was not AI-enabled as it was intended for a non-decision task. The use of RFID (radio frequency identification) chips on Procter & Gamble products for tracking through the supply chain, introduced in 1999 by Kevin Ashton, is considered the first IoT device.

Taking a keen interest in this, LG announced its first-ever smart refrigerator in the year 2000. In 2007, the first iPhone was launched, and by 2008, there were more connected devices than there were people on Earth.

In 2009, Google started testing its first driver-less car, and by 2011, Google's Nest Smart was launched. The use of IoT devices has extended to healthcare also where an AIoT (AI-enabled IoT) device can read human health-related data like heartbeat and can process the data to know whether the person is having heart issues and, based on this, can generate a warning message. The current study is working on the reading of IoT device data specific to human health monitoring in order to judge whether the person is having health issues. These IoT devices are fitted in rooms, not being worn by the person. With the introduction of 5G technology, IoT devices are now more advanced in terms of data handling and communicating with the server.

2.1.1.4.1 Edge Device    An edge device [12] that is part of the network layer is responsible for device-to-server connectivity. This is required to be able to have better connectivity as local devices use protocols like Bluetooth [13], Wi-Fi [14], Zigbee [15], and NFC [16], whereas the cloud uses the protocols like AMQP, MQTT, CoAP, and HTTP. Edge devices can be visualized as a smart gateway that is able to translate, sort, and move the data securely between the two sources. This is required in order to adapt to different protocols efficiently and effectively.

*2.1.1.4.1.1 Bluetooth*    In order to provide wireless connectivity for a shorter range (approximately 10 m) of devices, Bluetooth technology was introduced by Ericsson in 1994. It is a low-powered technology that is capable of transmitting and receiving signals in a noisy environment with low bandwidth (1–3 Mbps) connectivity. It is an industrial, unlicensed, scientific and medical (ISM) band ranging from 2.4 to 2.485 GHz. It follows the parent–child model with a maximum of seven children for a parent. The parent in one piconet [17] can also be a child in another piconet and can switch roles too. In the iIoT [18] environment, short bursts of data keep on interacting, and the setup required for this to handle hundreds of sensors is the strength of Bluetooth as opposed to WiFi.

With the increasing need for better connectivity and faster data transmission, Bluetooth 5 [19] has been introduced with four times the range, a broadcast messaging capacity boosted by 800% as compared to Bluetooth 4 [20], as well as twice the speed.

*2.1.1.4.1.2 WiFi*    WiFi has a better reach as compared to Bluetooth in terms of range and bandwidth. It has a range of approximately 50 m, with a transmission frequency between 2.4 and 5 GHz. However, it consumes more power as compared to Bluetooth. The longest-ever transmission range for data using WiFi is approximately 418,429 m. Just like LAN, there are different versions of WiFi: 802.11a, 802.11b, 802.11g, 802.11n, and 802.11ac. For each of these standards, the cost is a major factor as different hardware configurations are required for it. Considering the needs of IoT, two standards are developed: WiFi Hallow (802.11ah) and HEW (802.11ax).

*2.1.1.4.1.3 Zigbee*    Bluetooth has two divisions: traditional and low energy (LE). The two divisions are mainly based on the power consumption issue. Traditional operates on 1 W of energy, whereas LE can operate with 10–100 mW of energy. However, to increase the transmission range, another protocol was needed, and this brought on Zigbee. It is a wireless technology developed as an open global market connectivity standard with low power consumption. The Zigbee connectivity standard operates on the IEEE 802.15.4 physical board radio specification and works within unlicensed radio bands, including 2.4 GHz, 868 MHz, and 900 MHz. Due to the mesh topology used, it has higher latency and is therefore not suitable for iIoT.

2.1.1.4.2 Cloud Computing    The term "cloud" in cloud computing [9] is used to indicate data access and storage on remote servers. The architecture of the cloud can be divided into three categories [21]: cloud as an infrastructure, cloud as a platform and cloud as a service. They are popularly known as IAAS, PAAS and SAAS. The idea is to serve different requirements based on the user's needs. IAAS provides the raw cloud; i.e., the infrastructure is provided to the user such as server, processing, storage etc. In the case of PAAS, the user gets the complete platform to build and run the applications. It provides all requirements such as servers, operating systems, storage etc. The SAAS is a software distribution model in which the services are available to the end user over the Internet. Users can directly use such services as an online editor and co-compiler and need no installation in their system. The storage space [22] for users in the cloud is handled using two different approaches: NAS and SAN. The former, network access service, has a RAID configuration with a single storage device, while the latter, known as a storage area network, has multiple storage devices. The major difference between the two is that NAS has a single point of failure, which is not the case with SAN. Moreover, the data can be stored in either raw format or in files using the file system. The architecture of a cloud includes several key modules [23]: a resource provisioning module, a user interaction interface, and a system resource management module [24–25] with a services catalog.

## 2.1.2 Network Security Attributes of Cloud Computing

### 2.1.2.1 Authentication [26]

In order to authorize an entity, it is required to authenticate the identity of that entity. This can be done either through a password system, PIN (personal identification number) or biometrics. In addition, message authentication is also used for authentication. Here, entity can be machine to machine, person to person or mixed. Transport layer sockets (TLS) are one way for such authentication [27].

### 2.1.2.2 Authorization [28]

After successful authentication, the next step is to authorize the entity with the rightful service/resource. For instance, users can withdraw only the allowable limit once from an ATM for which they have been authorized [29].

### 2.1.2.3 Auditing [30]

Although an entity has been granted the requested service/resource after authentication, it is wise to audit the entity, so as to make sure there is no fraudulent activity.

### 2.1.2.4 Confidentiality (Privacy) [31]

This is related to avoiding/ensuring that there is no data breach. An unauthorized entity should not be able to disclose personal information including ID and password.

### 2.1.2.5 Availability

This is related to resource management and is the same as resource management in the operating system. The requested resource must be allocated to the authorized entity if available. At the same time, if an entity has left, the used resource must be deallocated. This is like a garbage collector in the Java programming language. Load-balancing hardware and software are dedicated to this task [32].

### 2.1.2.6 Non-Repudiation [33]

Non-repudiation is related to the validity and legitimacy of the message. Here, authentication is used for message validation. For security purposes, it is mandatory for the entity to commit itself by endorsing its signature [34–35]. For this purpose, User Identity Management Protocol (U-IDMP) [36].

### 2.1.3 Security Protocols

### 2.1.3.1 Predicate Encryption

Predicate encryption is another paradigm of encryption where the sender-receiver generates a key based on predicate calculus [37]. To evaluate the encrypted data, the secret token related to the predicate is evaluated using $f(a) = 1$, where $f$ is the predicate function. If the equation/condition is satisfied, the encrypted data is decrypted and confirms that the data is coming from the rightful sender. Although this is an effective mechanism, it is at the same time a complex one. This is why it is not widely accepted in the industry. But this does provide a new direction to solve traditional problems like network audit logs [38], sharing of medical records [39], untrusted remote storage [40] etc.

### 2.1.3.2 Dynamic Auditing Protocol for Data Storage in Cloud Computing

The ideal scenario in cloud computing is that the user and cloud owner can do the auditing to check for smooth and legal functioning. But this is not effective because the auditing needs to be guaranteed as unbiased. For this reason, this third party must be an expert auditor who can perform non-biased auditing. The auditing protocol should have the following properties—dynamic auditing and batch auditing—and, most importantly, confidentiality must be maintained at all levels of auditing.

### 2.1.3.3 Fully Homomorphic Encryption

There are two types of homomorphic encryption [41]: partial homomorphic encryption (PHE) and full homomorphic encryption (FHE). PHE is able to provide a single operation over the encrypted data, whereas FHE is able to perform multiple operations over the encrypted data, including the addition and multiplication of the data. The additive homomorphic encryption is done using Pailler [42] and Goldwasser–Micalli cryptosystems, whereas the multiplicative homomorphic encryption is achieved using the RSA and El Gamal cryptosystems. The interesting fact is that both operations are performed only on the encrypted data, and these operations are unaware of the secret key used for the purpose of the decryption.

### 2.1.4 Private Information Retrieval (PIR)

In this case [43–45], the user has the freedom to retrieve the data from the database without actually knowing the database from which the data is being retrieved. This is the weaker version of the 1-out-of-$n$ obvious transfer. The trivial solution is to send the entire database copy to the user, and in fact, this is a solution in terms of quantum settings. As far as a nontrivial solution is considered, we have two ways to achieve this: make the server computationally bounded or assume multiple non-cooperating servers, each having a copy of the database.

## 2.2 PROTOCOLS OF CLOUD COMPUTING

### 2.2.1 HTTP

The Hyper Text Transfer Protocol (HTTP) is based on message passing in the form of request–response. It is a half-duplex TCP connection, making this a connection-less protocol. The HTTP follows the REST [46, 47] guideline, which is responsible for the web services guidelines. Cloud IoT Core supports HTTP 1.1. The request to the server can be made for the creating, updating, reading and deleting operations on the data. This can be achieved by methods like HTTP PUT, GET, POST and DELETE. The CRUD (create-read-update-delete) operations let users directly interact and modify the target resources [48]. HTTP also provides a mechanism for clients and servers known as content negotiation [49]. The data must be encoded using base64 and requires more network and CPU resources for this task.

### 2.2.2 MQTT

The MQTT (Message Queue Telemetry Transport) [50–52] protocol is intended for use in sensor networks. Since it is mainly designed for sensors, it is best suited for the IoT and cloud. It was developed by IBM and is a lightweight and machine-to-machine communication method. The basic idea behind this protocol is that sensors are not intended for processing but rather for data transfer to the intended central location. It uses full-duplex communication and is a connection-oriented protocol.

## 2.3 CONCLUSION

The Internet of Things (IoT) has drastically improved and changed many parts of our life, presenting both previously unheard-of benefits and difficulties. Healthcare, agriculture, manufacturing, transportation, and smart cities are just a few of the sectors that have been transformed by IoT, which has increased efficiency, production, and convenience. For corporations, governments, and individuals alike, the capacity to connect to and communicate with objects and devices, to gather and analyze data in real time and to automate operations has opened up new opportunities. Smart homes, wearable technology, connected autos and intelligent supply chains are just a few of the applications that have been made possible by IoT breakthroughs. By delivering personalized experiences, maximizing resource use and enabling predictive maintenance, these advances have raised our quality of life. By facilitating smart energy management, waste reduction, and precision agriculture, among other things, IoT has also contributed to environmental sustainability.

## REFERENCES

[1] Ashton, K. (2009). That 'Internet of Things' Thing. *RFID Journal, 22*(7), 97–114.

[2] Ding, S., Ward, H., & Tukker, A. (2023). How Internet of Things Can Influence the Sustainability Performance of Logistics Industries–A Chinese Case Study. *Cleaner Logistics and Supply Chain, 6,* 100094.

[3] Koohang, A., Sargent, C. S., Nord, J. H., & Paliszkiewicz, J. (2022). Internet of Things (IoT): From Awareness to Continued Use. *International Journal of Information Management, 62,* 102442.

[4] Sinha, B. B., & Dhanalakshmi, R. (2022). Recent Advancements and Challenges of Internet of Things in Smart Agriculture: A Survey. *Future Generation Computer Systems, 126,* 169–184.

[5] Friess, P., & Ibanez, F. (2022). Putting the Internet of Things Forward to the Next Nevel. In *Internet of Things Applications-From Research and Innovation to Market Deployment* (pp. 3–6). River Publishers.

[6] Wójcicki, K., Biegańska, M., Paliwoda, B., & Górna, J. (2022). Internet of Things in Industry: Research Profiling, Application, Challenges and Opportunities—A Review. *Energies, 15*(5), 1806.

[7] Salih, K. O. M., Rashid, T. A., Radovanovic, D., & Bacanin, N. (2022). A Comprehensive Survey on the Internet of Things with the Industrial Marketplace. *Sensors, 22*(3), 730.

[8] Mishra, S., & Tyagi, A. K. (2022). The Role of Machine Learning Techniques in Internet of Things-Based Cloud Applications. *Artificial Intelligence-Based Internet of Things Systems,* 105–135.

[9] Bharany, S., Sharma, S., Khalaf, O. I., Abdulsahib, G. M., Al Humaimeedy, A. S., Aldhyani, T. H., & Alkahtani, H. (2022). A Systematic Survey on Energy-Efficient Techniques in Sustainable Cloud Computing. *Sustainability, 14*(10), 6256.

[10] Gazis, V., Görtz, M., Huber, M., Leonardi, A., Mathioudakis, K., Wiesmaier, A., Zeiger, F., & Vasilomanolakis, E. (2015, August). A Survey of Technologies for the Internet of Things. In *2015 International Wireless Communications and Mobile Computing Conference (IWCMC)* (pp. 1090–1095). IEEE.

[11] Chaudhary, H. A. A., Guevara, I., John, J., Singh, A., Margaria, T., & Pesch, D. (2022). Low-Code Internet of Things Application Development for Edge Analytics. *In IFIP International Internet of Things Conference* (pp. 293–312). Springer.

[12] Wang, Z., Zhou, Z., Zhang, H., Zhang, G., Ding, H., & Farouk, A. (2022). AI-Based Cloud-Edge-Device Collaboration in 6G Space-Air-Ground Integrated Power IoT. *IEEE Wireless Communications, 29*(1), 16–23.

[13] Barua, A., Al Alamin, M. A., Hossain, M. S., & Hossain, E. (2022). Security and Privacy Threats for Bluetooth Low Energy in IoT and Wearable Devices: A Comprehensive Survey. *IEEE Open Journal of the Communications Society, 3,* 251–281.

[14] Khanh, Q. V., Hoai, N. V., Manh, L. D., Le, A. N., & Jeon, G. (2022). Wireless Communication Technologies for IoT in 5G: Vision, Applications, and Challenges. *Wireless Communications and Mobile Computing, 2022*, 1–12.

[15] Lazaro, A., Villarino, R., & Girbau, D. (2018). A Survey of NFC Sensors Based on Energy Harvesting for IoT Applications. *Sensors, 18*(11), 3746.

[16] Shree, S. S., & Poovathy, J. F. G. (2022, August). Communication Technologies in IoT and Related Concepts: A Review. In *2022 Third International Conference on Intelligent Computing Instrumentation and Control Technologies (ICICICT)* (pp. 310–314). IEEE.

[17] Kalanandhini, G., Aravind, A. R., Vijayalakshmi, G., Gayathri, J., & Senthilkumar, K. K. (2022, May). Bluetooth Technology on IoT Using the Architecture of Piconet and Scatternet. In *AIP Conference Proceedings* (Vol. 2393, No. 1, p. 020121). AIP Publishing LLC.

[18] Arnold, L., Jöhnk, J., Vogt, F., & Urbach, N. (2022). iIoT Platforms' Architectural Features–A Taxonomy and Five Prevalent Archetypes. *Electronic Markets, 32*(2), 927–944.

[19] Mohamed, K. S. (2022). *Bluetooth 5.0 Modem Design for IoT Devices* (pp. 45–73). Springer.

[20] Padiya, S. D., & Gulhane, V. S. (2022). Analysis of Bluetooth Versions (4.0, 4.2, 5, 5.1, and 5.2) for IoT Applications. In *Implementing Data Analytics and Architectures for Next Generation Wireless Communications* (pp. 153–178). IGI Global.

[21] Ullah, A., Nawi, N. M., & Ouhame, S. (2022). Recent Advancement in VM Task Allocation System for Cloud Computing: Review from 2015 to2021. *Artificial Intelligence Review*, 1–45.

[22] Huawei Technologies Co., Ltd. (2022). Storage Basics in Cloud Computing. In *Cloud Computing Technology* (pp. 197–250). Springer Nature.

[23] Priyadarshini, I., Bhola, B., Kumar, R., & So-In, C. (2022). A Novel Cloud Architecture for Internet of Space Things (IoST). *IEEE Access, 10*, 15118–15134.

[24] Chyad, H. S., Mustafa, R. A., & George, D. N. (2022). Cloud Resources Modelling Using Smart Cloud Management. *Bulletin of Electrical Engineering and Informatics, 11*(2), 1134–1142.

[25] Malik, S., Tahir, M., Sardaraz, M., & Alourani, A. (2022). A Resource Utilization Prediction Model for Cloud Data Centers Using Evolutionary Algorithms and Machine Learning Techniques. *Applied Sciences, 12*(4), 2160.

[26] Dolan, E., & Widayanti, R. (2022). Implementation of Authentication Systems on Hotspot Network Users to Improve Computer Network Security. *International Journal of Cyber and IT Service Management, 2*(1), 88–94.

[27] Pohlmann, N. (2022). Transport layer security (TLS)/Secure Socket Layer (SSL). In *Cyber-Sicherheit: Das Lehrbuch für Konzepte, Prinzipien, Mechanismen, Architekturen und Eigenschaften von Cyber-Sicherheitssystemen in der Digitalisierung* (pp. 439–473). Springer Fachmedien Wiesbaden.

[28] Mihailescu, M. I., & Nita, S. L. (2022). A Searchable Encryption Scheme with Biometric Authentication and Authorization for Cloud Environments. *Cryptography, 6*(1), 8.

[29] Halpert, B. (2011). *Auditing Cloud Computing: A Security and Privacy Guide* (Vol. 21). John Wiley & Sons.

[30] Yang, C., Xiao, J., Liu, Y., & Liu, Y. (2022). Provable Cloud Data Transfer with Efficient Integrity Auditing for Cloud Computing. *Wireless Communications and Mobile Computing, 2022.*

[31] Abdulsalam, Y. S., & Hedabou, M. (2022). Security and Privacy in Cloud Computing: Technical Review. *Future Internet, 14*(1), 11.

[32] Tabassum, N., & Mujeed, S. (2022). The Availability and Load Balancing in Cloud Computing. *International Journal for Electronic Crime Investigation, 6*(1), 22–22.

[33] Chen, F., Wang, J., Li, J., Xu, Y., Zhang, C., & Xiang, T. (2022). TrustBuilder: A Non-Repudiation Scheme for IoT Cloud Applications. *Computers & Security, 116*, 102664.

[34] Divya, K. S., Roopashree, H. R., & Yogeesh, A. C. (2022). Non-Repudiation-Based Network Security System using Multiparty Computation. *International Journal of Advanced Computer Science and Applications, 13*(3).

[35] Liu, S. G., Liu, R., & Rao, S. Y. (2022). Secure and Efficient Two-Party Collaborative SM9 Signature Scheme Suitable for Smart Home. *Journal of King Saud University-Computer and Information Sciences, 34*(7), 4022–4030.

[36] Mahalle, P. N., & Railkar, P. N. (2022). *Identity Management for Internet of Things*. CRC Press.

[37] Shahzad, K., Zia, T., & Qazi, E. U. H. (2022). A Review of Functional Encryption in IoT Applications. *Sensors, 22*(19), 7567.

[38] Chen, C. M., Chaudhry, S. A., Yeh, K. H., & Aman, M. N. (2022). Security, Trust and Privacy for Cloud, Fog and Internet of Things. *Security and Communication Networks, 2022*, 1–2.

[39] Karumanchi, M. D., Sheeba, J. I., & Devaneyan, S. P. (2022). Integrated Internet of Things with Cloud Developed for Data Integrity Problems on Supply Chain Management. *Measurement: Sensors, 24*, 100445.

[40] Chen, Q., Jiang, M., Guo, Y., Zhang, D., Jia, W., & Zheng, W. (2022). Efficient Multibit Function Encryption for Data Security in Internet of Things. *Security and Communication Networks, 2022.*

[41] Halder, S., & Newe, T. (2022). Enabling Secure Time-Series Data Sharing Via Homomorphic Encryption in Cloud-Assisted iIoT. *Future Generation Computer Systems, 133*, 351–363.

[42] Chor, B., Kushilevitz, E., Goldreich, O., & Sudan, M. (1998). Private Information Retrieval. *Journal of the ACM (JACM), 45*(6), 965–981.

[43] Yu, X., Bai, H., Yan, Z., & Zhang, R. (2022). VeriDedup: A Verifiable Cloud Data Deduplication Scheme with Integrity and Duplication Proof. *IEEE Transactions on Dependable and Secure Computing, 20*(1), 680–694.

[44] Ke, P., & Zhang, L. F. (2022, June). Two-Server Private Information Retrieval with Result Verification. In *2022 IEEE International Symposium on Information Theory (ISIT)* (pp. 408–413). IEEE.

[45] Lu, Y., & Jafar, S. A. (2023). On Single Server Private Information Retrieval with Private Coded Side Information. *IEEE Transactions on Information Theory.*

[46] Karmakar, A., Raghuthaman, A., Kote, O. S., & Jayapandian, N. (2022, April). Cloud Computing Application: Research Challenges and Opportunity. In *2022 International Conference on Sustainable Computing and Data Communication Systems (ICSCDS)* (pp. 1284–1289). IEEE.

[47] Bhimani, P., & Panchal, G. (2018). Message Delivery Guarantee and Status Update of Clients Based on IOT-AMQP. In *Intelligent Communication and Computational Technologies* (pp. 15–22). Springer.

[48] Sommer, P., Schellroth, F., Fischer, M., & Schlechtendahl, J. (2018, August). Message-Oriented Middleware for Industrial Production Systems. In *2018 IEEE 14th International Conference on Automation Science and Engineering (CASE)* (pp. 1217–1223). IEEE.

[49] Katsikeas, S., Fysarakis, K., Miaoudakis, A., Van Bemten, A., Askoxylakis, I., Papaefstathiou, I., & Plemenos, A. (2017, July). Lightweight & Secure Industrial IoT Communications Via the MQ Telemetry Transport Protocol. In *2017 IEEE Symposium on Computers and Communications (ISCC)* (pp. 1193–1200). IEEE.

[50] Ngethe, M. I., Kiplimo, Y. C., & Aoki, S. (2022, November). Implementation of Message Queuing Telemetry Transport Protocol in Model Rocket. In *Proceedings of the Sustainable Research and Innovation Conference* (pp. 29–32).

[51] Pearson, B., Zhang, Y., Zou, C., & Fu, X. (2022, May). FUME: Fuzzing Message Queuing Telemetry Transport Brokers. In *IEEE INFOCOM 2022- IEEE Conference on Computer Communications* (pp. 1699–1708). IEEE.

[52] Hegedus, C., Varga, P., & Frankó, A. (2018, May). Secure and Trusted Inter-Cloud Communications in the Arrowhead Framework. In *2018 IEEE Industrial Cyber-Physical Systems (ICPS)* (pp. 755–760). IEEE.

# CHAPTER 3

# Optimal Configuration of IOT Cluster with Full Connectivity with Minimum Transmission Power Using SA and BO Algorithms

Sowjanya Kotte and Satish Kumar Injeti

*Kakatiya Institute of Technology and Science and*
*National Institute of Technology, Warangal,*
*Telangana, India*

## 3.1 INTRODUCTION

The Internet of Things (IoT) has developed into an essential component of our contemporary way of life [1]. Things, things, and more things, including devices that serve us daily, are required to do so efficiently to communicate so as to bring comfort with relatively little human interaction and intervention. When it comes to communication between the nodes, efficiency in the use of energy is of the utmost significance. Therefore, it is necessary to come up with various strategies to ensure efficiency so that no energy is wasted between signal transmission and reception and so that time is not wasted among the various nodes. Nevertheless, a decreased amount of transmission energy causes problems with connectivity. As a result, in recent years, researchers have been looking for possible solutions, working on developing the most effective solutions in which nodes are known to send messages with minimal power and bringing them together to form a network that is completely connected [2, 3]. Energy-efficient antennas have been used in wireless local area networks (WLANs) to reduce power consumption, as documented in [4]. Another option is the wireless transfer of harvested power to the nodes for their power requirements [5]. IoT networks are becoming more and more diverse, creating new issues that necessitate the renewed study of prior solutions, as well as the development of entirely new ones, and also presenting a survey that focuses on WSN battery life extension through control approaches and cluster selection [6]. The lack of efficiency in centralized connection methods is due to the additional communication overhead and delay required to gather and synchronize the transfer of information among coordinated nodes. However, it's critical to have a mathematical model for calculating how much power each node needs. A centralized control system for a wireless sensor network (WSN) is a viable alternative since it provides full-area coverage with little energy requirements, and, because of its powerful processing abilities, the central unit can decide after gathering all the necessary information. WSNs can also benefit from a centralized hub, which provides numerous networking advantages, including optimal node placement and deployment, energy-conscious clustering, and data aggregation. Particle swarm optimization (PSO) is one of the techniques employed, and some of these ideas have been compiled. It has been shown that PSO is simple to implement, computationally efficient, and rapidly converging [7]. Otherwise, as discussed, the most efficient placement of sensor nodes might require a tedious and computationally demanding process [8]. Network life can be extended by using clustered WSNs. Researchers typically build simple networks with clustered topology without any obstacles in mind [9]. Due to a spike in interest in wireless data collection, an enormous sensor deployment in diverse areas is unavoidable. Because of the high density of sensors and the fact that each one is self-contained, recharging them is difficult due to the associated logistical issues. As a result, a clustered WSN's energy efficiency becomes a critical factor in ensuring its long-term viability and reliability. Network dependability and energy efficiency are negatively impacted by communication overhead. Through the use of data aggregation, it is possible to reduce the energy required to communicate with a remote base station while still achieving the same level of performance [10]. Sensors in close proximity form a cluster for data gathering based on an efficient method for network structure.

Using PSO, a clustering technique can be developed that helps to reduce energy consumption in networks. These nodes have a much longer lifespan when selected by the PSO algorithm, which takes into account their remaining energy when selecting cluster heads (CHs) [11]. Particle swarm optimization has been applied to a routing protocol to reduce energy consumption. The authors explained how PSO can outperform the genetic algorithm when it comes to calculating cheaper energy paths [12]. Furthermore, they have considered the deployment of nodes to maximize coverage. Using the PSO algorithm, they are able to increase coverage without increasing the number of nodes [13]. In [14], each node's transmission power calculated using particle swarm optimization (PSO) to avoid establishing unconnected zones among sensor clusters. There is evidence that the proposed PSO algorithm is more energy efficient than the more usual use of nodes with only a single transmission power. Authors [15] proposed a game-theory-based adaptive power transmit control algorithm for IoT wireless sensor networks. Energy-Efficient Transmission Range Optimization Model for WSN-Based Internet of Things proposed in [16]. The Electrostatic Discharge Algorithm (ESDA) is a new algorithm that has been designed, implemented and utilized to reduce the amount of energy that a sensor node requires while simultaneously ensuring that each node is fully connected [17].

From the literature survey, it is evident that seeking a better solution for this particular engineering optimization problem is still open for further research and that no such novel optimization algorithms were explored. This made us attempt to implement Smell Agent Optimization (SAO)–Based Butterfly Optimization (BO) algorithms to minimize energy consumptions by identifying the appropriate transmission power while simultaneously guaranteeing that the entire network is properly linked. To evaluate the savings in energy, a comparison will be made with other existing meta-heuristic optimization techniques from the literature.

## 3.2 WIRELESS SENSOR NETWORKS

### 3.2.1 Clustered WSNs

Extending the life of a WSN network is made possible through the use of clustering. In clustered WSNs, most classic routing approaches are based on the premise that no obstacles exist [9]. Sensor networks (WSN) are becoming increasingly popular for a variety of purposes, including generating reports on factors such as temperature and humidity, as well as light and chemical activity. This trend is expected to continue in the future. Observers (such as base stations) collect the sensor data that is sent forth.

Recharge WSNs are challenging because of its dense deployment and independent nature. As a result, improving the project's energy efficiency is a top priority. Data aggregation in these networks reduces communication network overhead, resulting in significant energy savings [10]. Sensors can be split into tiny groups termed "clusters" to assist data aggregation through an effective network organization. There is a headset and several member nodes in each cluster [18]. The flow of data in a networked cluster is shown in Figure 3.1A.

### 3.2.2 Energy Saving in WSNs

Due to the limited energy capacity of wireless sensors, they remain a research priority. A WSN energy efficiency study was first conducted by Heinzelman et al. over a decade ago using clustering, and beam forming to save needless transmissions has been recommended by them. There have been several advancements in sensor nodes since that time, including additional capabilities. As a result, despite the research field's maturity, this movement toward IoT will necessitate further research [19, 20].

The development of sensors and energy models is the first stage in coming up with ideas for ways to save energy. The CPU, the sensing unit and the communication unit are the three subsystems that use battery power, according to [21]. In addition, the authors claim that many wireless node events can be tweaked to reduce power waste. Packet overhead, idle listening, overhearing, over-emitting, collisions and state transitions are some of the most common causes of network congestion. By determining the best transmission power for each node in the network, researchers hope to minimize state transitions and connect all sensor nodes in a single cluster. For the time being, we won't be considering any of the other energy-wasting activities.

It may be possible to save energy by changing sensor states, even though doing so requires some of the sensor's energy. Energy savings can be achieved, for example, by putting the nodes into sleep mode, which disables the vast majority of their functions [22]. Because the focus of this research is on network connectivity, it will not take into account the various node states. Once the network link is established for stationary sensors, the next phase of the network goal can then be to change modes.

### 3.2.3 Problem Emergence

The primary goal of this research is to locate each sensor node in a WSN in such a way that it consumes the least amount of power possible. While transmitting minimum power, sensors on the network's edge tends to link to inward nearby sensors. As a result, sensors that are located between the network's edges and its core tend to provide complete connectivity

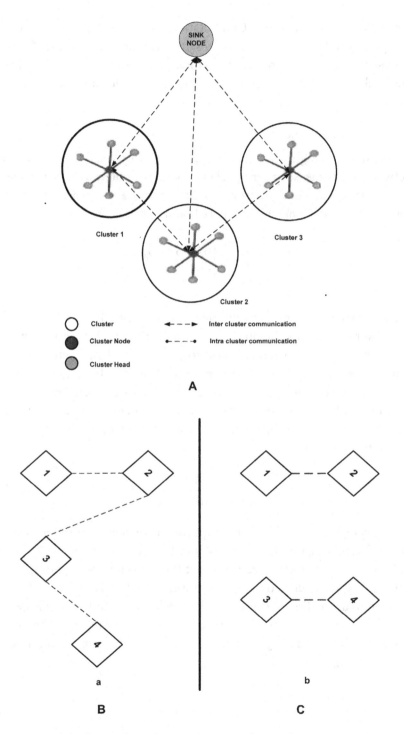

FIGURE 3.1 (A) Clustered wireless sensor networks topology. (B) System model. (C) (a) Fully connected network; (b) disconnected network.

throughout all dimensions. Computationally, it becomes hard to check every conceivable location that each sensor can do to guarantee effectiveness as the network increases. Therefore, meta-heuristic search strategies are used to identify the best answer. The cost of calculation is sometimes sacrificed to achieve the best possible result.

### 3.2.4 Modeling of System

In this study, a single group of $N$ wireless sensors is used to create a mesh network. Each measurement packet should be routed to a sink node to achieve this goal. Both sensor and sink nodes are contained within a square in the global neighbor matrix $\Gamma$, and it is defined as:

$$\Gamma_{ij}(\gamma) = \begin{cases} 0, if \ \rho_j < \rho_{th} \\ 1, if \ \rho_j \geq \rho_{th} \end{cases} \tag{3.1}$$

where $\gamma_i$ symbolizes the transmitting power of the node $i$, and $\rho_j$ specifies the power received by the node $j$. Receiver sensitivity is measured by $\rho_{th}$. Following. Eq. (3.1), a signal is said to be connected between two nodes when the sensitivity of the receiver is insufficient to handle the received power. As depicted in Figure 1.1B, the signal intensity in each node's circular area is sufficient to ensure connectivity. Each circle's signal intensity is $\rho_{th}$, This indicates that the signal will be able to be received by any receiver within this circle area.

$$\frac{P_R}{P_t} = \frac{A_r}{d^2} \frac{A_t}{\lambda^2} \tag{3.2}$$

A receiver's signal power $P_R$ is proportional to the transmitter's output power $P_t$, and $d$ is the receiver's distance from the transmitter. $A_r$ and $A_t$ indicate the relative effective regions of the receiving and sending antennas, and $\lambda$ represents the signal's wavelength being sent in Eq. (3.2), referred to as the Friis formula [14]. For each sensor node, a single isotropic broadcast and reception antenna is employed to represent the effective area of antenna's $A_{\text{isotropic}}$ because this work does not concentrate on antenna design for sensors.

$$A_{\text{isotropic}} = A_r = A_t = \frac{\lambda^2}{4\pi} \tag{3.3}$$

So Eq. (3.2) is further simplified as:

$$\frac{P_R}{P_t} = \left(\frac{\lambda}{4\pi}\right)^2 \tag{3.4}$$

Eq. (3.1) is used to calculate the global neighbor matrix, and then the algorithm decides the connected pair of nodes as described in the next section.

## 3.2.5 Checking of Network Full Connectivity

For a system to be considered fully connected, it must have at least one active connection link and be capable of forming an uninterrupted path, as illustrated in Figure 3.1C(a). Fake fully connected networks are generated when every node has a single connecting link and cannot be connected individually, as depicted in Figure 3.1C(b). Full connectivity can be readily achieved and checked in small networks with a few nodes. However, the sheer number of nodes in a real IoT application makes figuring out how well each one is connected computationally is visually difficult.

The first step in determining connectivity is to calculate the Laplacian matrix of the global neighbor matrix $\Gamma$. $n$ is the total number of nodes, and $deg(n_i)$ is the number of other nodes connected to the $i^{th}$ node, $n_i$:

$$L = \left(l_{ij}\right)_{nXn'} \tag{3.5}$$

$$l_{ij} = \begin{cases} deg(n_i) \text{ if } i = j \\ -1 \text{ if } i \neq j \text{ and } \Gamma_{ij} = 1 \\ 0 \text{ otherwise} \end{cases} \tag{3.6}$$

$$deg(n_i) = \Gamma^2_{ij} \longleftrightarrow i = j \tag{3.7}$$

There are nodes connected to $i^{th}$ node if $i = j$, and the square of their neighbor matrix is equal to the number of nodes connected to node $i$. Eigenvalues of the Laplacian matrix are obtained using the following equation:

$$L.E = \psi.E \tag{3.8}$$

Where $E$ is a $n \times 1$ eigenvector that meets all of the following conditions in Eq. (3.8). To construct a vector, each eigenvalue can be combined as $\psi$:

$$\psi = \left[\psi_1, \psi_2, \psi_3, \ldots\ldots, \psi_n, \right]^t \tag{3.9}$$

A fully connected state can only be achieved by having an $\psi_2$ that is positive, as shown by the notation $\psi_1 < \psi_2 < \psi_3 < \cdots < \psi_n$. It is also called "algebraic connectivity of $\Gamma$" and can be determined by looking at its second-smallest Laplacian eigenvalue $\psi_2$ and by checking to see whether there is at least one connection between nodes. There must be sufficient transmission power for a fully connected network under these conditions.

## 3.3 INVESTIGATED OPTIMIZATION ALGORITHMS

### 3.3.1 Butterfly Optimization Algorithm (BOA)

The foraging and mating behavior of the butterfly is modeled in a meta-heuristic algorithm called BOA. When compared to other meta-heuristics, BOA is distinguished by the fact that each butterfly has its distinct scent. The following is a possible formulation for the fragrance:

$$f = cI^a \tag{3.10}$$

According to this formula, $c$ represents the sensory modality, and $I$ is the stimulus intensity; $a$ denotes the power exponent depending on the extent of fragrance absorption $f$.

Sensory modality index $c$ can theoretically be taken at any value in the range $[0,\infty]$. When it comes to the BOA, its value is decided by the specificity of the optimization problem. In the optimal search phase of the algorithm, the sensory modality $c$ can be expressed as follows:

$$c(t+1) = c(t) + \left[ 0.25 \middle/ c(t).\text{Maxit} \right] \tag{3.11}$$

Maxit is the most iterations allowed, and $c$ is fixed to 0.01. In addition, the algorithm contains two crucial stages: a global search phase and a local search phase. For the global search movement of butterflies, we can formulate the mathematical model:

$$X_N^d(t+1) = X_N^d(t) + \left(r^2.\text{gbest} - X_N^d(t)\right).f_N \tag{3.12}$$

where $r$ is a random number in the range $[0,1]$, and $X_N^d$ is the $i$th butterfly's solution vector. In this case, .gbest is the current best solution among all the existing solutions for the $i$th butterfly, and $f$ indicates the fragrance. Local searches can be expressed as:

$$X_N^d(t+1) = X_N^d(t) + \left(r^2.X_j^d(t) - X_k^d(t)\right).f_N \tag{3.13}$$

where $X_j^d$ and $X_k^d$ are solutions of $j^{th}$ and $k^{th}$ butterflies, which are randomly selected from the solution space, respectively. This indicates that the butterfly performs a random walk if $X_j^d$ and $X_k^d$ are in the same iteration. The solution will be more diverse if this kind of random walk is allowed to take place.

A butterfly's search for food and a mate can take place on a local and a global scale. For this reason, a probability switch $p$ is established to convert between the traditional global search and the intensive local search. A random number in the range $[0,1]$ is generated by the BOA in each iteration and compared with the probability switch $p$ to decide whether the search should be global or local.

## 3.3.2 Smell Agent Optimization (SAO) Algorithm

It is through their sense of smell that most people get their first impressions of the world. The majority of living creatures can detect the presence of toxic chemicals in their surroundings utilizing their sense of smell. It's natural to think about creating SAO with the help of human olfaction. However, as it turned out, olfaction is used by the majority of biological agents for the same main function in the process of hunting, mating, and avoiding danger. This caused a widespread smell agent to be developed as a result of an algorithm for maximizing efficiency [23].

### 3.3.2.1 Steps of the SAO Algorithm

The SAO is structured around three unique modes. Using the processes outlined in the previous paragraph, these modes are derived. Detecting odor molecules and determining whether or not to look for the source is the initial phase of operation for the agent. In the second step of the evolution process in the SAO algorithm, the agent uses the first mode's choice to follow the molecules in search of the smell's source. Using the third option prevents the agent from becoming confined within a small area if its trail is lost.

### 3.3.2.2 Sniffing Mode

We start the procedure with an initial position that was chosen at random of scent molecules as smell molecules spread out in the agent's direction. For example, if the number of smell molecules is $N$, and $d$ represents the number of decision variables (number of thresholds) in hyperspace, then, using Eq. (3.8):

$$
x =
\begin{bmatrix}
x_1^1 & x_1^2 & \cdots & x_1^{d-1} & x_1^d \\
x_2^1 & x_2^2 & \cdots & x_2^{d-1} & x_2^d \\
\vdots & \vdots & \vdots & \vdots & \vdots \\
x_{N-1}^1 & x_{N-1}^2 & \cdots & x_{N-1}^{d-1} & x_{N-1}^d \\
x_N^1 & x_N^2 & \cdots & x_N^{d-1} & x_N^d
\end{bmatrix}
\tag{3.14}
$$

$$
x_N^d = x_{min,d} + \left( x_{max,d} - x_{min,d} \right) * rand
\tag{3.15}
$$

To find its optimal position in the search space, the agent uses Eq. (3.14) to build a position vector (1). $x_{max,d}$ and $x_{min,d}$ are maximum and minimum limits for the decision variable where the value of rand () ranges from 0 to 1.

It is determined that the molecules of odor will diffuse from the source/origin at an initial velocity determined by Eq. (3.15).

$$
v_N^d = v_{min,N} + \left( v_{max,N} - v_{min,N} \right) * rand()
\tag{3.16}
$$

Every odor molecule represents a potential solution in the geometric number space. Using the vector's position in Eq. (3.14) and the molecules' velocity in Eq. (3.16), we are able to locate these potential solutions' positions (smell molecule). Due to the Brownian spread of the smell molecules, Eq. (3.17) is used to update the scent molecules' velocity.

$$
x_N^d (t+1) = x_N^d (t) + v_N^d (t+1) * \Delta t
\tag{3.17}
$$

Assuming that, during the optimization process, the agent takes only one step at a time, $t$ is considered to be 1. For example, until the last iteration is reached, the algorithm's gradually increase their iteration by 1. As a result, the scent molecules have moved to Eq. (3.18) as their new location.

$$
x_N^d (t+1) = x_N^d (t) + v_N^d (t+1)
\tag{3.18}
$$

Each fragrance molecule's diffusion velocities are correlated with how quickly they evaporate and move around in the search space. Since the fragrance molecules spread out unevenly before they get to the agent's site, Eq. (3.19):

$$
v_N^d (t+1) = v_N^d (t) + v
\tag{3.19}
$$

$$v = r_1 \sqrt{3KT\Big/m} \tag{3.20}$$

In Eq. (3.20), $v$ denotes the component of the velocity that is updated throughout time. The temperature and mass of smell particles, $T$ and $m$, respectively, affect the kinetic energy of agents. The smell constant represented by $k$ normalizes this effect. The algorithm's stability is unaffected by temperature $T$ or mass $m$, which are both connected with the initialization of scent molecules. The ideas of $m$ and $T$ are derived from the ideal theory of gas. For the sake of saving time, experimental results show that $m$ and $T$ have values of 0.175 and 0.825, respectively. The new sites of the scent molecule in Eq. (3.17) are evaluated for their suitability. This signifies the end of the sniffing mode and the ability to locate the agent $x_{\text{best}}^d$ agent.

### 3.3.2.3 Trailing Mode

When an agent is tasked with locating the source of an unpleasant odor, this mode mimics the actions of the agent. The molecule may detect a new location with a greater concentration of agents than its current location while seeking a smell source, and the agent advances to this new location using Eq. (3.21).

$$x_N^d(t+1) = x_N^d(t) + r_2 * olf * \left( x_{\text{gbest}}^d(t) - x_N^d(t) \right)$$
$$- r_3 * olf * \left( x_{\text{worst}}^d(t) - x_N^d(t) \right) \tag{3.21}$$

where $r_2$ and $r_3$ are random numbers in the (0,1) range. Relatively speaking, both $r_2$ and $r_3$ penalize the impact of $olf$ on $x_{\text{gbest}}^d(t)$ and $x_{\text{worst}}^d(t)$.

Sniffing mode provides a way for the agent to find its current position $x_{\text{gbest}}^d(t)$ agent and the point with the worst fitness $x_{\text{worst}}^d(t)$. This allows the agent to track the scent's route more effectively. Eq. (3.21) shows how this information can be used to improve the algorithm's balance between exploration and exploitation. Olfaction ability is largely influenced by the size of one's olfactory lobes, as well as one's psychological and physical state; therefore, the value of $olf$ should be carefully chosen. Local searches benefit from low values of $olf$, while global searches benefit from high values of $olf$, since the former shows more strength in SAO's ability to detect scents on a global search.

### 3.3.2.4 Random Mode

Due to the discrete nature of smell molecules, their concentrations and intensities can change over time if they are spread out over a vast area relative to the search space. As a result, trailing becomes more difficult, and the scent is lost, making it difficult for an agent to follow. The agent may be unable to continue trailing at this moment, resulting in a local minimum. When this occurs, the agent enters a random mode:

$$x_N^d(t+1) = x_N^d(t) + r_4 * SL \qquad (3.22)$$

Random number $r_4$ penalizes the value of $SL$ by stochastically increasing the step length of $SL$. The molecule performs a step at random using Eq. (3.22) if the agent loses its track or if the trailing mode is unable to obtain the best fitness or locate the source of the smell.

As a result, the molecule will always try to retain its position on the search path that has the most concentration of the smell molecules. As previously noted, this information is used when trailing in Eq. (3.21) as the agent keeps track of its current location, $x_{gbest}^d(t)$ agent and worst positions $x_{worst}^d(t)$ agent, although the agent is restricted to searching only within the viable region by the optimization problem.

## 3.4 RESULTS AND DISCUSSIONS

The transmission power of −30 [dBm] has been chosen as the minimum for the experiments. The maximum power is set to offer a connection across a distance of 28.284 [m] within the random distribution area, while the transmission frequency is set to give the lowest attenuation value in the 915 Hz range [MHz], which is generally utilized in WSN applications. Finally, the sensitivity, which is defined as the minimum received power necessary for information recovery, is set at −60 [dBm]. Table 3.1 lists all the parameters values used in this investigation. There are only 10 possible

TABLE 3.1   WSN Parameters Used for the Simulation

| Parameter | Value |
| --- | --- |
| Total number of sensor nodes | 20 |
| Power range of sensor transmission | −30 [dBm] |
| power frequency of sensor transmission ($f$) | 915 [MHZ] |
| Sensor's random locations area (LXL) | 20 [m] X 20 [m] |
| Sensitivity of sensor ($\rho_{th}$) | −60 [dBm] |

scenarios according to [14]. However, scenarios 1 and 3, scenarios 2 and 5, scenarios 4 and 6 and scenarios 7 and 9 are identical. As a result, in this paper total scenarios are reduced from 10 to 6. The experiments were carried out on the same platform. MATLAB® R2022a, running on Windows 10 (64-bit), with an Intel® Core®) i5-5000 processor clocked at 2.9 GHz and 8 GB of RAM, was used to compare the output of each algorithm.

The SOA and BOA methods have been developed and applied to the scenarios studied in [14]. There were six different scenarios in the paper, each with 20 sensors dispersed across a 20 m² area. Various well-known algorithms, such as Particle Swarm Optimization (PSO), Simple Method (SM), Electro Static Discharge Algorithm (ESDA), Differential Evolution (DE), Genetic Algorithm (GA), Electromagnetism-like algorithm (EM), Black Hole (BH) algorithm, Sine Cosine Algorithm (SCA) and Salp Swarm Algorithm (SSA), have been examined for comparison purposes. However, it's worth noting that there are only ten possibilities in [14]. And it is observed that the power transmission range of deployed sensors by investigated methods is within the considered range of −30 [dBm]. In order to solve any optimization problem, it is essential to first set the algorithm's parameters. Parameter sensitivity analysis is done before the SOA and BOA algorithms are executed and then values are allocated, as shown in Table 3.2.

For a fair comparison, each scenario has been run 20 times by SOA and BOA algorithms, and the best results were presented in Table 3.3. From Table 3.3, it is clear that the BOA results are marginally better than the ESDA results. But the results of SOA are magnificent when compared to BOA, ESDA, and all other existing results. The best results obtained by SOA for all scenarios are bolded in Table 3.3. The reason was very clear,

TABLE 3.2   CCPSOBOA Algorithm Parameters

| Algorithm | Parameter | Description | Assigned Value |
|---|---|---|---|
| HCCPSOBOA | $\Phi_1, \Phi_2$ | Control parameters | 2.05 |
| | $N$ | Total number of agents | 50 |
| | $d$ | Dimension | 20 |
| | Maxit | Total number of maximum iterations | 1000 |
| | $c$ | Sensory modality index | 0.01 |
| | $a$ | Power exponent | 0.1 |
| | $p$ | Probability switch | 0.5 |
| | $V_{max}, V_{min}$ | Velocity limits for agents | 5, −5 |

TABLE 3.3    Results Comparison Using Different Algorithms.

| Scenario | Minimum Transmission Power Achieved [dBm] | | | | | | | | | | |
|---|---|---|---|---|---|---|---|---|---|---|---|
| | SAO | BOA | ESDA | PSO | SM | DE | GA | BH | EM | SSA | SCA |
| Scenario 1 | **-5.866** | -5.184 | -5.044 | -3.624 | 2.827 | -4.026 | -0.343 | Inf | Inf | -4.074 | 4.353 |
| Scenario 2 | **-8.613** | -7.857 | -7.683 | -6.669 | -2.699 | -6.758 | -1.090 | -6.798 | 7.214 | -5.841 | 7.636 |
| Scenario 3 | **-6.947** | -6.504 | -6.260 | -3.353 | 2.827 | -5.725 | -2.499 | -5.112 | 5.878 | -5.161 | 7.610 |
| Scenario 4 | **-5.949** | -5.415 | -5.044 | -5.113 | 3.842 | -4.014 | -0.529 | -4.281 | Inf | -3.389 | 8.473 |
| Scenario 5 | **-7.973** | -7.458 | -7.288 | -6.669 | -2.744 | -6.475 | -1.639 | -6.031 | 3.445 | -3.400 | 5.682 |
| Scenario 6 | **-5.390** | -4.763 | -4.507 | -5.226 | 3.865 | -3.363 | -1.766 | Inf | Inf | -0.541 | 6.532 |

except that, for SOA, all other experimented algorithms were performed alone according to their evolution strategy. The best values marked by SOA are −5.866 [dBm], −8.613 [dBm], −6.947 [dBm], −5.949 [dBm], −7.973 [dBm] and −5.390 [dBm] for scenarios 1 to 6, respectively, and among all algorithms BH and EM are poorly performed. The main reason is the SOA algorithm that takes advantage of the different phases during convergence for solving high-dimensional optimization problems.

Sketches of convergence curves obtained from the implemented SOA and BOA algorithms for six scenarios are shown in Figure 3.2. The number of iterations and the objective function value are shown on the $x$- and $y$-axes respectively. The following observations can be drawn from Figure 3.2. For scenario 1, the SOA algorithm converged the best solution at the 728th iteration, while BOA converged at 466. For scenario 2, SOA and BOA are converged at 755 and 527; for scenario 3, SOA and BOA are converged at 707 and 509; for scenario 4, SOA and BOA are converged at 730 and 649; for scenario 5, SOA and BOA are converged at 860 and 781; and for scenario 6, SOA and BOA are converged at 870 and 395, respectively. The average convergences for SOA and BOA are at 775 and 554 iterations, respectively. The average convergence time for BOA is 5.22 s, whereas SOA is 10.54 s because of the strong evolutionary process. Table 3.4 summarizes the SOA- and BOA-derived sensor transmission powers for the various scenarios under consideration. Each sensor has a different transmission power than the other sensors. The transmission power varies from scenario 1 to scenario 6 depending on the scenario. The average minimum and maximum sensor transmission power from scenarios 1–6 are −20.5 dBm and −23.9 dBm for SOA, −20.1 dBm and −23.8 dBm for BOA algorithms.

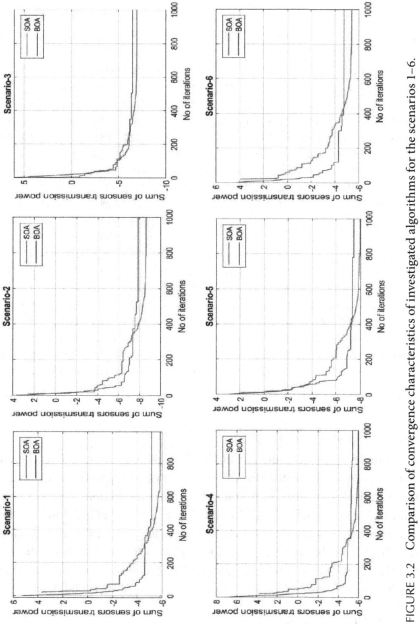

FIGURE 3.2   Comparison of convergence characteristics of investigated algorithms for the scenarios 1–6.

TABLE 3.4    Each Sensor Transmission Power for Six Different Scenarios Obtained by BOA and SOA

| | BOA | | | | | | SOA | | | | | |
|---|---|---|---|---|---|---|---|---|---|---|---|---|
| | 1 | 2 | 3 | 4 | 5 | 6 | 1 | 2 | 3 | 4 | 5 | 6 |
| Sensor 1 | −17.6 | −18.7 | −21.8 | −26.3 | −25.7 | −14.7 | −17.9 | −19.2 | −21.9 | −26.7 | −25.9 | −15.1 |
| Sensor 2 | −21.7 | −25.7 | −28.8 | −15.7 | −28.7 | −16.4 | −22.0 | −26.2 | −28.9 | −16.1 | −28.9 | −16.8 |
| Sensor 3 | −16.7 | −21.7 | −28.8 | −28.6 | −22.7 | −25.7 | −17.0 | −22.2 | −28.9 | −29.0 | −22.9 | −26.1 |
| Sensor 4 | −28.7 | −16.7 | −28.8 | −28.2 | −18.7 | −19.2 | −29.0 | −17.2 | −28.9 | −28.6 | −18.9 | −19.6 |
| Sensor 5 | −25.7 | −19.7 | −21.8 | −15.7 | −22.6 | −19.2 | −26.0 | −20.2 | −21.9 | −16.1 | −22.8 | −19.6 |
| Sensor 6 | −13.0 | −25.7 | −22.8 | −16.4 | −17.6 | −22.7 | −13.3 | −26.2 | −22.9 | −16.8 | −17.8 | −23.1 |
| Sensor 7 | −18.7 | −21.7 | −28.8 | −16.7 | −16.1 | −25.7 | −19.0 | −22.2 | −28.9 | −17.1 | −16.3 | −26.1 |
| Sensor 8 | −16.7 | −16.4 | −14.9 | −28.7 | −28.7 | −22.7 | −17.0 | −16.9 | −15.0 | −29.1 | −28.9 | −23.1 |
| Sensor 9 | −21.7 | −19.2 | −28.8 | −16.7 | −28.7 | −28.7 | −22.0 | −19.7 | −28.9 | −17.1 | −28.9 | −29.1 |
| Sensor 10 | −21.7 | −22.7 | −25.8 | −14.7 | −28.7 | −13.7 | −22.0 | −23.2 | −25.9 | −15.1 | −28.9 | −14.1 |
| Sensor 11 | −28.7 | −28.6 | −28.8 | −17.6 | −25.7 | −21.4 | −29.0 | −29.1 | −28.9 | −18.0 | −25.9 | −21.8 |
| Sensor 12 | −28.7 | −28.7 | −28.8 | −28.7 | −25.7 | −28.5 | −29.0 | −29.2 | −28.9 | −29.1 | −25.9 | −28.9 |
| Sensor 13 | −21.7 | −16.2 | −9.7 | −28.2 | −28.7 | −19.7 | −22.0 | −16.7 | −9.8 | −28.6 | −28.9 | −20.1 |
| Sensor 14 | −21.7 | −25.7 | −28.8 | −18.7 | −16.2 | −22.7 | −22.0 | −26.2 | −28.9 | −19.1 | −16.4 | −23.1 |
| Sensor 15 | −28.7 | −22.7 | −25.8 | −22.7 | −16.2 | −22.7 | −29.0 | −23.2 | −25.9 | −23.1 | −16.4 | −23.1 |
| Sensor 16 | −10.7 | −28.7 | −21.8 | −22.7 | −19.2 | −19.7 | −11.0 | −29.2 | −21.9 | −23.1 | −19.4 | −20.1 |
| Sensor 17 | −21.7 | −22.7 | −28.8 | −19.2 | −28.7 | −19.6 | −22.0 | −23.2 | −28.9 | −19.6 | −28.9 | −20.0 |
| Sensor 18 | −28.7 | −28.7 | −22.8 | −15.7 | −19.2 | −22.7 | −29.0 | −29.2 | −22.9 | −16.1 | −19.4 | −23.1 |
| Sensor 19 | −16.7 | −22.7 | −17.7 | −16.4 | −18.7 | −19.2 | −17.0 | −23.2 | −17.8 | −16.8 | −18.9 | −19.6 |
| Sensor 20 | −21.7 | −8.1 | −6.8 | −5.4 | −25.7 | −17.6 | −22.0 | −8.6 | −6.9 | −5.8 | −25.9 | −18.0 |
| Avg. Trans. Power | −21.6 | −22.0 | −23.8 | −20.1 | −23.1 | −21.1 | −22.3 | −22.5 | −23.9 | −20.5 | −23.3 | −21.5 |

## 3.4.1 Computational Complexity

The complexity of computation of HCCPSOBOA is $O(t(N \times D))$ where $t$ denotes the quantity of iterations, $D$ demonstrates the quantity of variables, and $N$ indicates the number of solutions. This computation's complexity is comparable to that of CCPSO, BOA, GA, DE, EM and SCA. However, the computational complexity of SSA is $O(t(N \times \log(N)))$ in the average case and $O(t(N^2)$ in the worst case, and for BH is $O(t(N^2 \times D))$. This indicates that the complexity of the computational SCA and BH is worse than that of other algorithms due to the sorting of solutions in every iteration.

## 3.5 CONCLUSIONS

The SOA and BOA approaches are presented in this paper to determine the transmission power of various sensor nodes to conserve sensor energy while maintaining all nodes fully connected. The SOA approach could save as much as 1 dBm of total network transmission power when compared to a sensor system that uses a continuous power supply. The proposed SOA and BOA algorithms have been compared with PSO, DE, GA, BH, SSA, EM and SCA in the literature, and the findings are magnificently satisfactory. The SOA has outperformed other examined algorithms in all six scenarios. The SOA has always been able to find a solution in every scenario (i.e., to find a fully connected network). Other wireless technologies, such as Wi-Fi, WiMAX, Zigbee, and Bluetooth, may be supported in the future by adding additional frequencies. Energy saving and network connection are also evaluated by incorporating transmission rates and power usage into the order. And the search for a better solution for this engineering optimization problem is still on because a lot of efficient hybrid variants of optimization algorithms are still evolving.

## REFERENCES

[1] V. Rodoplu and T. H. Meng, "Minimum Energy Mobile Wireless Networks," *IEEE Journal on Selected Areas in Communications*, vol. 17, no. 8, pp. 1333–1344, Aug. 1999. http://dx.doi.org/10.1109/49.779917.

[2] X. Li and H. Jiang, "Artificial Intelligence Technology and Engineering Applications," *The Applied Computational Electromagnetics Society Journal (ACES)*, vol. 32, no. 05, pp. 381–388, Jul. 2021, [Online]. Available: https://journals.riverpublishers.com/index.php/ACES/article/view/9611.

[3] A. A. Aziz, Y. A. Şekercioğlu, P. Fitzpatrick, and M. Ivanovich, "A Survey on Distributed Topology Control Techniques for Extending the Lifetime of Battery Powered Wireless Sensor Networks," *IEEE Communications Surveys and Tutorials*, vol. 15, no. 1. pp. 121–144, 2013. http://dx.doi.org/10.1109/SURV.2012.031612.00124.

[4] S. Jahanbakhsh, M. Ojaroudi, and S. Kazemi, "Small Low Power Rectenna for Wireless Local Area Network (WLAN) Applications," *The Applied Computational Electromagnetics Society Journal (ACES)*, vol. 30, no. 3, pp. 332–337, 2015.

[5] X. Jin, J. M. Caicedo, and M. Ali, "Near-Field Wireless Transfer to Embedded Smart Sensor Antennas in Concrete," *The Applied Computational Electromagnetics Society Journal (ACES)*, vol. 30, no. 03, pp. 261–269, Aug. 2021, [Online]. Available: https://journals.riverpublishers.com/index.php/ACES/article/view/10587.

[6] A. A. Aziz, Y. A. Şekercioğlu, P. Fitzpatrick, and M. Ivanovich, "A survey on Distributed Topology Control Techniques for Extending the Lifetime of Battery Powered Wireless Sensor Networks," *IEEE Communications Surveys and Tutorials*, vol. 15, no. 1. pp. 121–144, 2013. http://dx.doi.org/10.1109/SURV.2012.031612.00124.

[7] R. V. Kulkarni and G. K. Venayagamoorthy, "Particle Swarm Optimization in Wireless-Sensor Networks: A Brief Survey," *IEEE Transactions on Systems, Man and Cybernetics Part C: Applications and Reviews*, vol. 41, no. 2, pp. 262–267, Mar. 2011. http://dx.doi.org/10.1109/TSMCC.2010.2054080.

[8] R. M. Shubair, S. A. Jimaa, and A. A. Omar, "Robust Adaptive Beamforming Using Least Mean Mixed Norm Algorithm," *The Applied Computational Electromagnetics Society Journal (ACES)*, vol. 23, no. 3, pp. 262–269, Jun. 2022, [Online]. Available: https://journals.riverpublishers.com/index.php/ACES/article/view/16151.

[9] H. P. Gupta, S. V. Rao, A. K. Yadav, and T. Dutta, "Geographic Routing in Clustered Wireless Sensor Networks Among Obstacles," *IEEE Sensors Journal*, vol. 15, no. 5, pp. 2984–2992, May 2015. http://dx.doi.org/10.1109/JSEN.2014.2385734.

[10] O. Younis, M. Krunz, and S. Ramasubramanian, "Node Clustering in Wireless Sensor Networks: Recent Developments and Deployment Challenges," *IEEE Network*, vol. 20, no. 3, pp. 20–25, May 2006. http://dx.doi.org/10.1109/MNET.2006.1637928.

[11] Latiff, Nurul Mu'azzah Abdul et al. "Energy-Aware Clustering for Wireless Sensor Networks using Particle Swarm Optimization." 2007 IEEE 18th International Symposium on Personal, Indoor and Mobile Radio Communications (2007): 1–5

[12] S. Sarangi and B. Thankchan, "A Novel Routing Algorithm for Wireless Sensor Network Using Particle Swarm Optimization," *IOSR Journal of Computer Engineering*, vol. 4, pp. 26–30, 2012.

[13] S. Khezri, K. Faez, and A. Osmani, "Modified Discrete Binary PSO Based Sensor Placement in WSN Networks," in *Proceedings—2010 International Conference on Computational Intelligence and Communication Networks, CICN 2010*, pp. 200–204, 2010. http://dx.doi.org/10.1109/CICN.2010.49.

[14] G. L. da Silva Fre, J. de Carvalho Silva, F. A. Reis, and L. Dias Palhao Mendes, "Particle Swarm Optimization Implementation for Minimal Transmission Power Providing a Fully-Connected Cluster for the Internet of Things," in *IWT –015 - 2015 International Workshop on Telecommunications*, Institute of Electrical and Electronics Engineers Inc., Aug. 2015. http://dx.doi.org/10.1109/IWT.2015.7224573.

[15] K. Yadav and S. A. Saad, "Indian Journal of Science and Technology Game Theory Based Adaptive Transmit Power Control Algorithm for IoT Wireless Sensor Networks," *Indian Journal of Science and Technology*, vol. 14, no. 7, pp. 690–697, Sep. 2021. http://dx.doi.org/10.17485/IJST/v14i7.1258.

[16] M. J. Piran, S. Verma, V. G. Menon, and D. Y. Suh, "Energy-Efficient Transmission Range Optimization Model for WSN-Based Internet of Things," *Computers, Materials and Continua*, vol. 67, no. 3, pp. 2989–3007, Mar. 2021. http://dx.doi.org/10.32604/cmc.2021.015426.

[17] M. A. Alanezi, H. R. E. H. Bouchekara, M. S. Javaid, and M. S. Shahriar, "A Fully Connected Cluster with Minimal Transmission Power for IoT Using Electrostatic Discharge Algorithm," *Applied Computational Electromagnetics Society Journal*, vol. 36, no. 3, pp. 336–345, 2021. http://dx.doi.org/10.47037/2020.ACES.J.360313.

[18] A. A. Abbasi and M. Younis, "A Survey on Clustering Algorithms for Wireless Sensor Networks," *Computer Communications*, vol. 30, no. 14–15, pp. 2826–2841, Oct. 2007. http://dx.doi.org/10.1016/j.comcom.2007.05.024.

[19] M. Abdelaal and O. Theel, "Recent Energy-Preservation Endeavours for Longlife Wireless Sensor Networks: A Concise Survey," in *IFIP International Conference on Wireless and Optical Communications Networks, WOCN*, IEEE Computer Society, Oct. 2014. http://dx.doi.org/10.1109/WOCN.2014.6923052.

[20] W. R. Heinzelman, A. Sinha, A. Wang, and A. P. Chandrakasan, "Energy-Scalable Algorithms and Protocols for Wireless Microsensor Networks," in *ICASSP, IEEE International Conference on Acoustics, Speech and Signal Processing—Proceedings*, Institute of Electrical and Electronics Engineers Inc., 2000, pp. 3722–3725. http://dx.doi.org/10.1109/ICASSP.2000.860211.

[21] M. Abdelaal and O. Theel, "Recent Energy-Preservation Endeavours for Longlife Wireless Sensor Networks: A Concise Survey," in *IFIP International Conference on Wireless and Optical Communications Networks, WOCN*, IEEE Computer Society, Oct. 2014. http://dx.doi.org/10.1109/WOCN.2014.6923052.

[22] L. D. P. Mendes, J. J. P. C. Rodrigues, and M. Chen, "A Cross-Layer Sleep and Rate Adaptation Mechanism for Slotted ALOHA Wireless Sensor Networks," in *2010 International Conference on Information and Communication Technology Convergence, ICTC 2010*, 2010, pp. 213–217. http://dx.doi.org/10.1109/ICTC.2010.5674661.

[23] A. T. Salawudeen, M. B. Mu'azu, Y. A. Sha'aban, and A. E. Adedokun, "A Novel Smell Agent Optimization (SAO): An Extensive CEC Study and Engineering Application [Formula Presented]," *Knowledge-Based Systems*, vol. 232, Nov. 2021. http://dx.doi.org/10.1016/j.knosys.2021.107486.

# CHAPTER 4

# IoT Optimization for Smart Cities and Mobility in Smart Cities

Nisha Devi[1] and Neha Kishore[2]

1 *Department of Electronics and Communication Engineering,*
*Maharaja Agrasen University, Baddi, HP, India*

2 *Department of Computer Science and Engineering,*
*Maharaja Agrasen University, Baddi, HP, India*

## 4.1 INTRODUCTION

The capacity of computers to function equally effectively while processing numbers or symbols has given rise to a class of computer systems. The most well-known of these systems are expert systems. Artificial intelligence (AI) refers to the body of knowledge from which these systems are developed [1]. The goal of AI is to enable computers to reason similarly to humans. This change will enhance the digital revolution of each sector. The world may become autonomous by linking everything to digital platform. Machine learning and data analysis are two modules which are require to make the physical objects and environment autonomous. Data analysis would analyze all the data that is created over time to figure out the previous patterns and to be more effective in the future, whereas machine learning would develop strategies to assist learning in various devices of the network to make them automated and self-standing [2]. The integration of machine learning and data analysis into sensors and embedded systems for smart systems is now a focus for the growth of industry. IoT's anticipation of a world filled with implanted intelligent devices, sometimes referred to as "smart objects," is one of the foremost concepts driving this movement,

 DOI: 10.1201/9781003364856-4

and these components are interconnected through the Internet or other communication mediums like Bluetooth, infrared etc. [3]. The following subsections discuss AI, IoT and its applications.

### 4.1.1 Artificial Intelligence

AI is the study of giving robots intelligence so that they can do jobs that previously needed the human intellect. AI-based systems are advancing quickly in terms of capabilities, applicability, adaptability and processing speed. The ability of machines to perform less common activities is constantly improving. All of the data produced in each of these fields contributes to intelligence. To reveal the underlying principles of this data, analysis is crucial. AI is a method for effectively using data such that it is meaningful, intelligible to the people who offer it, and customizable. It is the study of developing tools and strategies for analyzing data and interpreting meaningful information out of it [2].

### 4.1.2 Internet of Things (IoT)

IoT is basically the combination of two words, "Internet" and "things," in which the Internet is a worldwide network of interconnected computer networks that serves multiple people across the world and that works on TCP/IP protocol. Different personal, public, educational, corporate, ministerial, security agencies networks are connected by a vital range of electromagnetic, wireless and optical networking technologies [4]. IoT can predict and respond to the environmental changes as it is a broad open network of smart objects that can self-organize, share information and resources, respond to events, and modify their behavior in response to environmental changes. IoT can provide anytime/anywhere connection for everything [5, 6].

### 4.1.3 Application of IoT

Figure 4.1 shows the applications of IoT in various components of smart cities. It includes smart door access control system, smart lighting for home and office, automated gate and garage, smart thermostats and humidity controllers, traffic management, smart lighting on streets, pollution monitoring and reporting, smart parking solutions etc. in industrial, health sector, agriculture, home automation, transportation, logistic management etc. The IoT also provides access to a number of inventive and

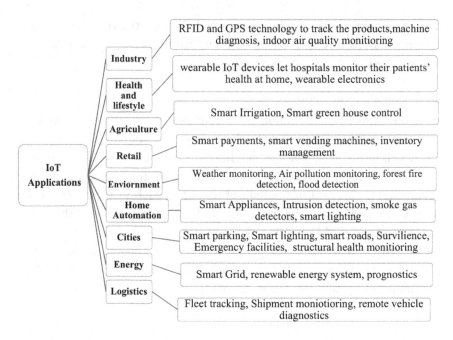

FIGURE 4.1 Applications of IoT.

comprehensive applications for smart cities, which significantly contribute to lowering energy consumption and other environmental consequences.

The ensuing sections of this chapter are structured as follows: In Section 4.2, a brief introduction about the smart cities is followed by common issues in smart cities, the role of IoT in smart cities and IoT optimization over the smart cities. Section 4.3, discusses smart mobility in smart cities, its global and regional prospective and smart mobility consequences over Himachal Pradesh, followed by the conclusion and future scope.

## 4.2 SMART CITIES

The smart city is a technologically advanced metropolitan area that deploys different electrical devices and sensors to get information, which is utilized to deal with the resources, services and assets and which is further utilized to improve multiple operations across the city.

### 4.2.1 Common Problems of Smart Cities

The idea of a "smart city" has become more important on the agendas of policy makers as a way to improve the quality of life offered to inhabitants via the search for and identification of intelligent solutions. Cities must improve the quality and efficiency of their resources and services offered due to population increase and high rates of urbanization, while also fostering sustainable and long-term economic growth. Smart cities face certain common problems:

1. Inadequate infrastructure to support smart cities

2. Data privacy and openness

3. Coordination between the private and public sectors

4. Inability to carry out initiatives for smart cities

5. Political incompatibility and a lack of legislative will

6. Lack of technical skills

7. Security and hackers

8. Imbalance between quality of life and invasion of privacy

9. Community education and their support in the development of the smart city

### 4.2.2 Role of IoT in Smart Cities

Modern advancements in AI and IoT play a significant role in the growth of smart cities. Both of these are based on applications such as smart healthcare, transportation, system infrastructure, environmental management, governance, sustainability and quality of life. An idealized form of urban development is represented by smart cities [7]. The concept of an intelligent city is typically based on a number of factors, including commercialization, logistics and transportation, healthcare, tourism etc. These sectors of the smart city can benefit from the IoT by raising the level of the city's intelligence, improving interactions between objects and humans, optimizing the use of general resources and raising business opportunities with improved information access to the citizens. As a result of the technology's potential to reduce harmful effects on ecology and men as well as to promote ecological sustainability by lowering carbon emissions, energy utilization, traffic management, and infrastructure deterioration, the integration of the IoT in a smart city can also give residents suitable holistic living conditions [8].

### 4.2.3 Optimization of Smart Cities through IoT

The stress on smart cities throughout the world has increased as a result of rising population and urbanization. To overcome these stressors, smart cities need optimization over the previous technologies and require smart health systems, smart home appliances, smart industries, smart infrastructural facilities, smart embedded system and smart transportation.

Figure 4.2 shows the IoT optimization applications for smart cities: smart agriculture, smart grid, smart city services, smart health, smart transportation, smart industry etc.

#### 4.2.3.1 Energy Optimization with IoT

A smart city is one that has several energy-consuming devices both within and outside it and is completely networked. Energy optimization is therefore necessary to make the best use of the available energy sources. To improve the energy efficiency in smart cities, a model based on IoT, 5G,

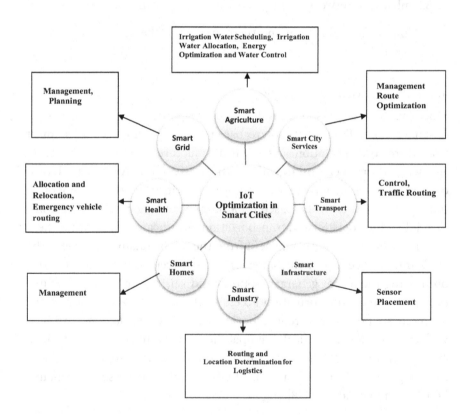

FIGURE 4.2   Applications for optimization in IoT-based smart cities.

and cloud computing is required. Energy-saving sensors with IoT capabilities can be used, and 5G enables quick communication with intelligent energy-consuming devices. The data produced by intelligent IoT devices can be kept in the cloud via a 5G communication channel. Through the application, smart device functionality is tracked. In the case of any problem, control management obtains information from the cloud via a communication channel and can fix the problem [9].

### 4.2.3.2 Smart Transportation Optimization with IoT

The majority of smart cities experience severe traffic problems every day. The traffic control system is a major issue for smart cities, even though certain areas are automated and cost-efficient. Every intersection with a traffic signal has an IoT sensor-integrated camera to keep an eye on the movements of passing vehicles. Additionally, the cloud processes the optimized vehicle flow data. An algorithm is performed using the information from the different signal corners to determine the direction of the flow of traffic and to manage the signal lights. IoT sensors are used to send the alarm notice to the closest traffic control facility when traffic is heavy [10].

### 4.2.3.3 Smart Agriculture Using IoT

IoT combines a number of current cutting-edge products and technologies, including wireless sensor networks (WSN), cognitive radio ad hoc networks, cloud computing, big data and user applications. The use of IoT technologies for smart agriculture is inevitable and will enhance productivity, provide hygienic and green food, endorse food traceability and decrease human efforts with increased production capacity. Various common sensors are used in the smart agricultural industry, depending on the necessary activity. Location sensors, mechanical sensors, electrochemical sensors, optical sensors and air flow sensors are just a few of the basic categories that may be used to classify sensors. These sensors are used to gather data on the atmospheric composition, air temperature/pressure/humidity, soil moisture/temperature, air humidity, plant moisture, precipitation, wind velocity/direction and sun radiation. These autonomous sensors supply data with a high degree of dependability, demonstrate great energy efficiency and provide independency [11].

### 4.2.3.4 IoT-Based Smart Health Care

The term "smart health" describes the use of technology to give people better medical treatment. This might take the form of creating instruments for improved illness diagnostics or using algorithms for better scheduling and providing better healthcare. In order to provide better healthcare services, it is essential to dispatch emergency vehicles at the appropriate time to a person in need. The allotment and movement of emergency vehicles is greatly facilitated by the IoT. A real-time indicator of the position of the vehicle as well as the volume of traffic in a certain region is made possible by the connection offered by IoT through vehicle-to-vehicle and vehicle-to-infrastructure communication. The best path for rescue vehicles to take and how best to deploy them to help those in need may then be decided using this information.

### 4.2.3.5 Smart Home Optimization

Home energy management has been the main application of optimization. In order to optimize a smart home, there are many requirements to maintain comfort, restrictions on power flow, time of operation, the maximum power that may be present or consumed and the availability of switchable appliances. Smart meters and IoT technologies are used to manage and monitor individual appliances as well as to schedule them. The microgrid, which controls the sources that are turned on and off from the homes' electrical supply and is used to collect data, is made possible by IoT devices. The data collected from these IoT devices may be analyzed to improve energy consumption patterns, which will save costs for the client and also enhance comfort.

### 4.2.3.6 Smart Infrastructure for Smart Cities

The management and improvement of public services, such as cultural activities, tourism and education, which are involved in enhancing the general quality of life of citizens, are also included in the smart living domain. This includes all elements related to developing smarter city infrastructures (e.g., smart homes, smart buildings etc.). IoT enables the rapidly expanding implementation of a variety of facilities for smart buildings, including tools for monitoring the structural integrity of buildings, tools for managing air conditioning and rainwater drainage, security systems for controlling verified access to buildings, video surveillance and human movement tracking.

## 4.3 SMART MOBILITY FOR THE SMART CITY

A smart city is a developed area that uses information and communication technology, business strategies and solutions to boost productivity, share knowledge with the public and enhance the welfare of its residents.

Utilizing information and communication technology, the smart city mission is to enhance both economic development and societal well-being [12]. One of the key tenets of the idea of a smart city is smart mobility. The potential for integrating technology into the transportation sector is growing as a result of the use of numerous technological solutions in every area of transportation and traffic science [13]. Information and communication technologies are developing at a rapid rate as determinants of a smart city. One of the greatest issues facing local authorities today is urban mobility [14]. Local councils are required to create ecologically friendly and sustainable solutions for urban transportation due to the rising number of private automobiles, traffic accidents, crowded roads in the traffic network, less public space and stagnant economies. The idea of "smart mobility" proposes that travel times may be optimized using a variety of recent and historical data, together with information and communication technology, which reduces the amount of space used, traffic jams, accidents and the emission of dangerous gases. Smart mobility indicators must be established as part of the planning process for sustainable urban mobility. During the design and implementation stages, the widely adopted notion of smart mobility (a holistic concept) is concentrated on the demands of city residents and their quality of life and health. The chosen metrics should be quantifiable by indicators in order to serve as guidance for accomplishing the sustainable goals [15]. The indicators track how quickly information and communication technologies are being adopted. In order to promote improved transportation options and their synchronization, apps and systems that draw on the gathering and analysis of big data are referred to as "smart mobility." The transition to zero-emission vehicles, the introduction of new sharing (car/travel) models, the facilitation of connectivity between vehicles and with other pertinent traffic data (pedestrians, infrastructure etc.), also known as "V2X" or "vehicle to everything," and automated vehicles are all part of the smart mobility revolution [16].

There are a number of key requirements for creating a strong future smart city, which are also thought of as the foundation for innovative and sustainable technology. The idea of future smart cities is essential for raising the standard of living and well-being of its inhabitants. A smart city is a wide notion, and for conventional cities, taking little steps is more effective. However, creating a new city using technology-based planning to create a smart city from the start will be a superior alternative. An innovative Mobility as a Service program is required to smoothly and intelligently combine multiple transport modes and provide effective mobility services to travelers depending on their demands, given the growing number of transport services available in cities and technology improvements [17].

### 4.3.1 Connected and Autonomous Vehicles (CAVs) in Smart Cities

Vehicles having different sensors to collect data from the surroundings are referred to as CAVs. A computer built into the vehicle then processes the data and enables the vehicle to operate automatically. More exceptional road safety is anticipated for drivers and vulnerable road users with more accessibility and less environmental effect with the deployment of CAVs. Promoting autonomous and environmentally friendly mobility depends on connectivity [18]. Mobility is viewed as a method of granting access to crucial services rather than as a goal in and of itself. Even in the most densely populated locations, the use of networked autonomous vehicles will expand road capacity and relieve congestion. However, as CAVs gain popularity, drivers lose control of their vehicles. This increases the security risk since it makes it easier for adversaries to launch effective attacks. The growing connectivity of cars, meanwhile, exposes more possible security holes and creates more entry points for cyber attacks. The development of CAV must necessarily contend with significant attack and security vulnerabilities. Potential vehicle vulnerabilities are becoming more visible due to the expansion of wireless vehicle connectivity, including Bluetooth, VANET and cellular networks. As a result, cyber attacks may be used to take advantage of these vulnerabilities and negatively affect the performance and functionality of CAVs [19, 20].

### 4.3.2 Global Perspective

Significant changes in the mobility industry have been made possible by the interaction of climate change, traffic congestion and the digital revolution. "Mobility as a Service" is the new business paradigm that is anticipated to rule in the twenty-first century. It combines shared, electric, connected and autonomous automobiles. It is now more important to consider how people move from one location to another rather than the actual vehicle. The International Transport Forum estimates that, if current efforts keep their current pace, global transportation activity would more than quadrupled by 2050 [21]. To address this, transportation policy makers must reconsider how public space is allocated and modify it to accommodate more people. Urban and legislative improvements, such as adding parking spaces, paving bicycle lanes, and advancing the development of public transportation networks, will be necessary for future solutions [22]. By 2030, the market for smart mobility is expected to be valued around USD 250.3 billion, with a CAGR of 20.09% from 2022 to 2030 [23].

Every year, traffic in Israel becomes worse. Data from WAZE shows that traffic rose by 27% in October 2021 compared to February 2020 (just before COVID 19 appeared in Israel for the first time). Israel is the OECD country with the worst traffic, according to statistics. Infrastructure for mass transportation is still being built at a far slower rate than the rate at which the number of private automobiles is rising. In Israel, the yearly cost of traffic congestion is estimated to be 40 billion NIS (about 11.5 billion EUR), and in 2030 that cost is projected to rise to 50 billion NIS (14.25 billion EUR). The TomTom index estimates that the average Israeli motorist wastes 150–200 hours per year in traffic [24]. In order to accelerate the adoption of innovative business and technological concepts, the Finnish government is establishing regulatory requirements. The Act advances Finland's goal of offering Mobility as a Service and building a digital mobility future that depends on data interoperability and open interfaces. It is a component of the larger Transport Code initiative [25]. Smart mobility is one of the cornerstones of the smart city, focusing on the utilization of transport systems to assist urban traffic and sustainable mobility [26].

### 4.3.3 Regional Perspective

By the end of this decade, the market for advanced transportation facilities is expected to grow by a staggering USD 320 billion, according to Market Research Future (MRFR) 2022 research. The government is leaning toward cutting-edge technological tools like the IoT, AI, 5G Internet access, cloud engineering and the like as work on smart city projects advances [27].

According to Niti Aayog, by 2030, 40% of buses in India will be electric; additionally, businesses in India that provide and cater to the demand of EV (electrical vehicle) buses support this aim [28]. According to the prime minister of India, 100 smart cities will be built. The goal of the smart cities project is to build future-proof towns that can provide their own water and power needs by recycling waste. An increasing number of urban residents will undoubtedly be catered to by smart cities. Mumbai, Bengaluru and Delhi have routinely ranked among the top ten most congested cities in the world according to TomTom for the past four years. According to IQAir, a global pollutant survey conducted in 2019 revealed that 21 of the 30 most polluted cities were in India, moving the nation up to the fifth spot overall. These are only a few examples of the signs that smart transportation solutions are necessary [29, 30].

### 4.3.4 Smart Cities Development in Himachal Pradesh

The Draft Electric Vehicle Policy, a comprehensive strategy to create and promote sustainable transportation systems for making Himachal Pradesh a worldwide center for the development of electric mobility, was adopted by the Himachal Pradesh cabinet [31]. The only goal of the draft electric vehicle policy is to switch to battery electric cars (BEVs) by at least 15% by 2025. The Himachal Road Transport Corporation (HRTC) now operates 50 electric taxis and 75 electric passenger transport buses, mostly in the smart city of Shimla and a few smaller cities [32]. The installation of a suitable number of charging stations at diverse places is the first and most important condition for the Electric Vehicle Policy-2021 to be effective. The implementation of policies like the zero emission level can help make hill towns and tourist hotspots pollution free.

## 4.4 CONCLUSION

The integrated Mobility as a Service concept and the smart mobility revolution might be significant in addressing the rising problem of traffic congestion in smart cities. With the exception of the COVID-19 era, travel demand has increased with traffic congestion. The demand for products and services, as well as the number of employees and, consequently, commuters, has grown as a result of growth and densification. Road excursions are becoming more and more popular, but so are travel by rail, air and sea. Since s vehicle offers point-to-point transportation, it meets the majority of trip demands in many cities. The demand for automobile travel frequently exceeds the capacity of the roads at specific times of the day, with detrimental effects such as air pollution, injury, property damage, lost time and fuel waste. Emergent technologies have grown in popularity in an effort to alleviate negative impacts and to steer urban transportation in a greener, safer path. Examples include electric autos, shared bikes and scooters. Smart mobility has come and will remain no matter what obstacles it faces. Industry participants would be better able to contribute to India's success story of smart mobility by adopting a positive, action-oriented approach and being open to exploring unexplored ground. However, current construction must take into account the requirements of a constantly expanding urban population and design solutions that can adjust to the rate and dynamic nature of urban transportation demands.

# REFERENCES

[1] Simmons, A. B., & Chappell, S. G. (1988). Artificial intelligence-definition and practice. *IEEE Journal of Oceanic Engineering, 13*(2), 14–42.

[2] Ghosh, A., Chakraborty, D., & Law, A. (2018). Artificial intelligence in Internet of things. *CAAI Transactions on Intelligence Technology, 3*(4), 208–218.

[3] Fortino, G., & Trunfio, P. (2014). *Internet of things based on smart objects: Technology, middleware and applications.* Springer.

[4] Nunberg, G. (2012). The advent of the internet: 12th April, courses.

[5] Kosmatos, E. A., Tselikas, N. D., & Boucouvalas, A. C. (2011). Integrating RFIDs and smart objects into a unified internet of things architecture. *Advances in Internet of Things: Scientific Research, 1*, 5–12. http://dx.doi.org/10.4236/ait.2011.11002.

[6] Madakam, S., Lake, V., Lake, V., & Lake, V. (2015). Internet of Things (IoT): A literature review. *Journal of Computer and Communications, 3*(05), 164.

[7] Glasmeier, A., & Christopherson, S. (2015). Thinking about smart cities. *Cambridge Journal of Regions, Economy and Society, 8*(1), 3–12.

[8] Rejeb, A., Rejeb, K., Simske, S., Treiblmaier, H., & Zailani, S. (2022). The big picture on the internet of things and the smart city: A review of what we know and what we need to know. *Internet of Things, 19*, 100565.

[9] Humayun, M., Alsaqer, M. S., & Jhanjhi, N. (2022). Energy optimization for smart cities using IoT. *Applied Artificial Intelligence*, 1–17.

[10] Liu, C., & Ke, L. (2022). Cloud assisted Internet of things intelligent transportation system and the traffic control system in the smart city. *Journal of Control and Decision*, 1–14.

[11] Quy, V. K., Hau, N. V., Anh, D. V., Quy, N. M., Ban, N. T., Lanza, S., Randazzo, G., & Muzirafuti, A. (2022). IoT-enabled smart agriculture: Architecture, applications, and challenges. *Applied Sciences, 12*(7), 3396.

[12] Rosayyan, P., Paul, J., Subramaniam, S., & Ganesan, S. I. (2023). An optimal control strategy for emergency vehicle priority system in smart cities using edge computing and IOT sensors. *Measurement: Sensors, 26*, 100697.

[13] Brčić, D., Slavulj, M., Šojat, D., & Jurak, J. (2018, May). The role of smart mobility in smart cities. In *Fifth International Conference on Road and Rail Infrastructure (CETRA 2018)* (pp. 17–19).

[14] Savastano, M., Suciu, M. C., Gorelova, I., & Stativă, G. A. (2023). How smart is mobility in smart cities? An analysis of citizens' value perceptions through ICT applications. *Cities, 132*, 104071.

[15] https://www.ippi.org.il/smart-mobility-shaping-a-new-world-2/.

[16] Eiza, M. H., Cao, Y., & Xu, L. (Eds.). (2020). *Toward sustainable and economic smart mobility: Shaping the future of smart cities.* World Scientific.

[17] Rajabi, E., Nowaczyk, S., Pashami, S., Bergquist, M., Ebby, G. S., & Wajid, S. (2023). A knowledge-based AI framework for mobility as a service. *Sustainability, 15*(3), 2717.

[18] Campisi, T., Severino, A., Al-Rashid, M. A., & Pau, G. (2021). The development of the smart cities in the connected and autonomous vehicles (CAVs) era: From mobility patterns to scaling in cities. *Infrastructures, 6*(7), 100.

[19] Wang, Z., Wei, H., Wang, J., Zeng, X., & Chang, Y. (2022). Security issues and solutions for connected and autonomous vehicles in a sustainable city: A survey. *Sustainability*, *14*(19), 12409.

[20] Ghosh, S., Zaboli, A., Hong, J., & Kwon, J. (2023). An integrated approach of threat analysis for autonomous vehicles perception system. *IEEE Access*, *11*, 14752–14777.

[21] Voda, A. I., & Radu, L. D. (2019). How can artificial intelligence respond to smart cities challenges? In *Smart cities: Issues and challenges* (pp. 199–216). Elsevier.

[22] Yeh, S., Gil, J., Kyle, P., Kishimoto, P., Cazzola, P., Craglia, M., Edelenbosch, O., Fragkos, P., Fulton, L., Liao, Y., Martinez, L., McCollum, D. L., Miller, J., Pereira, R. H. M., & Teter, J. (2022). Improving future travel demand projections: A pathway with an open science interdisciplinary approach. *Progress in Energy*, *4*(4), 043002.

[23] Market size of Smart Mobility retrieved Oct. 2022 from https://www.glo benewswire.com/news-release/2022/08/12/2497710/0/en/SmartMobility-Market-Size-to-Worth-Around-USD-250-3-Bn-by-2030.html.

[24] TomTom index retrieved Oct. 2022 from https://www.ippi.org.il/smart-mobility-shaping-a-new-world-2/.

[25] Mobility as a Service retrieved Oct. 2022 from https://data.europa.eu/en/news-events/news/smart-mobility-finland.

[26] Rey-Moreno, M., Periáñez-Cristóbal, R., & Calvo-Mora, A. (2023). Reflections on sustainable urban mobility, mobility as a service (MaaS) and adoption models. *International Journal of Environmental Research and Public Health*, *20*(1), 274.

[27] Smart mobility and transportation for atamanirbhar bharat retrieved Oct. 2022 from https://timesofindia.indiatimes.com/blogs/voices/smart-mobility-and-transportation-for-atmanirbhar-bharat/.

[28] Status Co analysis of various electric mobility segments retrieved Oct. 2022 from https://www.niti.gov.in/sites/default/files/2021,04/FullReport_Status_quo_analysis_of_various_segments_of_electric_mobility-com pressed.pdf.

[29] Smart Cities in India retrieved Oct. 2022 from https://economictimes.india times.com/news/india-unlimited/smart-cities.

[30] Electric vehicles retrieved Oct. 2022 from https://www.financialexpress. com/auto/industry/smart-mobility-transition-challenges-electric-cars-internet-connected-cars-smart-scooters/2282780/.

[31] Smart mobility in Himachal Pradesh retrieved Oct. 2022 from https://www. google.com/search?q=smart+mobility+in+Himachal&rlz=1C1CHBF_enIN 890IN891&oq=smart+mobility+in+Himachal&aqs=chrome.69i57j0i22i30j 0i39l4.12260j0j4&sourceid=chrome&ie=UTF-8.

[32] Electrical Vehicles in Himachal Pradesh retrieved Oct. 2022 from https:// www.outlookindia.com/website/story/india-news-himachal-pradesh-to-convert-15-per-cent-of-transport-to-electric-vehicles-by-2025/403317.

# CHAPTER 5

# Application of the Internet of Things in E-Waste Management

Smriti Snehil,[1] Ojaswi Vindhyachalam[2]
and Kamalesh Kumar Singh[1]

1 Department of Metallurgical Engineering, Indian Institute of
  Technology, Banaras Hindu University, Varanasi, India

2 Faculty of Law, Banaras Hindu University, Varanasi, India

## 5.1 INTRODUCTION

With the development and advancement of new technologies, contemporary electrical and electronic equipment, collectively known as e-products, is being discarded in massive amounts at regular intervals. On the one hand, this discarded equipment contains harmful and carcinogenic elements such as lead, nickel, cadmium and substances such as furans, halides etc. that present serious threats to human life and the environment. On the other hand, it hosts many precious metals such as gold, silver, platinum, palladium and valuable metals like copper, aluminum, iron etc., which are the main motivation factor to recycle the electronic waste. The recycling of e-waste gives the opportunity to recover theses valuable metals to put back them into their respective use and support the concept of a circular economy.

The handling the electronic waste involving proper identification, segregation and disposal becomes significantly important in deciding the fate of electronic waste.

DOI: 10.1201/9781003364856-5

Before deep diving into understanding the scope and mechanism of the management of electronic waste using modern artificial intelligence techniques, let us understand the terms and concepts associated with them.

"Electronic waste," or "e-waste," is a term that incorporates all kinds of electrical and electronic equipment and their parts that have been discarded after use. In other words, the electronic products that are nearing the end of their useful lives are collectively known as "e-waste." Some examples of e-waste are discarded e-products, such as computer monitors, keyboards, printers, calculators, circuit boards, cathode ray tubes, memory chips, cords and cables, fans, etc. E-waste is one of the most rapidly growing waste streams in the world. According to e-waste collection reports, the total e-waste generated across the globe has reached over 50 million tons. Just in 2019, the e-waste generated across the globe was approximately 53.6 million tons [1]. It is predicted [2] that the global e-waste generation in 2030 will be 75 million tons and approximately 111million tons in the 2050. This ever growing waste stream cannot be ignored and calls for the utmost care in its handling and processing. E-waste is either sent for recycling or simply thrown into a landfill. The recycling rates are improving gradually but are still low in developing countries.

A proper e-waste management system can contribute to minimize the landfill proportion. Various approaches are in practice to handle e-waste management.

Processing e-waste involves three critical steps:

1. **Collection of E-Waste:** This first step involves the collection of e-waste from households and industries. Further, the dumped waste is collected from bins by recycling units for processing.

2. **Preprocessing:** The collected e-waste is segregated based on many factors such as remaining life, hazardousness and ability to be recycled. After segregation, the parts of the wastes are dismantled and shredded into pieces using hammer mills. This is the initial part of processing e-waste.

3. **End-Processing (Finishing):** This stage involves further processing of metals and non-metals. Recyclable and materials that can be kept and used in other applications are kept and anything remaining is discarded.

Due to poor collection rates, only 20% of e-waste is recycled, whereas 4% joins the residential waste stream. Seventy-six percent of e-waste is disposed of illegally, either in open air incineration or in land fill, which in either case is a hazardous practice for humankind and the environment. To maximize the disposal of e-waste in legal centers of processing, the collection rate is extremely important and depends on the tracking of the movement of e-waste.

There are two approaches—producers' responsibility and users' responsibility—which are basically complementary to each other. In either case, the collection rate is dependent upon the active participation of both the producers and the users. The producers' responsibility may be collective or individual. The producers' responsibility approach to take back the discarded electronic equipment started in Germany and the Scandinavian countries in the 1990s and became obligatory in most parts of the developed world. However, in developing countries, progress is slow. Hence a collective effort at all levels is crucial to bring back the discarded e-waste into the collection system. To make the efforts effective at the local level, e-waste collection facilities need to be established and monitored.

The monitoring and tracking of the generation and management of such massive amounts of harmful waste become crucial and thus need the intervention of technologies such as the Internet of Things (IoT) to reduce the harmful impact of e-waste.

## 5.2 INTERNET OF THINGS

The "Internet of Things" is a term used for digitally connected smart devices that are linked with Internet connectivity, sensors and other hardware tools to exert control via the web. Billions of devices in everyday use, such as cars, smart watches and electrical appliances all comprised of computer chips and connected with high-bandwidth communication tools and sensors, collect data and respond intelligently to users [3].

There are five major components of Internet of Things: (1) devices, (2) connectivity, (3) analytics and data management, (4) cloud and (5) user interface. These components together are responsible for the functioning of Internet of Things services.

Devices that are comprised of sensors form the backbone of the Internet of Things system. Sensors detect all types of changes, including the most minute ones in the environment. The main purpose of sensors is to collect data from the surroundings. A wide range of sensors, such as temperature and humidity sensors, gyro sensors and wireless and Bluetooth sensors,

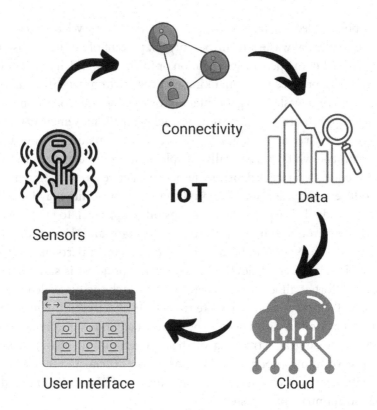

FIGURE 5.1 Components of Internet of Things.

measure various physical phenomena. Connectivity of the sensors or the devices can be established in a variety of ways including Bluetooth and satellites. Communication involves the transmission and reception of data that enables IoT devices to perform the functions they are designed for. After the establishment and connection of the IoT devices, the sensors function on collecting data from their surroundings, which is stored on the cloud. An IoT cloud is a web-based network that stores the data collected by the sensors of devices. The wide range of data collected on the cloud is then analyzed to leverage and automate processes. Now that the surrounding data has been collected and analyzed, it needs to be presented to the user for application. "User interface" is the term collectively used for the features that are used to interact with the computer systems. It includes screens, buttons, tabs etc.

IoT has a diverse range of applications including smartphones, home appliances and automobiles. Here are some of the most common applications of IoT:[4]

- **Self-Driven Cars:** IoT plays a major role in enabling the self-driving feature in cars. Cars have remote sensors, cameras and radar and are wirelessly connected to the cloud, which provides information about the movement of the car as well as the road on which it is being driven.

- **Agriculture:** Scaling up of various agricultural techniques has been facilitated with the help of Internet of Things. Smart irrigation, livestock tracking and prediction farming are some of the most prominent approaches that use IoT.

- **Healthcare:** The healthcare unit, especially during the pandemic, saw various significant applications of IoT. Telemedicine, vaccine cold chain monitoring and inventory management during the manufacturing process saw extensive usage of IoT. Medical research and maintaining patient records also witnessed streamlining due to the noteworthy capability of IoT to manage massive amounts of data.

- **Supply Chain Management Upgradation:** Supply chain management (SCM) is the entire process that consolidates the process of delivering products and services to customers right from the procurement of raw materials. IoT facilitates the process by introducing smart routes and enabling trackers to keep track of the product at every step.

- **Smart City:** One of the major and most diverse applications of IoT is the development of the smart city. Incorporating the IoT technologies to fulfill infrastructural requirements and using it to tackle some key concerns like traffic, electricity and waste management and to make living more convenient is the concept of smart cities.

IoT uses real-time data and thus has an enormous number of applications in day-to-day life. With the evolution of technologies, new products are being launched and discarded on a regular basis, ultimately leading to the generation of electronic waste in massive quantities. Evidently, one of the major concerns becomes the management of this electronic waste worldwide. IoT has seen its application in solving this issue to a significant extent. In the next section, the use of Internet of Things for the management of electronic waste is elaborated on.

FIGURE 5.2    Applications of Internet of Things.

## 5.3 ELECTRONIC WASTE MANAGEMENT USING IOT

Electronic waste generation is an ever increasing phenomenon in this technology-driven world. Thus management and proper disposal of the useless products become crucial [5]. The Internet of things and other domains of artificial intelligence, especially big data, can create a sustainable architecture for the proper management of electronic waste [6].

The chart in Figure 5.3 is a representation of how an electronic waste management system utilizes IoT techniques to keep track of and collect e-waste. Waste bins are one of the most essential components of waste management systems as they start the cycle of e-waste management. These bins utilize smart bin sensor technology, which senses location with real-time data, monitors the temperature of bins and checks the level of the

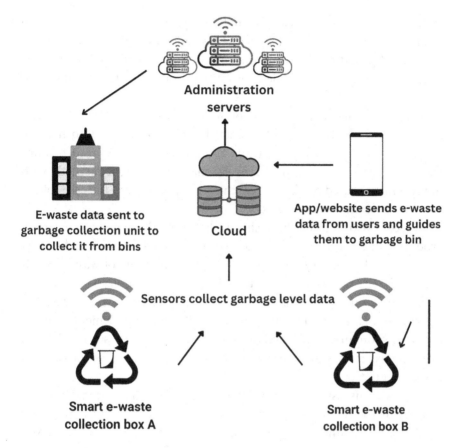

E-waste data sent to garbage collection unit to collect it from bins

Cloud

App/website sends e-waste data from users and guides them to garbage bin

Sensors collect garbage level data

Smart e-waste collection box A

Smart e-waste collection box B

FIGURE 5.3   Working of IoT-based e-waste management system.

bins for the routine collection of waste. The use of these "smart bins" helps garbage collection units to prioritize areas that require cleanup, thus contributing to the efficient pickup of garbage [17]. These smart waste bins are installed in different areas of the cities, the information about which is shared on cloud by the sensors.

The cloud sends the collected data to the administrative servers to analyze and take action accordingly. Based on requirements, the administrative units take a decision on whether a cleanup is required at a particular destination. If there is a need for removal, garbage trucks are sent to the respective areas for collection of the e-waste. Mobile applications and websites can also be integrated to the system to leverage connectivity benefits with the consumers directly. Consumers willing to get their electronic waste removed can use mobile apps for uploading and sharing information about their garbage [7]. These apps can guide consumers to smart bins, give them detailed information about the category of garbage collected and also enable collection units to collect waste from the right places.

E-waste management generally follows this process [8]. Many countries have successfully utilized and leveraged applications of IoT to manage electronic waste efficiently, Australia and Malaysia being two such countries. They have adapted their conventional management methods with improvements based on their research and requirements. The cases of the two countries are discussed next.

In recent years, studies have shown that Australia is one of the largest producers of e-waste globally because of the colossal usage of technology throughout the country. Managing such huge amounts of waste is challenging. So the waste either ends up being discarded carelessly or recycled under dangerous conditions. The improper disposal of waste may lead to the contamination of air, water and soil with harmful elements such as lead and cadmium. High levels of hazardous chemicals such as lead in drinking water have many harmful effects and can cause nervous system damage in the long run.

To tackle this issue, various rules and regulations have been developed recently by the Australian government in partnership with the State and Territory Governments [9]. In collaboration, the governments developed various schemes including the National Television and Computer Recycling Scheme. The role of the NTCRS is collecting raw materials from homes, offices and other institutions. This scheme offers access to electronic waste collection and recycling services without any charges. The collection, transport and recycling process is overseen and facilitated by the Australian government. Recycling processes yield a range of components that are utilized further for processing into usable components. There are also some amounts of invaluable materials that are eliminated and disposed of to landfill.

Under this scheme however, only desktops, laptops, printers and other computer peripherals can be recycled.

Malaysia, being one of the prominent producers of electronic waste, implemented some local legislative frameworks and rules to collect, transport and dispose of e-waste [10]. Households and industries are the major contributors of electronic waste in Malaysia. Various institutions are responsible for overseeing the e-waste collected in Malaysia.

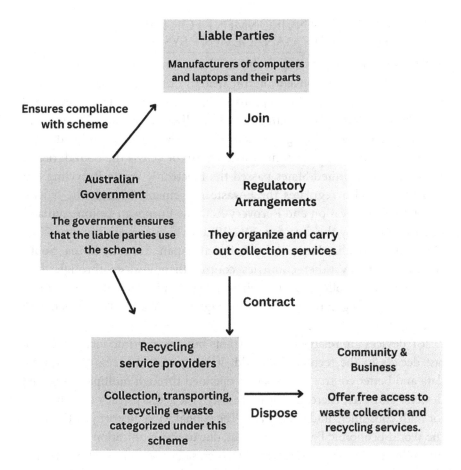

FIGURE 5.4 Roles and responsibilities of various bodies in a typical model.

Recovery facilities accept both industrial and household e-waste streams in Malaysia for both partial and full recovery of electronic waste [9]. Many partial recovery facilities work on the segregation of reusable EEE and its components and yield useful parts for use in other applications. Typical reusable equipment consists of projectors, desktops and laptops, DVD players, hard disks and the like.

For effective classification and segregation of complex e-waste stream, Ramya et. al. combined two algorithm approaches, FHGO (Fractional Henry Gas Optimization) and Horse Herd Optimization, and achieved an accuracy level of 0.95 through this model [11]. Taking into account factors like consumer behavior, buyback price and peer pressure, Guo and Zhong developed a customer-centric IoT based on a closed loop supply chain model [12] for e-waste.

## 5.4 REGULATORY ENVIRONMENT FOR IOT-BASED E-WASTE MANAGEMENT SYSTEM

The world took the growing problem of electronic waste seriously in the 1980s [13]. The Basel Convention [14], held in 1989, was a major step taken to address and prevent the shipping of hazardous waste from developed countries to developing countries. Gradually, the bigger economies of the world followed to bring out their own legislation to control and regulate the movement of electronic waste within or across the boundaries of their land. The United States passed the Electronic Waste Recycling Act in 2004 and also regulates the e-waste movement through the federal Resource Conservation and Recovery Act. The European Union regulates its 24 members by the directive 2012/19EU, which came out in year 2019. Similarly, Australia, New Zealand, Brazil, Japan, Taiwan, China, South Africa and many other countries control their e-waste through their own legislation, following the spirit of the Basal Convention of United Nations. India regulates its e-waste through the E-Waste Management and Handling Rules 2016.

IoT devices are relatively new entrants but are in prime focus since the last decade in the technology world. It has provided access to real-time data and better control over systems operated through multiple connected devices. However, there is a clear security risk about privacy and the data for both consumers and enterprises. The Global Risks Report [15] (2020) of the World Economic Forum states that, due to communication between the linked devices and enormous data transfer, safety, security and privacy are the major concerns for the users of IoT devices. IoT technology has the inherent ability to generate and collect extensive personal data. Practically, IoT environment has two broad challenges: IoT cybersecurity and IoT privacy.

In the United States, the Cybersecurity Improvement Act [13] 2019 guides product manufacturers to ensure a minimum security level for the IoT products manufactured. The National Institute of Standards and Technology (NIST) looks into issues of cybersecurity of the IoT equipment procured by the government. However, the private sector has not exerted pressure for compliance. The European Union and UK have their NIS (Network and Information System) directive, 2018 which provides cybersecurity to national IoT infrastructure through NIS regulations governing digital service providers.

IoT privacy in the EU is protected through the General Data Protection Regulation [14] (GDPR), i.e., Directive 95/46/EC, which ensures the safety

[18] of personal data. The United States does not have any specific law like GDPR but has separate federal and state laws like Gramm–Leach–Bliley Act (GLBA), The California Consumer Privacy Act (SB-1121) [6].

To address the challenges across the different corners of the world, the threat has been recognized and addressed through various initiatives to protect IoT devices and the inherent data within. Indian legislation tries to provide some security for the IoT environment through it E-Waste Management and Handling Rules 2016 and Information Technology Act [16] 2000. Further, framing uniform international legislation may be a good approach instead of dealing with IoT security at just the regional or national levels.

## 5.5 CONCLUSIONS

The stock of electronic waste throughout the world is growing due to rapid changes in technology and consumer demand for fast replacement. Due to the hazardous nature of e-waste, legislation is becoming more stringent. Under such circumstances, the application of the Internet of Things in waste management in general and in e-waste management in particular is a hope for achieving the optimum use, refurbishing, reuse and recycling of e-waste to support the circular economy.

It can be concluded that, since electronic waste is being generated at an ever increasing rate, its management and the utilization of the full potential of technology to extract "good from waste" is undeniably important. Hence the refinement and development of methodologies for the identification and recycling of electronic waste even more efficiently are what the developing and the developed countries should look to and work on in the near future.

## REFERENCES

[1] Rao, D., Singh, K., Morrison, C., & Love, J. Recycling Copper and Gold from e-Waste by a Two-Stage Leaching and Solvent Extraction Process. *Separation and Purification Technology*, 263 (2021) 118400. https://doi.org/10.1039/c9ra07607g.

[2] https://ewastemonitor.info/wpcontent/uploads/2020/11/FUTURE-E-WASTE-SCENARIOS_UNU_2019.pdf pp19.

[3] Bharadwaj, A. S., Rego, R., & Chowdhury, A. IOT Based Solid Waste Management System: A Conceptual Approach with an Architectural Solution as a Smart City Application. *2016 IEEE Annual India Conference (INDICON)* (2016). https://doi.org/10.1109/indicon.2016.7839147.

[4] Kang, K. D., Kang, H., Ilankoon, I. M. S. K., & Chong, C. Y. Electronic Waste Collection Systems Using Internet of Things (IOT): Household Electronic Waste Management in Malaysia. *Journal of Cleaner Production*, 252 (2020) 119801. https://doi.org/10.1016/j.jclepro.2019.119801.

[5] Islam, M. T., Huda, N., Baumber, A., Shumon, R., Zaman, A., Ali, F., Hossain, R., & Sahajwalla, V. A Global Review of Consumer Behavior Towards e-Waste and Implications for the Circular Economy. *Journal of Cleaner Production*, 316 (2021) 128297. https://doi.org/10.1016/j.jclepro.2021.128297.

[6] https://www.rfpage.com/applications-of-internet-of-things-iot/.

[7] Nirde, K., Mulay, P. S., & Chaskar, U. M. IoT Based Solid Waste Management System for Smart City. *2017 International Conference on Intelligent Computing and Control Systems (ICICCS)* (2017). https://doi.org/10.1109/iccons.2017.8250546.

[8] Pardini, K., Rodrigues, J. J., Kozlov, S. A., Kumar, N., & Furtado, V. IOT-Based Solid Waste Management Solutions: A Survey. *Journal of Sensor and Actuator Networks*, 8(1) (2019) 5. https://doi.org/10.3390/jsan8010005.

[9] A Systematic Approach to Garbage and Waste Management and Collection System Using IOT. *Strad Research*, 8(5) (2021). https://doi.org/10.37896/sr8.5/041.

[10] Yong, Y. S., Lim, Y. A., & Ilankoon, I. M. S. K. An Analysis of Electronic Waste Management Strategies and Recycling Operations in Malaysia: Challenges and Future Prospects. *Journal of Cleaner Production*, 224(16) (2019).

[11] Ramya, P. E-Waste Management Using Hybrid Optimization-Enabled Deep Learning in IoT Cloud Platform. *Advances in Engineering Software*, 176 (2023) 103353.

[12] Guo, R., & Zhong, Z. A Customer-Centric IoT-Based Novel Closed-Loop Supply Chain Model for WEEE Management. *Advanced Engineering Informatics*, 55 (2023) 101899.

[13] https://www.congress.gov/bill/116th-congress/house-bill/1668.

[14] http://www.basel.int/.

[15] World Economic Forum (weforum.org).

[16] Sharma & Sharma. *Information Technology Law and Practice, Universal LexisNex^{is}*, 7th edn. (2021) 272–277.

[17] Vishnu, S., Ramson, S. R., Senith, S., Anagnostopoulos, T., Abu-Mahfouz, A. M., Fan, X., Srinivasan, S., & Kirubaraj, A. A. IOT-Enabled Solid Waste Management in Smart Cities. *Smart Cities*, 4(3) (2021) 1004–1017. https://doi.org/10.3390/smartcities4030053.

[18] Kaneen, C. K., & Petrakis, E. G. M. Towards Evaluating GDPR Compliance in IoT Applications. *Procedia Computer Science*, 176 (2020) 2989–2998.

# CHAPTER 6

# Power of IoT in Smart Healthcare Systems

## Chinu[1] and Urvashi Bansal[2]

1 *Research Scholar, Department of Computer Science & Engineering,*
 *Dr. B. R. Ambedkar National Institute of Technology Jalandhar, India*

2 *Assistant Professor, Department of Computer Science & Engineering,*
 *Dr. B. R. Ambedkar National Institute of Technology Jalandhar, India*

## 6.1 INTRODUCTION

IoT devices play a vital role in improving the quality of life of patients by monitoring their body parameters to recognize their diseases and to help in sharing the data by using the Internet with healthcare providers. IoT has numerous applications in the healthcare sector, which is also called the Internet of Medical Things (IoMT). IoMT is a network of interconnected devices that store patient data and connects patients to doctors remotely and suggest solutions according to parameters measured by IoT-enabled devices. The healthcare industry is automated by using artificial intelligence and IoT. Nowadays with the help of IoMT, cost and time are saved. For regular checkups, there is no need to stand in long queues in hospitals. Patients can easily monitor their body parameters with smart wearables, and doctors can remotely check the stats of patient data through Internet-connected devices.

The Internet of Things has expanded human interaction options with the outside world while simultaneously enhancing freedom. IoT, with the aid of cutting-edge protocols and algorithms, has become a significant factor in advancing global communication. It links many gadgets, wearable technologies, household appliances and electronic gadgets to the Internet [1].

DOI: 10.1201/9781003364856-6

This chapter throws light on the concept of IoT in the healthcare domain. Section 6.2 explains the architecture of an IoT-based smart healthcare system. Section 6.3 explains the literature analysis of the usage of the Internet of medical things. Section 6.4 describes the various IoT-based devices used in the medical care system. The technical, ethical and economical barriers to building a better medical system are also the main emphasis of this study, as explained in Section 6.5. Lastly, we discuss the challenges and future scope of IoT in the healthcare domain.

## 6.2 ARCHITECTURE OF SMART HEALTHCARE USING IOT

One of the key sectors that have pioneered the use of the Internet of Things technologies is the healthcare sector. This is because IoT devices enable the combination of patient-centered care routines with substantial, long-term cost reductions. The Internet of Things concept is both robust and deep, and for all the pieces of the IoT puzzle to fit together flawlessly, they must all be a part of a carefully considered framework. IoT architecture enters the picture at this point, particularly in terms of IoT device management.

Although each Internet of Things (IoT) system is unique, all of them share a similar architecture as well as a general procedure. The things are the first component of the IoT, which are linked items with embedded sensors and actuators that allow them to detect their surroundings and capture data that is subsequently sent to IoT gateways. The IoT data collection systems and gateways that collect the vast amount of raw data, transform it into digitized streams, analyze it and preprocess it before analysis make up the next step [2].

Edge computing devices, which are in charge of further data processing and improved analysis, represent the third layer. Additionally, machine learning and visualization technologies may be used at this tier. The data is then moved to data centers, which may be installed locally or hosted on the cloud. This is where the data is kept, handled and thoroughly examined for meaningful ideas.

Figure 6.1 represents the architecture of the IoT used in smart healthcare systems. In this figure, we have discussed phase-wise analysis of architecture. In the first phase, different smart devices like sensors, actuators, monitors, detectors, video systems etc. are collected to gather the information. In the second phase, the data collected from different devices is unstructured, and we need to preprocess the data. Analog data must be combined and transformed into digital form to extract meaningful data

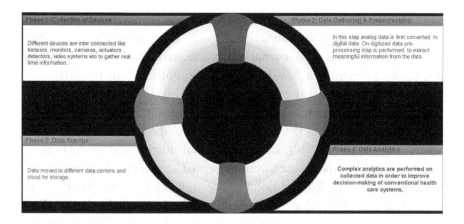

FIGURE 6.1  Architecture of IoT-based smart healthcare system.

for further processing. In the third phase, preprocessed data is transferred to different storage devices like a data center or the cloud after it has been digitized and aggregated. In the last phase, the final data is managed and examined. Advanced analytics are applied to this data in order to produce useful business insights for accurate decision making [3].

## 6.3  RELATED WORK

Oryema et al. have designed a message system that is interoperable for healthcare services [4]. Constrained application protocol and international standards of IoT are followed to design the message system. Ashfaq et al. discussed a review of IoT technologies used in the in-healthcare system. Various sensors used in IoT-based healthcare systems are discussed [5]. The authors discussed in-depth literature based on the Internet of medical things and explored machine learning and edge-computing-based approaches used in the smart healthcare system. Joyia et al. have prepared a detailed literature survey to discuss various challenges, applications, architecture and benefits of the Internet of medical things in their research work [6].

Kumar et al. have presented a novel healthcare framework using blockchain and IoT and have showed implementation using Healthcare 4.0 processes [7]. Simulations of various results presented in the paper validated the proposed approach. Although the error rate was lower, it affected overall system performance. Bao et al. have presented a smart healthcare system using IoT and cloud technology [8]. The authors proposed an easy-to-use keyword search mechanism to reduce the overhead of resource sharing on both the patient and the doctor sides. This research work also analyzed security mechanisms using encryption methods. Amin et al. proposed a cognitive healthcare framework that uses IoT and cloud technologies [9].

This framework is used in smart cities and provides a good platform for doctors and patients for healthcare-related problems. This research work also presented a case study based on the EEG technique used for brain-related problems. The results shown in the paper validate the proposed framework. Divel et al. have designed an IoT-based framework called Smart Log for infants [10]. Lack of essential nutrients in infants causes serious diseases. This research work presented an automatic nutrient monitoring system using IoT and cloud technology. A Bayesian-network-based algorithm is used to calculate the nutrition level in each food meal. Maji et al. have presented the ikardo automatic heart disease monitoring system. This system is another addition to a smart healthcare system based on IoT. The authors have presented a review of IoT-based voice-activated devices. This research work also presented challenges, applications and prospects of voice-activated IoT devices [11].

Elayan et al. have proposed a digital twin framework for heart disease prediction. An ECG classifier predicts heart disease and considers human body metrics for further analysis. Machine learning is employed by the author for better results. IoT-based wearable devices need verification of data for security purposes [3]. Chinaei et al. have discussed blockchain-based optimization methods for the verification of data at a low cost and low error rate [12]. Wu et al. proposed a lightweight and low-power wearable sensor that is IoT based and helps to identify vital signs related to the health of the patient [13]. Data encryption is applied for the security of data [14]. Verma and Sood have discussed fog- and IoT-based patient health monitoring systems in smart home applications. The proposed model used embedding data mining, distributed storage, and alert services at the edge to reduce the delay in transferring data through the cloud [15].

Balasundaram et al. proposed a multimodal device based on IoT for the diagnosis of patient parameters quickly in emergency cases like heart attacks, accidents, etc [16]. Hennebelle et al. proposed a smart healthcare framework known as HealthEdge in order to predict type 2 diabetes using IoT-edge computing system. This framework utilizes machine learning algorithms in order to evaluate the results [17]. Vishvanath et al. proposed an automatic glucose and temperature monitoring system using IoT. This device helps to maintain and organize patient data effectively anywhere at any time [18]. In order to create a privacy-preserving environment for the IoT-enabled healthcare system, this article presents a blockchain-based framework. The suggested design improves efficiency while securely generating and maintaining medical certifications [19].

## 6.4 IOT-BASED HEALTHCARE DEVICES

- **Continuous Glucose Monitoring:** This is very difficult for diabetic patients. IoT devices resolve this problem with the help of smart glucose monitoring devices [20]. Such devices maintain records automatically and also alert the patient if the glucose level exceeds the normal range.

- **Heart Rate Monitoring Devices:** To measure heart rate, patients must continually be hooked to devices using typical continuous cardiac monitoring systems, which limits their movement. IoT-enabled heart rate monitoring devices allow patients to move freely and continuously update the patient regarding heart rates.

- **Hand Hygiene Monitoring Devices:** These use sensors and remind people to sanitize their hands before entering hospital rooms.

- **Depression and Mood Monitoring Devices:** Such devices help doctors read the mental state of patients by measuring their blood pressure, heart rate, and even eye movements. These devices can detect depression symptoms, but sometimes they suffer from poor accuracy.

- **Disease Monitoring System:** IoT also helps to detect diseases. One example is the Parkinson's disease monitoring system. This device not only helps healthcare providers track the symptoms of the disease on daily basis but also gives liberty to patients to live their lives without spending long hours in hospitals [21]. Figure 6.2 shows examples of IoT devices used in the healthcare industry.

- **Connected Inhalers:** These devices avoid conditions that happen suddenly, like asthma attacks. This IoT-enabled device monitors the frequency of attacks by collecting and analyzing data from the environment sensed by sensors and provides relevant information to healthcare providers. The device also alerts patients to take inhalers when they forget to carry them [22].

- **Ingestible Sensors:** IoT-enabled devices like ingestible sensors help in the internal examination of the human body to keep track of the stomach to find the source of internal bleeding.

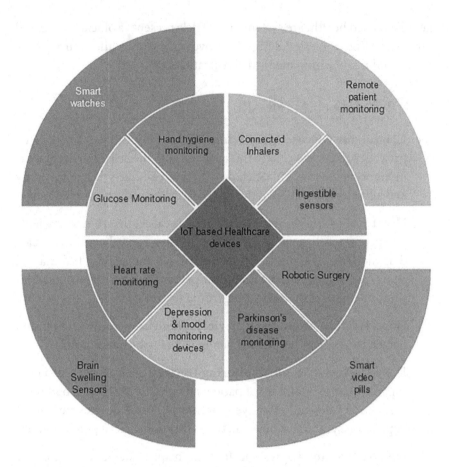

FIGURE 6.2  IoT based on smart healthcare devices.

- **Robotic Devices:** IoT-based small robotic devices help doctors during surgery.

- **Brain Swelling Sensors:** Such devices help surgeons check various parameters that are causing brain swelling and injuries by measuring pressure on the brain.

- **Smart Pills:** These travel inside the human body and collect information in the form of images and send them to devices like smart watches or wearable devices. With the help of the application, healthcare providers analyze gastrointestinal problems [23].

- **Remote Patient Monitoring Devices:** Remote devices collect patient data like blood pressure, sugar level, oxygen level and heart rate and share them remotely with healthcare providers.

## 6.5 CHALLENGES FOR IOT IN SMART HEALTHCARE SYSTEMS

In the healthcare system, IoT remotely provides support for patients as well as for healthcare providers. From the literature, we have found various challenges in the field of IoT. We have divided such challenges into three categories: technical, ethical and economical. Table 6.1 explains all the technical, ethical and economic challenges that have occurred in smart healthcare systems using IoT.

### 6.5.1 Technical Challenges

With the help of wearable sensors, patient health can be tracked very easily, but the main challenge is data, which is very big and which requires efficient algorithms and less complex infrastructure to process. Data generated with the help of sensors is unstructured and requires time for fast delivery. Moreover, IoT platforms should be user-friendly for both healthcare providers and patients.

- **Critical Processing and Response Time:** IoT devices used for smart healthcare require sensors to capture data from the patient's body. Data collected from IoT devices is unstructured and requires high-processing computing devices, which increases cost and time.

- **Connectivity Issues:** for faster and quick communication using IoT devices and reliable Internet connection are required for the remote monitoring of patients.

TABLE 6.1    Types of Challenges in IoT-Based Smart Healthcare Systems

| Technical Challenges | Ethical Challenges | Economic Challenges |
|---|---|---|
| Critical processing and response time | Privacy and security of data | High infrastructure resources cost |
| Heterogeneous devices | Ethics of devices | Devices maintenance cost |
| Nonuniformity of communication protocols | Ethics of practices | Big data |
| Stakeholder association and implementation | Ethics of data | |
| Connectivity issues | No open standards | |
| Device monitoring and sensing | | |
| Programming models for IoT networks | | |
| Data distribution and interoperability [24] | | |

- **Heterogeneous Devices:** IoT is nothing but the interconnection of devices. Devices can be any wearable devices that we are using in our homes, cars, office—anywhere. Interoperability is the main challenge due to the heterogeneous nature of the devices.

- **Nonuniformity of Communication Protocols:** Every vendor has protocols for devices, and, due to this nonuniformity, communication problems occur among the devices.

- **Stakeholder Association and Implementation:** Any person who is directly or indirectly related to IoT for the healthcare domain comes under the category of stakeholder. IoT systems should be improved by data collection from hospital staff, doctors, and patients through workshops and interviews. Collected data should be analyzed to improve the quality of IoT-based healthcare services. All doctors, patients and hospital staff should be trained for the proper use of IoT-based healthcare services [5].

- **Device Monitoring and Sensing:** Sensors play an important role in real-time sensing and monitoring of data. Sensors should be active all the time for real-time capturing of data. The main challenge is the maintenance of the energy efficiency of IoT tags and sensors. There is a lot of research scope in this area because handling the heterogeneity of sensors is the main challenge for the real-time capturing of data.

- **Programming Models for IoT Networks:** For effective implementation of IoT in the healthcare domain, dynamic programming models are required. These models not only maintain the workflow but also provide a user-friendly interface to end users [15].

- **Data Distribution and Interoperability:** Handling multi-model data is the biggest challenge in the technical domain. Effective techniques should be explored to model IoT data.

## 6.5.2 Ethical Challenges

- **Privacy and Security of Data:** Security is a major concern in a smart healthcare system using IoT. The personal information of both doctors and patients can be misused by hackers to create fake IDs. Hackers can buy drugs and medical equipment with their names and later sell them, which is unethical. Data ownership is also the main concern related to electronic devices. With the help of an intrusion detection system, we can ensure security to some extent.

- **Ethics of Data:** Informational privacy is a major issue for the design and implementation of H-IoT [25]. In both an ethical and a legal sense, health data is often seen as being highly sensitive. While confidentiality is essential to ensure that data cannot be linked to a specific person, the authors also contend that users should have complete control over their data and be able to track a third party every time.

- **Ethics of Practices:** IOMT can restrict the evaluation of a patient's state to a small number of easily quantifiable or measurable factors, which could lead to an excessively optimistic assessment of the technology's impact. By utilizing technology, it is possible to restrict the exchanges that provide medical professionals access to such information. As a result, providers must take action to prevent this from happening and to guarantee that a trustworthy relationship is established between patient and caregiver. For instance, rather than completely replacing dialogue, monitoring may be used to start a conversation [26].

- **Ethics of Devices:** Ethical considerations are challenging due to the variety of devices and application scenarios. Although technology can significantly improve healthcare, it also poses a threat to our expectation of personal and informational privacy because it makes it simple for outsiders to observe and assess the lives of users.

- **No Open Standards:** Lack of open standards for users and device manufacturers also becomes a major issue for IoT in the healthcare domain.

## 6.5.3 Economic Challenges

- **High Infrastructure and Resource Costs:** For the implementation of IoT in smart healthcare, we need to maintain the balance between technical specifications and cost. Memory storage capacity, low power consumption and processing capacity are what we need to balance the cost and technical requirements [15].

- **Maintenance Cost:** Since IoT-enabled devices use sensors to capture the data, sensors should be active persistently to fetch real-time data.

High cost is involved to maintain the sensors and devices for obtaining accuracy in the data.

- **Big Data:** IoT devices produce a huge volume of data that is unstructured. Techniques are required to structure the data efficiently in less time. Handling big data is a major challenge in the field of smart healthcare systems [15].

## 6.6 CONCLUSION

In this research work, various applications of IoT related to the healthcare domain have been discussed. The rise in demand, advancements in 5G connection and IoT technologies, and the rising popularity of healthcare IT software are all contributing factors to the growth of IoT-based healthcare systems. The patient's diagnosis, treatment and recovery are all heavily reliant on IoT. Predictive analytics and IoT data collection will enhance healthcare and lower human error rates. Data processing, resource management, security, privacy, interoperability, stakeholder engagement and actual implementation are just a few of the problems that IoT in healthcare faces. The largest obstacle to the success of IoT at the moment is security. Data handling and resource management are going to be difficult shortly because of the vast number of devices that are producing tremendous amounts of unstructured data. The ability of IoT systems in the healthcare sector to function together and generate value through stakeholder collaboration will determine their success or failure.

It's also likely that the initiatives of digital behemoths like Apple, Google and Samsung to make investments in bridging the gap between fitness monitoring apps and real medical treatment will aid in the process. Despite the drawbacks, the concept of IoT will continue to grasp and reshape the environment of medical care, and greater digital transformation in healthcare is inevitable. Therefore, it looks like the moment has come to move past the obstacles and start the transition to linked healthcare equipment.

## REFERENCES

[1] Pradhan, Bikash, Saugat Bhattacharyya, and Kunal Pal. "IoT-Based Applications in Healthcare Devices." *Journal of Healthcare Engineering* 2021 (2021). https://doi.org/10.1155/2021/6632599.

[2] AVsoft. "What is IoT Architecture? Explanation with Example of IoT Architecture." Accessed December 20, 2022. https://www.avsystem.com/blog/what-is-iot-architecture/.

[3] Wipro. "IoT in Healthcare Industry | IoT Applications in Healthcare—Wipro." Accessed November 19, 2022. https://www.wipro.com/business-process/what-can-iot-do-for-healthcare-/.

[4] Oryema, Brian, Hyun Su Kim, Wei Li, and Jong Tae Park. "Design and Implementation of an Interoperable Messaging System for IoT Healthcare Services." *2017 14th IEEE Annual Consumer Communications and Networking Conference, CCNC 2017* (2017): 45–51. https://doi.org/10.1109/CCNC.2017.7983080.

[5] Ashfaq, Zarlish, Abdur Rafay, Rafia Mumtaz, Syed Mohammad Hassan Zaidi, Hadia Saleem, Syed Ali Raza Zaidi, Sadaf Mumtaz, and Ayesha Haque. "A Review of Enabling Technologies for Internet of Medical Things (IoMT) Ecosystem." *Ain Shams Engineering Journal* 13, no. 4 (June 1, 2022). https:// doi.org/10.1016/J.ASEJ.2021.101660.

[6] Joyia, Gulraiz J., Rao M. Liaqat, Aftab Farooq, and Saad Rehman. "Internet of Medical Things (IOMT): Applications, Benefits and Future Challenges in Healthcare Domain." *Journal of Communications* 12, no. 4 (2017): 240–247. https://doi.org/10.12720/jcm.12.4.240-247.

[7] Kumar, Adarsh, Rajalakshmi Krishnamurthi, Anand Nayyar, Kriti Sharma, Vinay Grover, and Eklas Hossain. "A Novel Smart Healthcare Design, Simulation, and Implementation Using Healthcare 4.0 Processes." *IEEE Access* 8 (2020): 118433–118471. https://doi.org/10.1109/ACCESS.2020.3004790.

[8] Bao, Yangyang, Weidong Qiu, and Xiaochun Cheng. "Secure and Lightweight Fine-Grained Searchable Data Sharing for IoT-Oriented and Cloud-Assisted Smart Healthcare System." *IEEE Internet of Things Journal* 9, no. 4 (February 15, 2022): 2513–2526. https://doi.org/10.1109/JIOT.2021.3063846.

[9] Amin, Syed Umar, M. Shamim Hossain, Ghulam Muhammad, Musaed Alhussein, and Md Abdur Rahman. "Cognitive Smart Healthcare for Pathology Detection and Monitoring." *IEEE Access* 7 (2019): 10745–10753. https://doi.org/10.1109/ACCESS.2019.2891390.

[10] Sundaravadivel, Prabha, Kavya Kesavan, Lokeshwar Kesavan, Saraju P. Mohanty, and Elias Kougianos. "Smart-Log: A Deep-Learning Based Automated Nutrition Monitoring System in the IoT." *IEEE Transactions on Consumer Electronics* 64, no. 3 (2018): 390–398. https://doi.org/10.1109/TCE.2018.2867802.

[11] Spachos, Petros, Stefano Gregori, and M. Jamal Deen. "Voice Activated IoT Devices for Healthcare: Design Challenges and Emerging Applications." *IEEE Transactions on Circuits and Systems II: Express Briefs* 69, no. 7 (2022): 3101–3107. https://doi.org/10.1109/TCSII.2022.3179680.

[12] Elayan, Haya, Moayad Aloqaily, and Mohsen Guizani. "Digital Twin for Intelligent Context-Aware IoT Healthcare Systems." *IEEE Internet of Things Journal* 8, no. 23 (2021): 16749–16757. https://doi.org/10.1109/JIOT.2021.3051158.

[13] Chinaei, Mohammad Hossein, Hassan Habibi Gharakheili, and Vijay Sivaraman. "Optimal Witnessing of Healthcare IoT Data Using Blockchain Logging Contract." *IEEE Internet of Things Journal* 8, no. 12 (2021): 10117–10130. https://doi.org/10.1109/JIOT.2021.3051433.

[14] Wu, Taiyang, Fan Wu, Chunkai Qiu, Jean Michel Redoute, and Mehmet Rasit Yuce. "A Rigid-Flex Wearable Health Monitoring Sensor Patch for IoT-Connected Healthcare Applications." *IEEE Internet of Things Journal 7*, no. 8 (2020): 6932–6945. https://doi.org/10.1109/JIOT.2020.2977164.

[15] Lohiya, Ritika, and Ankit Thakkar. "Application Domains, Evaluation Data Sets, and Research Challenges of IoT: A Systematic Review." *IEEE Internet of Things Journal* 8, no. 11 (2021): 8774–8798. https://doi.org/10.1109/JIOT.2020.3048439.

[16] Verma, Prabal, and Sandeep K. Sood. "Fog Assisted-IoT Enabled Patient Health Monitoring in Smart Homes." *IEEE Internet of Things Journal* 5, no. 3 (2018): 1789–1796. https://doi.org/10.1109/JIOT.2018.2803201.

[17] Balasundaram, A., Sidheswar Routray, A. V. Prabu, Prabhakar Krishnan, Prince Priya Malla, and Moinak Maiti. "Internet of Things (IoT) Based Smart Healthcare System for Efficient Diagnostics of Health Parameters of Patients in Emergency Care." 18, no. 9 (2023). https://doi.org/10.1109/JIOT.2023.3246065.

[18] Hennebelle, Alain, Huned Materwala, and Leila Ismail. "HealthEdge: A Machine Learning-Based Smart Healthcare Framework for Prediction of Type 2 Diabetes in an Integrated IoT, Edge, and Cloud Computing System." *The 14th International Conference on Ambient Systems, Networks and Technologies (ANT)* 00 (2023): 331–338. https://doi.org/10.1016/j.procs.2023.03.043.

[19] Vishvanath, D., A. Ramchandra, and M. Koban. "IOT Based Temperature and Oxygen Level Monitoring and Data Visualization." *International Conference on Emerging Smart Computing and Informatics (ESCI)* (2023): 1.

[20] Namasudra, Suyel, Pratima Sharma, Ruben Gonzalez Crespo, and Vimal Shanmuganathan. "Blockchain-Based Medical Certificate Generation and Verification for IoT-Based Healthcare Systems." *IEEE Consumer Electronics Magazine* 12, no. 2 (March 1, 2023): 83–93. https://doi.org/10.1109/MCE.2021.3140048.

[21] Gia, Tuan Nguyen, Mai Ali, Imed Ben Dhaou, Amir M. Rahmani, Tomi Westerlund, Pasi Liljeberg, and Hannu Tenhunen. "IoT-Based Continuous Glucose Monitoring System: A Feasibility Study." *Procedia Computer Science* 109 (2017): 327–334. https://doi.org/10.1016/j.procs.2017.05.359.

[22] Gatouillat, Arthur, Youakim Badr, Bertrand Massot, and Ervin Sejdic. "Internet of Medical Things: A Review of Recent Contributions Dealing with CyberPhysical Systems in Medicine." *IEEE Internet of Things Journal* 5, no. 5 (October 1, 2018): 3810–3822. https://doi.org/10.1109/JIOT.2018.2849014.

[23] Ordr. "10 Internet of Things (IoT) Healthcare Examples." https://ordr.net/article/iot-healthcare-examples/.

[24] Intellectsoft. "IoT in Healthcare: Benefits, Use Cases, Challenges [Guide]." Accessed October 4, 2022. https://www.intellectsoft.net/blog/iot-in-healthcare/.

[25] IoT, Table 1 shows types of challenges in IoT based Smart Healthcare Systems, 2020.
[26] DZone IoT. "The Ethics of IoT Usage in Healthcare—DZone IoT." Accessed October 11, 2022. https://dzone.com/articles/the-ethics-of-iot-usage-in-healthcare.

# CHAPTER 7

# Verification Scheme for Malicious Routing in the Internet of Things

Bharti Sharma,[1] Sakshi Patni[2] and
Sumit Kumar Mahana[3]

1 MMICTBM (MCA), Maharishi Markandeshwar (Deemed
to be University), Mullana-Ambala, Haryana, India

2 Gachon University, Seongnam, South Korea

3 NIT Kurukshetra, India

## 7.1 INTRODUCTION

The Internet of Things (IoT) is a ubiquitous, worldwide network that supports and provides a system for the observation and management of the physical world through the gathering, processing and analysis of data produced by IoT sensor devices. The number of linked devices is expected to increase dramatically to 60 billion by 2022 [1–3]. Our everyday objects, including vehicles, refrigerators, fans, lights, mobile phones and other operational technologies, such as manufacturing infrastructures that are now becoming globally networked systems, are the key drivers of this expansion. It is clear that security will be a crucial enabler for the implementation and usage of the majority of IoT applications, particularly secure routing among IoT sensor nodes [4]. Methods must thus be created to provide safe routing connections for devices made possible by IoT technology. IoT is one of the most important technologies of the twenty-first century. The capacity to connect everyday objects, such as home appliances, cars, thermostats and baby monitors, to the Internet via embedded devices has

 DOI: 10.1201/9781003364856-7

made continuous communication among people, processes and things possible [5]. Minimal human engagement is required for exchanging and gathering data by physical objects thanks to low-cost computers, the cloud, big data, analytics and mobile technologies. In today's hyper-connected environment, digital technologies have the ability to record, monitor and change every interaction among linked things. Though they collide, the physical and digital worlds coexist [6].

By 2025, Internet nodes may reside in ordinary items—including, according to NIC, "food containers, furniture, paper documents, and more." Beginning with the notion that "public demand paired with technological improvements might promote widespread dispersion of an Internet of Things (IoT) that could, like the current Internet, contribute immensely to economic development," it identifies potential future prospects [7]. It is also emphasizing that risks may be associated with the broad use of such a device. In fact, it is stressed that "the IoT might transmit such dangers considerably more widely than the Internet has to date" if common devices start to pose information security issues [8, 9].

IoT and other networked computer systems have become indispensable components of daily life for people, as shown in Figure 7.1. The size of these networks, the heterogeneity at different tiers, the emergence of new network technologies and new business models are all still expanding [10–13]. The old network architecture and protocols are under pressure and sometimes even perform poorly in the face of new settings, which goes hand in hand with the increase in complexity. Therefore, new architectures are required to enable new applications, efficiently utilize network resources

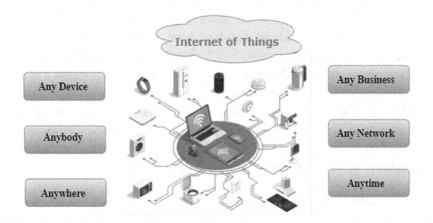

FIGURE 7.1   Internet of Things.

and satisfy current and foreseeable network demand. The Internet plays a massive role in today's day-to-day life. Be it home, school, bank or corporate office, we can find wireless networks everywhere [14–16]. Many network designs rely on heuristics and intuition, which are subsequently confirmed by simulations and tests. The same design cycle is repeated in the event that issues are discovered or performance is not adequate. We contend that design based on intuition and heuristics is not going to satisfy emerging requirements for network architecture and protocols because it is typically constrained in the range of system features that will be considered, can easily underestimate the significance of certain factors, and result in subpar performance or, even worse, not foresee potentially adversarial interactions, resulting in disastrous implementations. Instead, networks should be designed and controlled using methods that are methodical and logical in mathematics. New facets of Internet security have been revealed through the use of wireless networks. Information may now be sent using radio waves rather than cables, eliminating the need for wires. Information exposure grows and, with it, the vulnerabilities. As a result of the transmitted data being exposed, new security issues arise [17].

Commercial applications of IoT include oil well sensing, intelligent vehicle transportation systems, gaming and agriculture, as well as applications in smart homes, wearable technology, healthcare, the automobile industry, and smart grid technology. The principal area of concentration in IoT research is the security of the various IoT nodes to preserve the flawless operation of the IoT networks [18].

Designing, putting into practice and guaranteeing security on an IoT network are among the most popular IoT study topics, which have drawn several researchers from standardization organizations as well as from academia and business. Many ideas have been made so far with the goal of addressing the security issues with IoT. This chapter is focused on security routing protocols in IoT. Moreover, we developed a framework for a verification scheme for malicious routing.

The rest of this chapter is organized as follows: Section 7.2 defines the security issues in IoT. Section 7.3 focuses on the proposed methodology, the Verifiable Key Scheme (VKS). The results and discussion are presented in Section 7.4, followed by the Conclusion and Future Scope.

## 7.2 SECURITY ISSUES IN IOT

Security encompasses all the methods designed to safeguard, fix and ensure that data in computer systems is protected from hostile assaults. The potential of identity theft, computer system infection, personal data leakage and economic espionage are only a few examples of security issues mentioned in the daily headlines. The protection techniques used to safeguard network-based or Internet-connected devices are called "IoT security." IoT is an extensive phrase, and, as technology has continued to advance, it has only grown even more so. Nearly all modern electronics, including watches, thermostats and gaming consoles, have some kind of connectivity to the Internet or other devices [19].

To prevent these devices from being hacked, a range of methods, plans and resources known as "IoT security" is deployed. Ironically, the connection of IoT is what makes these gadgets more susceptible to hackers. Various security concerns are related to IoT security:

- **Data and Information Leakage:** In any IoT smart environment, personal information might easily be spilled, leading to security breaches in the absence of adequate security systems that shield data and information from malware and other hostile intruders [20].

- **Eavesdropping:** Malicious attackers may use unstable network connections to steal data as it is being transmitted between the connected IoT devices or as it moves within and across IoT-based smart environments, as well as across the Internet. This might lead to other, severe security breaches [21, 22].

- **IoT Device Security:** Due to a lack of specialized, globally recognized IoT security standards or security assessment frameworks, some devices might be manufactured with weak security baselines, including outdated and unpatched embedded operating systems and software; weak, guessable, or hard-coded passwords; insecure data transfer and storage; among others. Because of this, these IoT devices are vulnerable to a range of security threats and attacks [23].

- **Hacking:** The majority of the data and information that IoT devices in smart environments acquire may be kept on Internet-accessible platforms like the "cloud." It is well-known that many cloud-based IoT systems and devices have security flaws and are readily vulnerable to hacking and assaults since data transfer, such as video footage from cameras, may not even be encrypted when delivered over the Internet.

- **Ransomware and the Hijacking of IoT Devices:** Many IoT devices may soon be simple targets for ransomware attacks due to lax security, a lack of specific universally agreed on IoT security standards and evaluation frameworks, and the growing use of IoT devices [24].

- **Absence of Active Device Monitoring:** IoT device monitoring can be complex. This is due to the fact that the majority of the monitoring techniques and tools now in use, particularly those that concentrate on the cloud, were historically intended to monitor time-series metric data without a focus on contemporary IoT devices or their operations. In IoT-based smart settings, it is difficult to have complete network visibility due to a lack of active IoT device monitoring solutions. Additionally, not many technologies are available that can be used to directly monitor specific the IoT devices deployed in IoT-based smart settings [25, 26].

- **Lack of Effective and Reliable Security Protocols:** Inadequate IoT security standards, evaluation frameworks and protections might result in security breaches in smart environments that compromise personal data exfiltration [26].

- **Denial of Service (doS/DDoS):** Hackers may attempt to perform a denial of service (doS/DDoS) on the sensors themselves or on existing hubs in IoT-based smart environment networks [7] due to technological advancements. Attackers can also get access to the network and use methods like Clear To Send (CTS) and Request To Send (RTS) to send mass messages to IoT devices, which can result in DoS attacks against genuine IoT devices [27–29].

## 7.3 PROPOSED FRAMEWORK FOR MALICIOUS ROUTING

The authors have suggested the Verifiable Key Scheme (VKS) model for participating IoT devices. Initially, from the existing network, a pool of authenticated IoT devices has been created, and separate keys have been allocated to them. A pool of authenticated nodes is chosen by sending false packets to the neighbor devices and requesting the shortest path, and the malicious device will drop the packet and come in under the suspected device. Suspected devices are further verified with the same scheme and by checking whether packets have been received at the destination. In this whole process, malicious devices are recognized. Then a list of verified devices is made, and new keys are allocated to them.

- **Cluster Head Creation:** As now an authentication list of IoT devices has been created, a cluster head will be chosen with a factor $x$. This factor $x$ depends on a number of parameters like proximity of the IoT device to other devices, battery power etc. The number of cluster

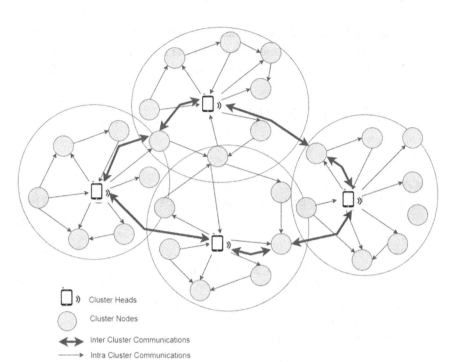

FIGURE 7.2   IoT device management in large network and scheme of transferring secure key.

heads depends on the participating nodes of the network. However, the cluster head communicates and asks for the shortest path only to the authenticated list of nodes. Each head circulates the authenticated list to the authenticated nodes (IoT devices) of its cluster, as shown in Figure 7.2.

- **Communication of Cluster Head:** Each cluster head communicates and shares its authenticated list with other cluster heads, so that, if an authenticated node enters another cluster head's network range, its request can be approved by the cluster head.

- **Middle Nodes:** These are nodes that are in the network range of two networks. These middle nodes are used for inter-cluster communication.

- **New Key Generation:** New key = ID of the IoT device given by the cluster head (I) + verified function (f). A (adjustment) = the total number of participating nodes of the complete network% authenticated list of the individual cluster.

- **Notifying Scheme:** In this scheme, if an authenticated scheme finds that the key is not new, it is understood that the node is malicious, and false data is sent to the node, the loss of which carries no weight and effect.

---

### Pseudo Code of the VKS Model

```
Key ()
{
  X=RNG();
  Function(f) = Aproxy(value of node, adjustment, X)
  {
  int apr, node;
  node=X+ node
  New key(nk) = node + adjustment;
  check the authenticated list
  if nk is already in the authenticated list, then
  adjustment++;
  calculate the nk value;
  return nk;
  }
}
New_generate_key(nk, sizeof network)
{
  y=nk % size of network;
  return l;
}
  Enter the value of l in authenticated list of nodes
  l is now a distinguished value for all the nodes
  participating.
At each device:
  verification(l)
     {
         Verify the l with the log table given by
         admin.
         If l matches the value in the authenticated
         nodes list, then
         Send a success message to the participating
         node
     else {
     Discard the device
  }
}
```

---

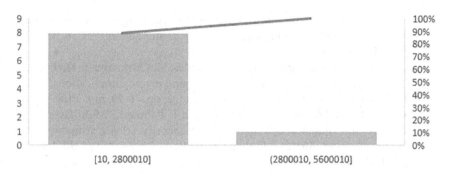

FIGURE 7.3   Traffic flow level vs. detection accuracy.

## 7.4 RESULTS AND DISCUSSION

The experiments were conducted in the Cooja simulator, which works well with Java 8. It requires Ubuntu (32-bit) as an operating system. A minimum ram of 2 GB, a processor of 2.5 GHz and Contiki-2 were taken as the setting of the simulator. In our simulation, we have used the network, simulation control, notes, mote output and timeline tools of Cooja.

Simulation was carried out taking more than two networks, and the number of packets was changed every time in each simulation. Packets vary from 10 to 500,000, as shown in Figure 7.3.

## 7.5 CONCLUSION AND FUTURE SCOPE

The VKS model is suggested for avoiding malicious routing of IoT devices and DDOS attacks. Key verification and new key generation protect against not only malicious against other vulnerabilities. The model is verified with the Cooja simulator, and pseudocode is provided in this chapter.

## REFERENCES

[1] M. S. Rahman, A. Basu, T. Nakamura, H. Takasaki, and S. Kiyomoto, "PPM: Privacy policy manager for home energy management system," *J. Wireless Mobility Network, Ubiquitous Computing Dependable Applications*, vol. 9, no. 2, pp. 42–56, 2018.

[2] D. Shin, V. Sharma, J. Kim, S. Kwon, and I. You, "Secure and efficient protocol for route optimization in PMIPv6-based smart home IoT networks," *IEEE Access*, vol. 5, pp. 11100–11117, 2017.

[3] B.-C. Chifor, I. Bica, V.-V. Patriciu, and F. Pop, "A security authorization scheme for smart home Internet of Things devices," *Future Generation Computer Systems*, vol. 86, pp. 740–749, Sep. 2018.

[4] A. Jacobsson, M. Boldt, and B. Carlsson, "A risk analysis of a smart home automation system," *Future Generation Computer System*, vol. 56, pp. 719–733, Mar. 2016.

[5] V. Sivaraman, H. Gharakheili, C. Fernandes, N. Clark, and T. Karliychuk, "Smart IoT devices in the home: Security and privacy implications," *IEEE Technology & Society. Magazine*, vol. 37, no. 2, pp. 71–79, Jun. 2018.

[6] M. Tao, J. Zuo, Z. Liu, A. Castiglione, and F. Palmieri, "Multi-layer cloud architectural model and ontology-based security service framework for IoT-based smart homes," *Future Generation Computer System*, vol. 78, pp. 1040–1051, Jan. 2018.

[7] A. Jacobsson and P. Davidsson, "Towards a model of privacy and security for smart homes," in *Proc. IᴱᴱE 2nd World Forum Internet Things*, Milan, Italy, pp. 727–732, Dec. 2015.

[8] J. C. S. Sicato, P. K. Sharma, V. Loia, and J. H. Park, "VPN filter malware analysis on cyber threat in smart home Network," *Applied Sciences*, vol. 9, no. 13, p. 2763, 2019.

[9] S. Chhabra and A. K. Singh, "Secure VM allocation scheme to preserve against co-resident threat," *International Journal of Web Engineering and Technology*, vol. 15, no. 1, pp. 96–115, 2020.

[10] B. Ali and A. Awad, "Cyber and physical security vulnerability assessment for IoT-based smart homes," *Sensors*, vol. 18, no. 3, p. 817, 2018.

[11] A. Hassan, "Implementation of lightweight cryptographic algorithms in IoT devices and sensor networks," in *Proceedings of the Future Technologies Conference*, Springer, Cham, pp. 130–146, 2023.

[12] A. K. Sangaiah, A. Javadpour, F. Ja'fari, H. Zavieh, and S. M. Khaniabadi, "SALA-IoT: Self-reduced internet of things with learning automaton sleep scheduling algorithm," *IEEE Sensors Journal*, http://dx.doi.org/10.1109/JSEN.2023.3242759.

[13] D. Airehrour, J. A. Gutierrez, and S. K. Ray, "SecTrust-RPL: A secure trust-aware RPL routing protocol for Internet of Things," *Future Generation Computer Systems*, vol. 93, pp. 860–876, 2019.

[14] S. Chhabra and A. K. Singh, "Security enhancement in cloud environment using secure secret key sharing," *Journal of Communication Software and Systems*, vol. 16, no. 3, pp. 296–306, 2020.

[15] A. O. Bang, U. P. Rao, P. Kaliyar, and M. Conti, "Assessment of routing attacks and mitigation techniques with RPL control messages: A survey," *ACM Computing Surveys (CSUR)*, vol. 55, no. 2, pp. 1–36, 2022.

[16] S. Chhabra and A. K. Singh, "Beyond lightning: A systematic review of information security in the age of cloud computing using key management," *International Journal of Computer Engineering and Applications*, vol. XI, no. XII, 10 Jan. 2018.

[17] N. Kshetri, "Can blockchain strengthen the Internet of Things?" *IT Professional*, vol. 19, no. 4, pp. 68–72, 2017.

[18] W. Wang, P. Xu, and L. T. Yang, "Secure data collection, storage and access in cloud-assisted IoT," *IEEE Cloud Computing*, vol. 5, no. 4, pp. 77–88, Jul. 2018.

[19] S. Suhail, C. S. Hong, Z. U. Ahmad, F. Zafar, and A. Khan, "Introducing secure provenance in IoT: Requirements and challenges," in *Proc. Int. Workshop Secure Internet Things (SIoT)*, pp. 39–46, Sep. 2016.

[20] S. Gali and V. Nidumolu, "An intelligent trust sensing scheme with meta-heuristic based secure routing protocol for Internet of Things," *Cluster Computing*, vol. 25, no. 3, pp. 1779–1789, 2022.

[21] L. Xiao, X. Wan, X. Lu, Y. Zhang, and D. Wu, "IoT security techniques based on machine learning: How do IoT devices use AI to enhance security?" *IEEE Signal Processing Magazine*, vol. 35, no. 5, pp. 41–49, Sep. 2018.

[22] B. Rakesh, "Novel authentication and secure trust based RPL routing in mobile sink supported Internet of Things," *Cyber-Physical Systems*, vol. 9, no. 1, pp. 43–76, 2023.

[23] A. K. Singh, S. Chhabra, R. Gupta, and D. Saxena, "RCDS: Reliable client detection system for multi-tenant cloud," *SN Computer Science*, pp. 1–14, 2023. Springer.

[24] A. O. Bang, U. P. Rao, P. Kaliyar, and M. Conti, "Assessment of routing attacks and mitigation techniques with RPL control messages: A survey," *ACM Computing Surveys (CSUR)*, vol. 55, no. 2, pp. 1–36, 2022.

[25] A. Seyfollahi, M. Moodi, and A. Ghaffari, "MFO-RPL: A secure RPL-based routing protocol utilizing moth-flame optimizer for the IoT applications," *Computer Standards & Interfaces*, vol. 82, p. 103622, 2022.

[26] G. Savithri, B. K. Mohanta, and M. Kumar Dehury, "A brief overview on security challenges and protocols in Internet of Things application," in *2022 IEEE International IOT, Electronics and Mechatronics Conference (IEMTRONICS)*, Toronto, ON, Canada, pp. 1–7, 2022, http://dx.doi.org/10.1109/IEMTRONICS55184.2022.9795794.

[27] S. Chhabra and A. K. Singh, "A comprehensive vision on cloud computing environment: Emerging challenges and future research directions," *arXiv preprint*, arXiv:2207.07955v1.

[28] C. Ge, W. Susilo, J. Baek, Z. Liu, J. Xia, and L. Fang, "A verifiable and fair attribute-based proxy re-encryption scheme for data sharing in clouds," *IEEE Transactions on Dependable and Secure Computing*, vol. 19, no. 5, pp. 2907–2919, 2021.

[29] Y. Chen, Y. Su, M. Zhang, H. Chai, Y. Wei, and S. Yu, "FedTor: An anonymous framework of federated learning in Internet of Things," *IEEE Internet of Things Journal*, vol. 9, no. 19, pp. 18620–18631, 1 Oct. 2022, http://dx.doi.org/10.1109/JIOT.2022.3162826.

# CHAPTER 8

# Agricultural Applications Using Artificial Intelligence and Computer Vision Technologies

Chitranjan Kumar Rai* and Roop Pahuja

*Department of Instrumentation and Control Engineering, Dr. B. R. Ambedkar National Institute of Technology, Jalandhar, Punjab, India*

## 8.1 INTRODUCTION

Agriculture's position in every country is determined by the quality and quantity of agricultural goods produced. In India, agriculture employs over half of the people but produces just 17.5% of the GDP [1]. Aside from providing employment, the sector also assures global food security. However, climate change, pests and developing infectious diseases jeopardize food security, poverty reduction, agriculture-driven development, crop yields etc. These variables account for a loss of 15–20% of total global production annually [2]. As a result, efficient and modern approaches are required in the agricultural area to address such a significant loss, particularly for disease prevention and control. Detection of plant diseases by visual observation, an intellectually driven procedure that may entail visual misconceptions, biases and mistakes, necessitates

* Corresponding author: chitranjanr.ic.18@nitj.ac.in

DOI: 10.1201/9781003364856-8

extensive human knowledge [3]. Through the use of computational image processing techniques, a new tool can be developed to help farmers identify and prevent diseases in their crops [4]. This technology can also help non-specialists, such as those who are not specialists in agriculture, to monitor and control disease. An image-based system for detecting plant diseases typically consists of five phases: image acquisition, preprocessing, image segmentation, feature selection and extraction, and disease classification [5]. Each stage is equally important and contributes differently to the disease diagnosis process based on the specific symptoms observed on the plant leaves. In order to differentiate infection from other infections that are similar based on distinct symptoms or easily apparent spots/lesions, the feature extraction step is essential in classifying different diseases.

Deep learning approaches, which have evolved from traditional machine learning, are representation learning methods that can automatically identify features from raw data without requiring considerable technical expertise in feature extraction. This benefit makes the techniques versatile for processing images from various agricultural settings. Convolutional neural networks (CNNs) are a popular deep learning method. CNNs are artificial neural networks that use mathematical operations and connection patterns. This includes convolution, initialization, pooling, activation, full connection etc. The increasing number of publicly available deep learning datasets and the availability of high-quality graphics processing units (GPUs) are some of the factors that have contributed to the development of deep learning techniques.

Furthermore, the advancement of transfer learning and the emergence of powerful frameworks such as TensorFlow, PyTorch, Theano and others are breaking down barriers between computer science and other sciences, including agriculture science. As a result, CNN techniques are increasingly being used in agricultural applications. Although the number of CNN applications being used in the agricultural sector has increased, the current state of these systems is not considered to be thoroughly analyzed. This means that the development and optimization of these systems remain unanswered. Although previous investigators have looked into the use of CNN-based machine vision technology in various applications, such as image classification, object detection, and semantic segmentation, they have not focused on the development of these systems for agriculture. Some studies have focused on using CNN-based systems in animal farming and plant disease detection, but none have focused on developing systems for entire agricultural applications. This study aims to review and investigate the various aspects of CNN-based computer vision systems used in agriculture.

## 8.2 COMPUTER VISION

Today's technological and innovative era is changing our lives rapidly. The potential of such technology is far beyond our wildest dreams. The introduction of modern technology like computer vision is making a significant contribution in all fields. Among various sectors, agriculture is the one that has started using computer vision in its style of operation. Every country stands out in the global market because of its agriculture industry, which is considered a boosting economy sector. Countries with abundant production dominate the export market. However, many countries have high labor costs, underdeveloped manufacturing processes, and a lack of automation, which increases the cost of goods produced.

Humans interpret the real world by using brain-processed vision to understand their environment. Computer vision is a field of computer science that uses computer systems or machines to achieve comparable results. As the world becomes more human, the sub-branch of computer vision seeks to educate computers in order to comprehend and understand the visual environment. With computer vision, computers can evaluate a series of images or videos and derive accurate item identification from them. The science of computer vision is making inroads into agriculture. Computer vision has pervaded the entire functioning of the agricultural sector, from increasing production through automation to cheaper production costs. With its automation and detection capabilities, computer vision has started to develop a stronghold in agriculture. Artificial intelligence is one of the most recent agricultural breakthroughs. Agriculture is rapidly going digital thanks to drones, robots, sensors, algorithms and machine learning. Thanks to the digital tools we use, we can quickly collect vast amounts of data and truly optimize crop care procedures on a daily basis.

### 8.2.1 Potential Applications of Computer Vision in Agriculture

Computer vision–artificial intelligence models have significantly contributed to the agricultural industry in areas such as quality analysis of seed and soil, irrigation management, weeding, plant disease detection, yield estimation, livestock farming etc. Some of the most notable contributions, as shown in Figure 8.1, that exist now are discussed next.

FIGURE 8.1  Applications of computer vision in agriculture.

### 8.2.1.1  Seed Quality Analysis

The primary objective of the commercial seed business is to make available seeds of appropriate quality at the right time, in the right quantity, and to the right farmers. In addition to being a time-consuming and tedious process, separating poor-quality seeds from best-quality seeds requires specialized equipment, an established infrastructure and significant amounts of time. By collecting morphological information from the seed lot, computer vision technologies can help increase the seed lot's quality. This process can then be used to assess seed development. Deep learning has primarily addressed the performance problems of classical computer vision, resulting in the widespread use of seed variety recognition. SeedSortNet, developed by Li et al. for seed sorting of maize and sunflower plants using the computer vision CNN model, showed promising results with an accuracy of 97.33% and 99.56%, respectively [6]. Taheri-Garavand et al. built a modified VGG16 model for automated chickpea variety identification using seed images [7]. Zhao et al. used seven models to detect surface flaws on seeds to increase breeding yield [8]. For the soybean datasets, the MobileNet-V2 model demonstrated good detection accuracy. Numerous studies have been conducted on the use of computer vision models in the seed business. These models have greatly improved seed business automation capabilities.

### 8.2.1.2 Soil Analysis and Irrigation Management

The primary focus of soil and irrigation management in agriculture is to maintain and enhance dynamic soil properties in order to increase crop yield [9]. The standard procedure for determining soil texture involves collecting soil samples, taking them to a laboratory, and then drying, crushing, and filtering the results before use. In recent years, there has been a significant increase in image processing performance and developments in the methods used to capture images. As a result, computer-vision-based image analysis methods have attracted much attention in various fields, including soil and irrigation science. This technique uses cameras to acquire images of the soil, which are then analyzed using simple software on a computer. Zhang et al. designed a soil texture classification method using wavelet transform techniques that differentiate different soil types [10]. Thus it is important to use computer vision technologies to integrate and utilize automated agricultural production management, crop irrigation and yield estimation. Zhang et al. identified and monitored central pivot irrigation systems using a CNN method for irrigation water distribution [11]. Kamyshova et al. offered a computer vision-based technology for optimizing crop watering using a phyto indicator system in low latency mode [12]. The research also provided an algorithm-based method for producing a maize irrigation map.

### 8.2.1.3 Weed Detection

Weeds are plants that are considered to be harmful in agriculture because they compete with crops for water and other nutrients available in the soil. Spraying pesticides where weeds are found decreases the danger of contamination to crops, people, animals and water resources. The intelligent identification and control of weeds are crucial to agricultural progress. Methods for detecting weeds in the field mainly involve computer vision technologies, such as standard image processing and deep learning

[13, 14]. But as computing power improves, deep learning algorithms like AlexNet, VGGNet, ResNet and others can use their enhanced ability to express image data to get more information about weeds' spatial and semantic features. This avoids the problems with traditional methods of feature extraction.

### 8.2.1.4 Crop Health Monitoring and Disease Detection

Advances in deep learning and computer vision have brought new, promising approaches to assessing the overall health status of crops. An intelligent decision support system for managing panic conditions and eliminating critical losses will eventually be able to quickly identify crop diseases, water stress and nutritional deficiencies, improving crop quality. Drones have become an essential component in precision agriculture and farming. The growing popularity of drone technology has led to a significant increase in the market for these types of aircraft. With their ability to fly and cover substantial distances, drones can collect massive amounts of data using an already installed camera. Due to the increase in public image datasets, such as PlantVillage and PlantDoc [15, 16], researchers have made various deep-learning models for crop health monitoring and disease detection [17, 18]. Various researchers have used the PlantVillage dataset extensively to address the challenges of disease identification using deep learning [19–22]. Several other studies show that pretrained models can identify diseases early and accurately using performance matrices such as accuracy, recall, precision, F1 score etc. [19, 23, 24]. It is important to note that it took some research to find out where the disease spots were that gave accurate information about diseases [18, 25, 26]. Several additional publications presented findings from their investigation into using deep-learning-based computer vision to detect water stress and crop nutritional deficiencies. Compared with manual operation, real-time crop growth monitoring and estimating eaten leaf area using computer vision technology can identify small changes in crops due to malnutrition and provide a solid and accurate basis for prompt management [27, 28]. These studies have resulted in productive steps toward achieving agriculture that is free of disease.

### 8.2.1.5 Computer Vision Systems in Livestock Farming

So far, we have concentrated on plants and crops, but agriculture is much more than maize, wheat, tomatoes and apples. Animals are another essential component of our agricultural systems and need more surveillance

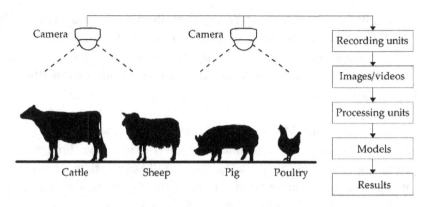

FIGURE 8.2 Schematic drawing of a computer vision system for monitoring animals [30].

than plants. The livestock market is one industry that makes extensive use of artificial intelligence. Through 2026, it is anticipated that investments in artificial intelligence will expand rapidly, with computer vision predicted to account for the most significant portion of this industry [29]. Figure 8.2 depicts the key components of a computer vision system, which comprise cameras, recording devices, processing units and models. Animals (e.g., cattle, sheep, pigs, poultry etc.) are watched in a computer vision system application by cameras set in permanent areas such as ceilings and corridors [30]. The new research was undertaken on a computer vision and deep learning system to monitor dairy cows with precision and real-time data. The algorithm effectively detected cows based on pelt patterns, assessed their location, comprehended the cows' activities and monitored mobility [31]. There have been many recent studies on the potential of noninvasive computer vision technologies for recognizing cattle behavior and found that computer vision systems are gradually replacing conventional direct observation methods [32].

### 8.2.1.6 Yield Estimation

Crop yield estimation and yield mapping are two essential processes in precision agriculture. This helps farmers use their available resources more effectively and gain access to more accurate representations of their fields. Farmers with accurate production estimates can more effectively manage their crop logistics, crop storage, and sales and account for losses. Farmers and other stakeholders must have the necessary yield estimation tools to make informed decisions about postharvest planning [33]. According to several research works, yield estimation using deep learning on image datasets outperforms conventional techniques. Unmanned aerial vehicle (UAV) images may provide a low-cost solution for obtaining high-precision remote data. Sanches et al. used datasets obtained from UAVs to estimate the potential of UAVs and to predict sugarcane field yields [34]. To estimate soybean production, You et al. used a mixture of CNNs and RNNs based on distant sensory images [35]. Another study by Russello used satellite images in conjunction with CNN to predict crop productivity [36]. Computer vision methods are more straightforward for orchard crops such as citrus, where estimations are made by counting the number of fruits before harvesting [37].

## 8.3 CONVOLUTIONAL NEURAL NETWORK ARCHITECTURE

CNN is a type of multilayer network that is helpful for finding patterns in images. CNNs generally have three layers: a convolutional layer, a pooling layer and a fully connected layer, as shown in Figure 8.3. The convolutional layer is the first layer used to extract essential features from the input images. The purpose of the pooling layer is to reduce the size of the feature map extracted after convolution and thereby to reduce the computational cost and estimation time. The fully connected layer consists of weights and biases and is usually placed before the output layer. Neurons in this layer have full connectivity, which helps map the representation between the input and the output.

This section summarizes and organizes several CNN architectures used for agricultural applications in the context of different computer vision tasks. Figure 8.4 depicts three different CNN architectures used to detect diseases in plant images. It should be noted that the CNN architectures

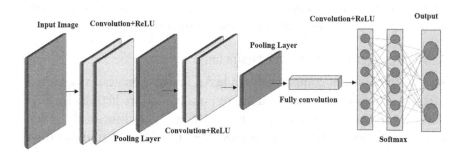

FIGURE 8.3   Architecture of convolution neural networks.

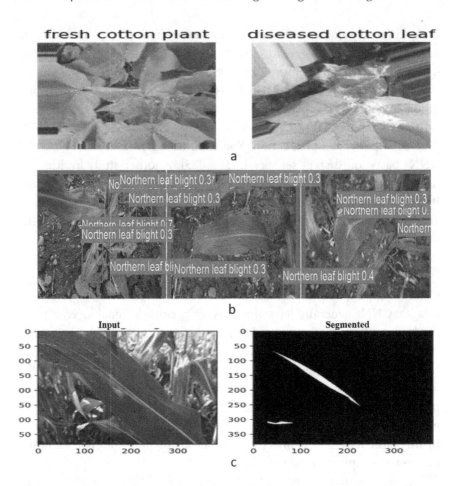

FIGURE 8.4   Illustration of three application computer vision tasks: (A) image classification, (B) object detection, and (C) semantic segmentation.

presented in the next section are not restricted. Other, more complex network configurations have not been used in farming.

## 8.3.1 Architecture for Image Classification

Among the different computer vision tasks, image classification architectures are the most common and are responsible for predicting classes of images. Early researchers investigated CNNs using feed-forward connections and shallow networks (e.g., AlexNet and LeNet) and found that these networks would not generalize well to some problematic issues [38, 39]. As a result, several convolutional layers were added to create extremely deep

TABLE 8.1    Convolutional Neural Network Architectures for Image Classification

| References | Objective and Application | Crop/Livestock | Year | Models Architecture | Accuracy |
|---|---|---|---|---|---|
| [44] | Weed classification | Maize, wheat, sugar beet | 2018 | AlexNet and VGGNet | 98.23% |
| [45] | Disease identification | Grape | 2022 | DeepLabV3 | 97.75% |
| [46] | Irrigation efficiency | Sunflower | 2022 | SFAO-Deep CNN | 92% |
| [47] | Seed classification | — | 2020 | VGG16 | 99.9% |
| [48] | Cattle vocal classification and livestock monitoring | Cattle | 2021 | CNN (author defined) | 81.96% |
| [49] | Cotton disease classification | Cotton | 2023 | Modified AlexNet | 97.98% |
| [50] | Fruit classification | Fruits | 2023 | XGBoost | 98.30% |

networks to boost performance (e.g., VGG16, ResNet50, InceptionV2, etc.) [24, 40–42]. Several novel ideas were proposed to improve computational efficiency (e.g., GoogLeNet, MobileNet) [17, 43]. The two most common architectures utilized for image classification agricultural applications were ResNet50 and VGG16. The former may be the best model for balancing processing speed and detection accuracy, making it popular. The latter was a well-known and early accurate model for handling large image datasets. A single network may sometimes fail to correctly classify images from complex agricultural landscapes. It is necessary to use multiple models to increase performance. In the combination of models, CNN is typically used as the first stage to pull out features, which other models then use to classify the images. Table 8.1 summarizes some of the research in this field.

## 8.3.2 Architecture for Object Detection

Object detection is a key in computer vision that focuses on classifying and localizing objects in video and images. Object detection architectures are composed of different types of networks, such as fast detection networks, shortcut connection networks and region-based networks. The first group mainly includes the single shot detector (SSD) family and the YOLO family [26, 51, 52]. The second group includes a two-stage object detector architecture (such as R-CNN, Fast-RCNN, Faster-RCNN, Mask-RCNN and others) that extracts regions of interest and then classifies objects using classifiers [22, 26, 53, 54]. These networks are effective from various perspectives, such as processing speed or accuracy. They are widely used in

TABLE 8.2    Convolutional Neural Network Architectures for Object Detection

| References | Objective and Application | Crop/Livestock | Year | Models Architecture | Accuracy |
| --- | --- | --- | --- | --- | --- |
| [57] | Yield prediction | Strawberry | 2019 | Faster RCNN model CNN | 84.1% |
| [58] | Automated muzzle detection and identification | Cattle | 2021 | YOLOv3-ResNet50 | 99.13% |
| [59] | Weed detection | Soyabean | 2020 | SSD, Faster R-CNN | 85% |
| [60] | Citrus disease detection | Citrus | 2022 | Two-stage deep-CNN | 94.37% |
| [61] | Seed grading | Corn | 2019 | Deep CNN | 98.2% |
| [62] | Plant health detection | Bell pepper and potato leaves | 2023 | YOLOv5 | 93% |
| [63] | Animal detection and counting | Deer | 2023 | YOLOv4 | 70.45% |

various agricultural applications. Most of them were used, but SSD, YOLO V3 and the faster R-CNN were used the most [41, 55, 56]. That's because the SSD and YOLO V3 were faster at processing, while the faster R-CNN was better at balancing speed and accuracy. Table 8.2 lists the earlier research on computer vision technologies using CNN for object detection.

### 8.3.3 Architecture for Semantic/Instance Segmentation

Image segmentation is a method used in computer vision that works at the pixel level to determine what a given image contains. Image recognition, which assigns one or more labels to a whole image, and object detection, which finds items inside an image by drawing a bounding box around them, are distinct from this process. Image recognition labels an entire image with one or more labels. The process of image segmentation provides information about the contents of a more granular image. Encoders and decoders are standard components of semantic models. Encoders are responsible for converting images into high-level semantics, while decoders are responsible for converting high-level semantics into interpretable images. In both cases, only the areas of interest are retained. Instance segmentation models are developed more slowly than semantic segmentation models because they need more computer resources and may be inefficient for real-time processing. Current instance segmentation methods have better accuracy than semantic segmentation models, regardless of processing speed. One widely used model, for instance segmentation, was

TABLE 8.3    Convolutional Neural Network Architectures for Image Segmentation

| References | Objective and Application | Crop/Livestock | Year | Models Architecture | Accuracy |
|---|---|---|---|---|---|
| [68] | Identifying irrigation system problems | — | 2020 | Mask R-CNN | — |
| [69] | Cattle segmentation | Cattle | 2019 | Mask R-CNN | 92% |
| [70] | Weed segmentation | Sugarbeet | 2020 | res-UNet | 98.3% |
| [71] | Livestock classification | Cattle | 2020 | Mask RCNN | 96% |
| [72] | Crop disease quantification | Corn | 2023 | DeepLabV3+ | 96% |
| [73] | Plant lesion segmentation | Potato, tomato | 2022 | CANet | 92% |
| [74] | Leaf disease segmentation | Tomato | 2022 | DS-DETR | 96.40% |

the mask R-CNN, which simultaneously carried out object classification, object detection and instance segmentation [64, 65]. This model was quite successful. Agricultural applications often use DeepLab, UNet and Mask R-CNN because of their efficient designs and performance [66, 67]. Some of the earlier work in image segmentation utilizing deep learning computer vision is summarized in Table 8.3.

## 8.4 ANALYSIS OF COMPUTER VISION TECHNOLOGY IN AGRICULTURE

Agriculture is the basis of contemporary human civilization and is vital to human life. As an emerging technology, computer vision technology paired with artificial intelligence algorithms for computer vision solutions will become essential for enhancing agricultural productivity and offer broad prospects in future agricultural applications and research. For automation and robotic farming, computer vision technology will be more effectively used in agriculture. Computer visual intelligence technology is applied in several areas of agricultural automation production management, including crop automation, growth monitoring, disease control, fruit picking and others. To further ensure agricultural productivity, quality and food security, computer vision technology will be used more broadly to solve existing agricultural issues. Future agricultural productivity, quality and economic growth will all benefit from the application of computer vision technology, which will also encourage the improvement of agriculture's production, efficiency, quality, ecology, safety and intelligence.

### 8.4.1 Benefits of Computer Vision in Agriculture

Despite the slow progress in digitization in the agriculture industry, the practical implementation of deep-learning-based artificial intelligence systems has gained significant momentum. Applications that use computer vision to identify diseases combine the knowledge of genetic resources with that of artificial intelligence. This enables farmers and extension workers to respond swiftly and save the crop.

- A deep learning-based computer vision system can be used to automate various tasks, such as plant health monitoring and weed detection. It can also be used to improve the efficiency of livestock management.

- Deep learning using computer vision techniques, UAV data and spectral information can aid in the development of more sophisticated intelligent systems.

- Despite the advantages of deep learning and computer vision, many challenges remain. Some of these include data quality issues and computation power requirements.

- The increasing automation in various agricultural activities is expected to continue attracting the interest of researchers in deep learning.

### 8.4.2 Challenges Faced by Computer Vision in the Field of Agriculture

Due to the rapid emergence of artificial intelligence, computer vision technology is expected to be widely used in the automation of agricultural production. However, it is also being used to manage individual crop production. Despite the technological advances in agriculture, computer vision technology still has a long way to go before it becomes widely used.

- Currently, there is a lack of comprehensive databases that can provide information about the agriculture sector. This is because the data collected during the development of research programs is not uniform and does not reflect the actual state of the agricultural industry. For example, computer vision systems can only identify a specific insect species when used for quality inspection. They do not yet apply to other agricultural field operations that manage and prevent diseases and pests.

- In addition to the databases and applications that need to be expanded, researchers have also discovered other issues that could affect the quality of the data collected. Some of these include poor response times for environmental systems and delays in image gathering.

- Computer vision technology is a field of study that involves the development of various computer-related technologies, such as artificial intelligence and pattern recognition. Some of the technical achievements in this area require much professional expertise. More practitioners and professionals will be needed if the technology is used in agricultural automation.

- Computer vision technology must fill many challenges and complementary gaps in agricultural automation. This technology is greatly needed for various capabilities in education and training, application promotion or scientific research.

- When using computer vision technology, the issue's unique characteristics must be considered to choose the appropriate image capture, processing and classification algorithms. This is necessary to ensure accurate results. When it comes to putting computer vision techniques into practice, no standard method or approach is invariably used.

## 8.5 CONCLUSION

The Indian economy is an agro-economy that is heavily reliant on agriculture. The agricultural sector supports not only the Indian economy but also the industrial sector and international commerce in imports and exports. Despite the fact that the agricultural sector's contribution to the Indian economy is decreasing, it is the sector with the most significant number of people employed across the nation. The impact of artificial intelligence across disciplines is growing all the time. Deep learning models are becoming more intelligent, and they can perform complicated jobs with ease. Agriculture is a sector that may benefit significantly from technological advancements. With some nations failing to satisfy demand and supply needs, it is critical to use technology to improve manufacturing and overall efficiency. Computer vision is making good progress in agriculture. Although there are hurdles, as with any technology on the market, AI-powered computer vision services must solve the relevant issues before the technology is fully adopted. Before using such modern technology, there are various considerations to consider. However, technological breakthroughs and upheavals are ushering us into a digital world. It is advisable to remain optimistic in order to maximize agricultural production using futuristic technology.

## REFERENCES

[1] Ministry of Agriculture & Farmers Welfare: *GoI: Annual report 2018–19*. Ministry of Agriculture & Farmers Welfare. 1–224 (2018).

[2] Deshpande, T.: State of agriculture in India. *PRS Legislative Research*. 1–29 (2017).

[3] Vishnoi, V.K., Kumar, K., Kumar, B.: *A comprehensive study of feature extraction techniques for plant leaf disease detection*. Springer (2021).

[4] Prasad, S., Kumar, P., Hazra, R., Kumar, A.: Plant leaf disease detection using Gabor wavelet transform. *Lecture Notes in Computer Science* (Including Subseries Lecture Notes in Artificial Intelligence and Lecture Notes in Bioinformatics). 7677 LNCS, 372–379 (2012). https://doi.org/10.1007/978-3-642-35380-2_44.

[5] Rai, C.K., Pahuja, R., Chabbra, J.K.: Implementation of virtual instrumentation system for estimation of eaten leaf area using digital image processing. *International Conference on Image Information Processing (ICIIP)*. 472–476 (2022). https://doi.org/10.1109/iciip53038.2021.9702652.

[6] Li, C., Li, H., Liu, Z., Li, B., Huang, Y.: SeedSortNet: A rapid and highly efficient lightweight CNN based on visual attention for seed sorting. *PeerJ Computer Science*. 7, 1–21 (2021). https://doi.org/10.7717/peerj-cs.639.

[7] Taheri-Garavand, A., Nasiri, A., Fanourakis, D., Fatahi, S., Omid, M., Nikoloudakis, N.: Automated in situ seed variety identification via deep learning: A case study in chickpea. *Plants*. 10 (2021). https://doi.org/10.3390/plants10071406.

[8] Zhao, G., Quan, L., Li, H., Feng, H., Li, S., Zhang, S., Liu, R.: Real-time recognition system of soybean seed full-surface defects based on deep learning. *Computers and Electronics in Agriculture*. 187, 106230 (2021). https://doi.org/10.1016/j.compag.2021.106230.

[9] Kushwaha, N., Elbeltagi, A., Mehan, S., Malik, A., Yousuf, A.: Comparative study on morphometric analysis and RUSLE-based approaches for microwatershed prioritization using remote sensing and GIS. *Arabian Journal of Geosciences*. 15 (2022). https://doi.org/10.1007/s12517-022-09837-2.

[10] Zhang, X., Younan, N.H., King, R.L.: Soil texture classification using wavelet transform and maximum likelihood approach. *International Geoscience and Remote Sensing Symposium (IGARSS)*. 4, 2888–2890 (2003).

[11] Zhang, C., Yue, P., Di, L., Wu, Z.: Automatic identification of center pivot irrigation systems from landsat images using convolutional neural networks. *Agriculture (Switzerland).* 8 (2018). https://doi.org/10.3390/agriculture8100147.

[12] Kamyshova, G., Osipov, A., Gataullin, S., Korchagin, S., Ignar, S., Gataullin, T., Terekhova, N., Suvorov, S.: Artificial neural networks and computer vision's-based phytoindication systems for variable rate irrigation improving. *IEEE Access.* 10, 8577–8589 (2022). https://doi.org/10.1109/ACCESS.2022.3143524.

[13] Wang, A., Xu, Y., Wei, X., Cui, B.: Semantic segmentation of crop and weed using an encoder-decoder network and image enhancement method under uncontrolled outdoor illumination. *IEEE Access.* 8, 81724–81734 (2020). https://doi.org/10.1109/ACCESS.2020.2991354.

[14] Krogh Mortensen, A., Dyrmann, M., Karstoft, H., Nyholm Jørgensen, R., Gislum, R.: Semantic segmentation of mixed crops using deep convolutional neural network. *CIGR-AgEng Conference.* 1–6 (2016).

[15] Hughes, D.P., Salathe, M.: An open access repository of images on plant health to enable the development of mobile disease diagnostics. *ArXiv.* (2015). https://doi.org/10.1111/1755-0998.12237.

[16] Singh, D., Jain, N., Jain, P., Kayal, P., Kumawat, S., Batra, N.: PlantDoc: A dataset for visual plant disease detection. *ACM International Conference Proceeding Series.* 249–253 (2020). https://doi.org/10.1145/3371158.3371196.

[17] Zhang, X., Qiao, Y.U.E., Meng, F., Fan, C., Zhang, M.: Identification of maize leaf diseases using improved deep convolutional neural networks. *IEEE Access.* 6, 30370–30377 (2018). https://doi.org/10.1109/ACCESS.2018.2844405.

[18] Ozguven, M.M., Adem, K.: Automatic detection and classification of leaf spot disease in sugar beet using deep learning algorithms. *Physica A: Statistical Mechanics and its Applications.* 535, 122537 (2019). https://doi.org/10.1016/j.physa.2019.122537.

[19] Chen, J., Chen, J., Zhang, D., Sun, Y., Nanehkaran, Y.A.: Using deep transfer learning for image-based plant disease identification. *Computers and Electronics in Agriculture.* 173, 105393 (2020). https://doi.org/10.1016/j.compag.2020.105393.

[20] Hassan, S.M., Maji, A.K., Jasiński, M., Leonowicz, Z., Jasińska, E.: Identification of plant-leaf diseases using cnn and transfer-learning approach. *Electronics (Switzerland).* 10 (2021). https://doi.org/10.3390/electronics10121388.

[21] Ferentinos, K.P.: Deep learning models for plant disease detection and diagnosis. *Computers and Electronics in Agriculture.* 145, 311–318 (2018). https://doi.org/10.1016/j.compag.2018.01.009.

[22] Zhang, Y., Song, C., Zhang, D.: Deep learning-based object detection improvement for tomato disease. *IEEE Access.* 8, 56607–56614 (2020). https://doi.org/10.1109/ACCESS.2020.2982456.

[23] Thangaraj, R., Anandamurugan, S., Kaliappan, V.K.: Automated tomato leaf disease classification using transfer learning-based deep convolution

neural network. *Journal of Plant Diseases and Protection.* 128, 73–86 (2021). https://doi.org/10.1007/s41348-020-00403-0.

[24] Wang, G., Sun, Y., Wang, J.: Automatic image-based plant disease severity estimation using deep learning. *Computational Intelligence and Neuroscience.* 2017 (2017). https://doi.org/10.1155/2017/2917536.

[25] Guo, Y., Zhang, J., Yin, C., Hu, X., Zou, Y., Xue, Z., Wang, W.: Plant disease identification based on deep learning algorithm in smart farming. *Discrete Dynamics in Nature and Society.* 2020 (2020). https://doi.org/10.1155/2020/2479172.

[26] Hammad Saleem, M., Khanchi, S., Potgieter, J., Mahmood Arif, K.: Image-based plant disease identification by deep learning meta-architectures. *Plants.* 9, 1–23 (2020). https://doi.org/10.3390/plants9111451.

[27] Gupta, H., Pahuja, R.: Estimating morphological features of plant growth using machine vision. 10 (2019). https://doi.org/10.4018/IJAEIS.2019070103.

[28] Rai, C.K., Pahuja, R.: Digital image processing-based virtual instruments for the detection and classification of eaten leaves. *Journal of East China University of Science and Technology.* 65, 877–885 (2022). https://doi.org/10.5281/ZENODO.7081544.

[29] *Global artificial intelligence in livestock farming market.* https://www.globenewswire.com/news-release/2021/07/30/2272238/0/en/Global-Artificial-Intelligence-in-Livestock-Farming-Market.html.

[30] Li, G., Huang, Y., Chen, Z., Chesser, G.D., Purswell, J.L., Linhoss, J., Zhao, Y.: Practices and applications of convolutional neural network-based computer vision systems in animal farming: A review. *Sensors.* 21, 1–42 (2021). https://doi.org/10.3390/s21041492.

[31] Tassinari, P., Bovo, M., Benni, S., Franzoni, S., Poggi, M., Mammi, L.M.E., Mattoccia, S., Di Stefano, L., Bonora, F., Barbaresi, A., Santolini, E., Torreggiani, D.: A computer vision approach based on deep learning for the detection of dairy cows in free stall barn. *Computers and Electronics in Agriculture.* 182, 106030 (2021). https://doi.org/10.1016/j.compag.2021.106030.

[32] Rony, M., Barai, D., Riad, Hasan, M.Z.: Cattle external disease classification using deep learning techniques. *20²¹ 12th International Conference on Computing Communication and Networking Technologies, ICCCNT 2021.* (2021). https://doi.org/10.1109/ICCCNT51525.2021.9579662.

[33] Wei, M.C.F., Maldaner, L.F., Ottoni, P.M.N., Molin, J.P.: Carrot yield mapping: A precision agriculture approach based on machine learning. *Ai.* 1, 229–241 (2020). https://doi.org/10.3390/ai1020015.

[34] Sanches, G.M., Duft, D.G., Kölln, O.T., Luciano, A.C. dos, S., De Castro, S.G.Q., Okuno, F.M., Franco, H.C.J.: The potential for RGB images obtained using unmanned aerial vehicle to assess and predict yield in sugarcane fields. *International Journal of Remote Sensing.* 39, 5402–5414 (2018). https://doi.org/10.1080/01431161.2018.1448484.

[35] You, J., Li, X., Low, M., Lobell, D., Ermon, S.: Deep Gaussian process for crop yield prediction based on remote sensing data. *Proceedings of the Thirty-First AAAI Confer- ence on Artificial Intelligence,* AAAI'17 AAAI Press, San Francisco, California, USA. 4559–4565 (2017).

[36] Russello, H.: Convolutional neural networks for crop yield prediction using satellite images. *IBM Centers for Advanced Studies*. (2018).

[37] Dorj, U.O., Lee, M., Yun, S.S.: An yield estimation in citrus orchards via fruit detection and counting using image processing. *Computers and Electronics in Agriculture*. 140, 103–112 (2017). https://doi.org/10.1016/j.compag.2017.05.019.

[38] Krizhevsky, A., Hinton, G.E.: ImageNet classification with deep convolutional neural networks. *NIPS*. 1–9 (2012).

[39] Ahila Priyadharshini, R., Arivazhagan, S., Arun, M., Mirnalini, A.: Maize leaf disease classification using deep convolutional neural networks. *Neural Computing and Applications*. 31, 8887–8895 (2019). https://doi.org/10.1007/s00521-019-04228-3.

[40] Yang, K., Zhong, W., Li, F.: Leaf segmentation and classification with a complicated background using deep learning. *Agronomy*. 10 (2020). https://doi.org/10.3390/agronomy10111721.

[41] Selvaraj, M.G., Vergara, A., Ruiz, H., Safari, N., Elayabalan, S., Ocimati, W., Blomme, G.: AI-powered banana diseases and pest detection. *Plant Methods*. 15, 1–11 (2019). https://doi.org/10.1186/s13007-019-0475-z.

[42] Esgario, J.G.M., Krohling, R.A., Ventura, J.A.: Deep learning for classification and severity estimation of coffee leaf biotic stress. *Computers and Electronics in Agriculture*. 169 (2020). https://doi.org/10.1016/j.compag.2019.105162.

[43] Chen, J., Zhang, D., Nanehkaran, Y.A.: Identifying plant diseases using deep transfer learning and enhanced lightweight network. *Multimedia Tools and Applications*. 79, 31497–31515 (2020). https://doi.org/10.1007/s11042-020-09669-w.

[44] Chavan, T.R., Nandedkar, A.V.: AgroAVNET for crops and weeds classification: A step forward in automatic farming. *Computers and Electronics in Agriculture*. 154, 361–372 (2018). https://doi.org/10.1016/j.compag.2018.09.021.

[45] Ji, M., Wu, Z.: Automatic detection and severity analysis of grape black measles disease based on deep learning and fuzzy logic. *Computers and Electronics in Agriculture*. 193, 106718 (2022). https://doi.org/10.1016/j.compag.2022.106718.

[46] Kumbi, A.A., Birje, M.N.: Deep CNN based sunflower atom optimization method for optimal water control in IoT. *Wireless Personal Communications*. 122, 1221–1246 (2022). https://doi.org/10.1007/s11277-021-08946-7.

[47] Gulzar, Y., Hamid, Y., Soomro, A.B., Alwan, A.A., Journaux, L.: A convolution neural network-based seed classification system. *Symmetry*. 1–29 (2020). https://doi.org/10.3390/sym12122018.

[48] Jung, D.H., Kim, N.Y., Moon, S.H., Jhin, C., Kim, H.J., Yang, J.S., Kim, H.S., Lee, T.S., Lee, J.Y., Park, S.H.: Deep learning-based cattle vocal classification model and real-time livestock monitoring system with noise filtering. *Animals*. 11, 1–16 (2021). https://doi.org/10.3390/ani11020357.

[49] Rai, C.K., Pahuja, R.: Classification of diseased cotton leaves and plants using improved deep convolutional neural network. *Multimedia Tools and*

*Applications.* 1–14 (2023). https://doi.org/10.1007/s11042-023-14933-w.

[50] Alharbi, A.H., Alkhalaf, S., Asiri, Y., Abdel-Khalek, S., Mansour, R.F.: Automated fruit classification using enhanced tunicate swarm algorithm with fusion based deep learning. *Computers and Electrical Engineering.* 108, 108657 (2023). https://doi.org/10.1016/j.compeleceng.2023.108657.

[51] Liu, W., Anguelov, D., Erhan, D., Szegedy, C., Reed, S., Fu, C.Y., Berg, A.C.: SSD: Single shot multibox detector. *Lecture Notes in Computer Science* (Including Subseries Lecture Notes in Artificial Intelligence and Lecture Notes in Bioinformatics). 9905 LNCS, 21–37 (2016). https://doi.org/10.1007/978-3-319-46448-0_2.

[52] Redmon, J., Divvala, S., Girshick, R., Farhadi, A.: You only look once: Unified, real-time object detection. *Proceedings of the IEEE Computer Society Conference on Computer Vision and Pattern Recognition.* 2016-Decem, 779–788 (2016). https://doi.org/10.1109/CVPR.2016.91.

[53] Girshick, R., Donahue, J., Darrell, T., Malik, J.: Region-based convolutional networks for accurate object detection and segmentation. *IEEE Transactions on Pattern Analysis and Machine Intelligence.* 38, 142–158 (2016). https://doi.org/10.1109/TPAMI.2015.2437384.

[54] Masood, M.H., Saim, H., Taj, M., Awais, M.M.: Early disease diagnosis for rice crop. *ICLR.* 1–5 (2020).

[55] Liu, J., Wang, X.: Tomato diseases and pests detection based on improved Yolo V3 convolutional neural network. *Frontiers in Plant Science.* 11, 1–12 (2020). https://doi.org/10.3389/fpls.2020.00898.

[56] Shill, A., Rahman, M.A.: Plant disease detection based on YOLOv3 and YOLOv4.2021. *International Conference on Automation, Control and Mechatronics for Industry 40, ACMI 2021.0.* 8–9 (2021). https://doi.org/10.1109/ACMI53878.2021.9528179.

[57] Chen, Y., Lee, W.S., Gan, H., Peres, N., Fraisse, C., Zhang, Y., He, Y.: Strawberry yield prediction based on a deep neural network using high-resolution aerial orthoimages. *Remote Sensing.* 11, 1–21 (2019). https://doi.org/10.3390/rs11131584.

[58] Shojaeipour, A., Falzon, G., Kwan, P., Hadavi, N., Cowley, F.C., Paul, D.: Automated muzzle detection and biometric identification via few-shot deep transfer learning of mixed breed cattle. *Agronomy.* 11 (2021). https://doi.org/10.3390/agronomy11112365.

[59] Sivakumar, A.N.V., Li, J., Scott, S., Psota, E., Jhala, A.J., Luck, J.D., Shi, Y.: Comparison of object detection and patch-based classification deep learning models on mid-to late-season weed detection in UAV imagery. *Remote Sensing.* 12 (2020). https://doi.org/10.3390/rs12132136.

[60] Syed-Ab-Rahman, S.F., Hesamian, M.H., Prasad, M.: Citrus disease detection and classification using end-to-end anchor-based deep learning model. *Applied Intelligence.* 52, 927–938 (2022). https://doi.org/10.1007/s10489-021-02452-w.

[61] Ni, C., Wang, D., Vinson, R., Holmes, M., Tao, Y.: Automatic inspection machine for maize kernels based on deep convolutional neural networks. *Biosystems Engineering.* 178, 131–144 (2019). https://doi.org/10.1016/j.biosystemseng.2018.11.010.

[62] Khalid, M., Sarfraz, M.S., Iqbal, U., Aftab, M.U., Niedbała, G., Rauf, H.T.: Real-time plant health detection using deep convolutional neural networks. *Agriculture (Switzerland)*. 13, 1–26 (2023). https://doi.org/10.3390/agriculture13020510.

[63] Rančić, K., Blagojević, B., Bezdan, A., Ivošević, B., Tubić, B., Vranešević, M., Pejak, B., Crnojević, V., Marko, O.: Animal detection and counting from UAV images using convolutional neural networks. *Drones*. 7, 179 (2023). https://doi.org/10.3390/drones7030179.

[64] Afzaal, U., Bhattarai, B., Pandeya, Y.R., Lee, J.: An instance segmentation model for strawberry diseases based on Mask R-CNN. *Sensors*. 21 (2021). https://doi.org/10.3390/s21196565.

[65] He, K., Gkioxari, G., Dollár, P., Girshick, R.: Mask R-CNN. *IEEE Transactions on Pattern Analysis and Machine Intelligence*. 42, 386–397 (2020). https://doi.org/10.1109/TPAMI.2018.2844175.

[66] Wang, C., Du, P., Wu, H., Li, J., Zhao, C., Zhu, H.: A cucumber leaf disease severity classification method based on the fusion of DeepLabV3+ and U-Net. *Computers and Electronics in Agriculture*. 189, 106373 (2021). https://doi.org/10.1016/j.compag.2021.106373.

[67] Gowroju, S., Aarti, Kumar, S.: Robust pupil segmentation using UNET and morphological image processing. *2021 International Mobile, Intelligent, and Ubiquitous Computing Conference, MIUCC 2021*. 105–109 (2021). https://doi.org/10.1109/MIUCC52538.2021.9447658.

[68] Albuquerque, C.K.G., Polimante, S., Torre-Neto, A., Prati, R.C.: Water spray detection for smart irrigation systems with Mask R-CNN and UAV footage. *2020 IEEE International Workshop on Metrology for Agriculture and Forestry, MetroAgriFor 2020—Proceedings*. 236–240 (2020). https://doi.org/10.1109/MetroAgriFor50201.2020.9277542.

[69] Qiao, Y., Truman, M., Sukkarieh, S.: Cattle segmentation and contour extraction based on Mask R-CNN for precision livestock farming. *Computers and Electronics in Agriculture*. 165, 104958 (2019). https://doi.org/10.1016/j.compag.2019.104958.

[70] Fawakherji, M., Potena, C., Prevedello, I., Pretto, A., Bloisi, D.D., Nardi, D.: Data augmentation using GANs for crop/weed segmentation in precision farming. *CCTA 2020—4th IEEE Conference on Control Technology and Applications*. 279–284 (2020). https://doi.org/10.1109/CCTA41146.2020.9206297.

[71] Xu, B., Wang, W., Falzon, G., Kwan, P., Guo, L., Sun, Z., Li, C.: Livestock classification and counting in quadcopter aerial images using Mask R-CNN. *International Journal of Remote Sensing*. 41, 8121–8142 (2020). https://doi.org/10.1080/01431161.2020.1734245.

[72] Divyanth, L.G., Ahmad, A., Saraswat, D.: A two-stage deep-learning based segmentation model for crop disease quantification based on corn field imagery. *Smart Agricultural Technology*. 3, 100108 (2023). https://doi.org/10.1016/j.atech.2022.100108.

[73] Shoaib, M., Shah, B., Hussain, T., Ali, A., Ullah, A., Alenezi, F., Gechev, T., Ali, F., Syed, I.: A deep learning-based model for plant lesion segmentation,

subtype identification, and survival probability estimation. *Frontiers in Plant Science.* 13, 1–15 (2022). https://doi.org/10.3389/fpls.2022.1095547.

[74] Wu, J., Wen, C., Chen, H., Ma, Z., Zhang, T., Su, H., Yang, C.: DS-DETR: A model for tomato leaf disease segmentation and damage evaluation. *Agronomy.* 12, 1–16 (2022). https://doi.org/10.3390/agronomy12092023.

# CHAPTER 9

# Artificial Intelligence-Based Smart Identification System Using Herbal Images

## Decision Making Using Various Machine Learning Models

Sanyam Sharma,[1,2] Subh Naman,[1,3] Jayesh Dwivedi[2] and Ashish Baldi[1*]

1 Pharma Innovation Lab, Department of Pharmaceutical Sciences and Technology, Maharaja Ranjit Singh Punjab Technical University, Bathinda, 15001, Punjab

2 Pacific Academy of Higher Education and Research University, Udaipur, Rajasthan

3 School of Pharmaceutical Sciences, CT University, Ferozepur Road, Ludhiana

## 9.1 INTRODUCTION

Ayurveda, the oldest and most conventional practice of Indian medicine, is essential for establishing specialized remedies and therapies. Drugs used in ayurveda are made of botanical ingredients and substances from

* Corresponding author: +91–8968423848, baldiashish@gmail.com

DOI: 10.1201/9781003364856-9

animals, metals or minerals. India is a rich source of traditional medicines and medicinal herbs, making it an ideal place to look for new ones. Contemplate ayurveda is an Indian traditional medical system that is still utilized today due to its effectiveness in treating a variety of disorders holistically. It emphasizes total unification of consciousness, mind, body and soul [1, 2].

Herbs differ from other plants in their color, texture, and odor. Herb identification is typically done using organoleptic techniques, which mainly rely on botanists. Based only on their unique characters, distinct herb species belonging to the same family are become harder to distinguish as a result of their identical physical characteristics. Contrary to humans, artificial-intelligence-assisted technology is supposed to be able to accurately distinguish various species [3].

Bioactive substances such as phenolics, anthocyanins, carotenoids and tocopherols can be derived through aromatic and medicinal plants with multiple therapeutic benefits and pharmacological effects [4]. However, just like other plant recognition, the work of physically recognizing medicinal and aromatic plants is challenging and time-consuming due to the inaccessibility of expert opinions. Many automatic plant or leaf recognition systems have been developed as a result of these issues, with the majority of them using machine learning techniques [5–7].

A branch of computer science called "artificial intelligence" aims to give machines additional intelligence. Learning is one of the fundamental prerequisites for any cognitive conduct. Most scientists today concur that intellect cannot exist without learning. Therefore, machine learning (ML) is one of the main subfields of artificial intelligence (AI) study and is really one of the fastest growing areas of the research [8]. Artificial intelligence was used by the system to start learning that anticipates new objects after learning based on previously trained/learned experience. It learns by extracting features, referring to particular quantifiable characteristics like more illuminating and exclusionary features [9]. Figure 9.1 depicts the basic steps of identification through machine learning models.

## 9.2 PRIOR ART

A mobile application called "MedLeaf" was developed by Laxmi and authors to help identify Indonesian plants based on their leaves. The feature extraction from the leaves from the library of 3502 photos from the 85 distinct species

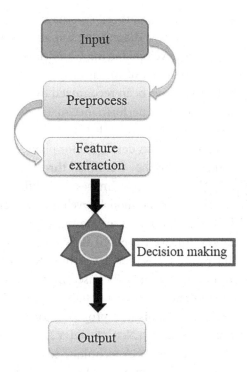

FIGURE 9.1  Workflow of machine learning models.

of Indonesian plants used geometrical characteristics and LBP. This model was developed using a PNN classifier. The accuracy of using a composite of features (85%) was shown to be superior to using a single feature alone [10].

By analyzing the photos of the leaves, Culman and coauthors developed an automated program for identifying nutrient deficiencies in oil palm plants. To create the datasets, they used 52 tagged photos of palm oil plant leaves. The datasets were then separated in a ratio of 6:1:2 into three categories: training datasets, model selection datasets, and test datasets. The development identification model has been used with ANN classification approaches. The performance matrices that the authors utilized to evaluate the effectiveness of the identification model included recall, precision, F1 score and accuracy. The authors came to the conclusion that the constructed model produced positive results in the performance metric tests. For improved use of the developed identification model, an android application has also been created based on this model [11].

Based on photographs of the tomato leaves, Elhassouny and Smarandache developed an automated tool for diagnosing tomato diseases. This identification model, which was developed using CNN classification techniques and was trained on 7176 photos of tomato leaves, was created. Ten distinct tomato plant diseases have been recognized by the model. Accuracy, the average loss curve and other performance matrices were used, and the results were reported to be satisfactory [12].

A mobile-based application was developed for plant leaf identification by Akiyama and coworkers where they examined three CNN models, namely MobileNetV2, Mobile Net and VGG19. Images of 33 different categories were used to build the database for the model development. For comparing the three CNN models, various performance metrics including F1 score, dropout rate and calculation time were used. In all performance metrics, authors found that the MobileNetV2 CNN model was the best of the three [13].

Tang and his group proposed a CNN-based model for diagnosing grape diseases. A unique technique comprised of lightweight CNN and the channel-wise attention (CA) mechanism is proposed for tiny and low-latency models. The backbones are ShuffleNet V1 and V2, with squeeze-and-excitation (SE) blocks employed as a CA technique to improve the ShuffleNet design. The proposed model is supported by an available dataset of 4062 photographs of grape leaves divided into four classes—three healthy and one diseased class. The experiments' findings demonstrated that the suggested technique has been successful and accurate to an acceptable degree [14].

On the basis of a leaf analysis, Yang and Guo compared various ML models for the diagnosis of plant disease. The authors came to the conclusion that machine learning models are a crucial and effective technique for obtaining results that can be verified quickly after analyzing a significant quantity of data [15].

Ferentinos presented a deep CNN model for disease identification of plants through analysis of leaves of plants. The training and development of the model was done on a freely available database of approximately 89,000 images. The photographs in the database consists of both types of images, i.e., in laboratory setting and under original cultivation conditions. Results of the developed model showed an accuracy of 99.71% with VGG CNN techniques [16].

De Luna and co-workers proposed an automatic system for the identification of plants of the Philippine region. Datasets were created from 12 different species of herbal plants. The ANN-based neural network was utilized for the development of this automated system for identification.

For training the datasets, 50 images were used. The datasets were trained with the developed neural network with the aid of Python and reached an accuracy of 98.16% identification of whole datasets. For testing the datasets, about 72 sample images were utilized. The trained neural network with the help of MATLAB® achieved an accuracy of 98.61% in identification of an unknown sample [17].

On datasets related to plants, Joseph and colleagues did a comparison study of a few traditional features extracted and deep CNN approaches. The HOG feature descriptor combined with KNN and the HOG-BOW mixed with SVM and MLP classifiers were contrasted against AlexNet and GoogleNet, respectively trained at scratch as well as utilizing fine-tuned variations as deep CNN architectures. Three plant-datasets-based picture identification systems were tested and found that they performed admirably. The authors came to the conclusion that enhanced deep CNN architectures routinely outperform conventional feature descriptor methods [18].

Based on the analysis of leaf pictures taken in their natural habitat, which can be subjected to a variety of lighting conditions and complex backgrounds, Putzu and coauthors presented a mobile app for the computerized identification of plant species. The main goal of this research was to construct and design a system that could recognize and segment the target leaf automatically. It is focused on saliency extraction to choose the targeted leaf and classification employing the region growing methodology, which utilizes both the data from the saliency map and the color features of every individual pixel [19].

A machine learning model, built on the k-NN technique, was developed by Munisami and his group. With an accuracy of 83.5%, the created system was evaluated on 640 leaves from 32 different species groups. Using color histogram approaches, accuracy was further raised to 87.3%. The developed model is also very user-friendly and robust [20].

For unsupervised feature visualizations of 44 plant species acquired at the Royal Botanic Gardens in Kew, England, Lee and his team created a CNN model. Instead of using a box approach, a deconvolutional network-based visualization technique (DN) was employed to gain understanding of the extracted features through the CNN model. It has been found that different order venations have been used to represent each type of plant. The authors came to the conclusion that experimental results employing these CNN features with different classifiers showed consistency and superiority as contrasted to state-of-the-art approaches that depend on hand-crafted characteristic [21].

## 9.3 MACHINE LEARNING: EXPANDING HORIZONS

The field of computer science with the fastest growth right now is machine learning, which has applications in fields as varied as marketing, healthcare, production, cybersecurity and mobility. Three elements are readily available and combined: (1) faster and more potent part of a computer, like multiple cores and broad sense GPU; (2) a computer program that utilizes these computational structures; and (3) essentially unlimited training data sets for a certain issue, like digital photos, digitalized files. Posts on social media or even other types of information are the primary cause of this literal "explosion" of the technique. ML is a type of AI that is capable of carrying out tasks without being particularly trained to do so. Instead, it employs a process known as "training to learn" from prior samples of the assigned task. Inference is the technique through which the task can be carried out on fresh data after training [22]. It is notably helpful for instances where the data is challenging to analyze, such as reviewing image and video recordings, and it especially helps in getting data from enormous amounts of continuously increasing data [23]. Computer vision is the science of analyzing and drawing conclusions from digital images and movies. It aims to automate tasks from an engineering standpoint that the human visual interface can do [24]. The two stages of a computer-vision-based machine learning process are feature extraction and classification.

### 9.3.1 Various Steps in Machine Learning Models

Data gathering using a cameras/mobile phones/smartphones is the first step in the framework for the creation of the ML-based picture identification model, as illustrated in Figure 9.2. To construct an online image database, collected appropriate photographs can be uploaded to a server. The image is further processed in order to make it suitable for applying a machine learning model. Various extraction techniques can be used to extract various characters in the context of color, shape and size. Following the use of features extraction techniques, the dimensionality reduction technique is further used to optimize the results. Additional machine learning models, including ANN, CNN, RNN and others, can be applied for system training and optimization. Each of these actions with specific response to herbal drugs is thoroughly explained in the next section.

## 9.4 CREATION OF IMAGE DATABASE

The easiest way to accomplish this is using a mobile phone equipped with a camera that has at least 10 pixels. Additionally, since cameras have superior

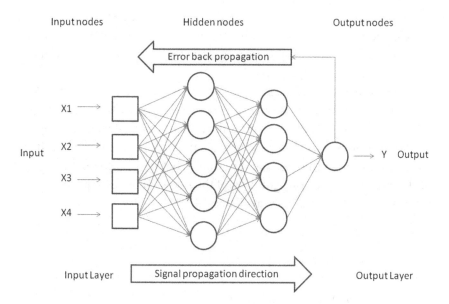

FIGURE 9.2    Basic representation of artificial neural network.

sensors and pixels than cellphones, they can also be employed. The background should be white or clear when clicking an image because pictures taken against a busy background may produce unneeded noise that affects our machine learning algorithm and ultimately produces inaccurate results. Herbs and spices can be photographed and posted to online image databases that can be accessed from anywhere, like Google Drive, Microsoft Community, and other sources. Based on the quality of the camera used to capture the photographs of the herbal/spices entity, the image dataset can be submitted in the form of a Zip file that is clearly classified into categories such as normal, high end, and moderate [25]. Clear categories for each sort of image should be present in the database.

According to Waldchen and Mäder, the photos in the Swedish Leaf, ICL, Leafsnap and Flavia databases were taken in a controlled environment. However, the number of images and the species utilized vary depending on the database. On the other hand, the ImageCLEF database provides a wide range of leaf pictures for leaf recognition in a natural context [7].

Using a k-NN classifier, Mzoughi and coworkers detected leaf photos in ImageCLEF 2011, which contained 5436 images from 71 varieties of plants. Due to the roughly comparable leaf shapes of each plant species in the dataset, the classification of this dataset is exceedingly difficult. Despite the similarities in the photos, the researchers were nevertheless able to classify the leaves with an accuracy of 82.1% by using various attributes on various leaf types [26, 27].

For leaf images from ImageCLEF, Pyramid histograms of oriented gradients, top-hat transformation and Haar wavelet transform, according to Ma and coworkers, produced a classification accuracy of 90%. The top-hat transformation was used to eliminate small items from a noisy backdrop, and PHOG is a common shape descriptor that defines the image by the local form and spatial configuration of the shape. Table 9.1 represents a list of the online server databases available [28].

TABLE 9.1    List of Online Server Databases

| S no. | Database Name | Outcomes and Features | References/Website Link |
|---|---|---|---|
| 1 | ImageCLEF11/Image-CLEF12/ ImageCLEF13 | Following are the total numbers of species and photos in each database: The 5436 photos in ImageCLEF11 represent 71 species; 11,572 images from 126 species make up Image-CLEF12; 26,077 images from 250 species make up Image-CLEF13. | [29–32] |
| 2 | PlantCLEF14, PlantCLEF15, PlantCLEF16,Plant-CLEF17 | 60,961 images from 500 species make up Plant-CLEF14; 113,205 images from 1000 species make up Plant-CLEF15; 121,205 images from 1000 species make up Plant-CLEF16; and 256,287 images from 10,000 species make up Image-CLEF17. | [29–32] |
| 3 | Flavia | This collection includes 1907 photos of 33 different plant species that are well aligned, noise-free, and have minimal to no differences in brightness and color. | [33] |
| 4 | ICL | Images of leaves that were entirely cultivated in China are included in the dataset. There are 220 plant species represented by 16,851 photos in total. | [34–36] |

| S no. | Database Name | Outcomes and Features | References/Website Link |
|---|---|---|---|
| 5 | Leafsnap | The 30,866 leaf photos in this dataset, which are all from the northeastern United States, represent 185 different species. Only 23,147 of the photos from the Smithsonian Collection are of a good caliber. The remaining pictures were taken with cellphones in a wide range of situations and conditions. | [30, 37, 38] |
| 6 | VITHERB | Images about the Vietnamese plant species | http://vietherb.com.vn/ |
| 7 | plant_leaves | Images of healthy plants' leaves | https://data.mendeley.com/datasets/hb74ynkjcn/1 |
| 8 | American Botanical Council | Herbal plant information catalogue | http://www.herbalgram.org/ |
| 9 | Image CLEF 2013 | Plant image database | https://www.imageclef.org/2013/plant |
| 10 | CIFAR-10 | Plant and other articles image database | https://www.cs.toronto.edu/~kriz/cifar.html |
| 11 | PLANT CV | Images of different species of plants | https://www.quantitative-plant.org/dataset |
| 12 | PlantVillage dataset | A set of images and labeled for diseased plant leaves | https://www.kaggle.com/datasets/emmarex/plantdisease |
| 13 | Pl@ntNet-300K | Datasets of different species of plants | https://zenodo.org/record/4726653#.YmowC_NBxQI |
| 14 | Database of leaf images | Datasets of different image of plants | https://data.mendeley.com/datasets/hb74ynkjcn/4 |
| 15 | DiaMOS Plant | Database for identifying and tracking plant disease | https://francescamalloci.com/category/projects/ |

## 9.5 FEATURE EXTRACTION

However, rather than starting with human prior knowledge, the essential step in conceptually understanding a software program is to extract useful and effective visual characteristics and build models from them. The majority of picture identification and retrieval systems are based on color, texture and shape because they are the most common visual features. But how well they function is heavily dependent on how they use picture attributes. The three different types of feature extraction methodologies are region-based, global and block-based features [39].

### 9.5.1 Color Features

Among the most significant aspects of captured image is color. Particular color properties are described in the context of a particular RGB space or model. Color spaces like RGB, HMMD, LUV and HSV have been used in literature. Color features can be retrieved from images or regions of interest once the color space has been defined. Color histogram, color coherence vector (CCV), color correlogram and color moments (CM) are just a few of the major color features present in color images [40].

#### 9.5.1.1 Color Histogram

A color histogram is a graphical description of the color distribution of a picture. A histogram's data is derived by recording the appearance of each conceivable color of the respective color model appearing in the image [40].

#### 9.5.1.2 Color Coherence Vector

The color coherence vector (CCV) approach is more complicated than the color histogram method. It works by determining whether each pixel is coherent or incoherent. In contrast to an incoherent pixel, which is a member of a tiny connected component, a coherent pixel is a component of a big connected component (CC). Establishing the criteria by which we determine whether a connected component is large is a critical step in making this strategy function [40].

#### 9.5.1.3 Color Moments

Color moments are measures that help separate photos based on their many color characteristics. The color moments provide a measurement for color similarity between photos once they've been calculated. For applications like image retrieval, these similarity values can be compared to the frequencies

TABLE 9.2    Advantages and Disadvantages of Different Color Method

| Color Method | Advantage | Disadvantage |
| --- | --- | --- |
| Histogram | Simple and basic calculation | High dimensionality, no spatial information, noise sensitivity |
| SCD | Scalability and compactness on demand | There is no spatial information, and if the data is compressed, it is less reliable. |
| DCD | Compact, robust and perceptive | Post-processing required for spatial data |
| CM | Robust, compact | It is not well enough to represent all color |
| Correlogram | Statistical information | The cost of calculation is extremely high, and it is susceptible to noise, rotation, and scale. |
| CSD | Statistical information | Very susceptible to rotation, noise and scale |

of images categorized in a database. Color moments of an image can be calculated/measured with the help of probability distribution. CM is one of the most basic yet powerful qualities among them [40]. Table 9.2 represents the different advantages and disadvantages of various color methods.

## 9.5.2 Shape Features

Shape is a key clue for humans to identify and differentiate real-world things, with the objective of encoding simple geometrical patterns including straight lines in various orientations. Contour-based and region-based approaches are the two primary categories of shape feature extraction methods. The former approach pulls features from the entire region, while the latter method calculates shape characteristics solely from the shape's boundary. Shape feature is a very important feature for feature extraction from an image. Various properties of shape feature are transition, scale invariance and rotation, identifiability (the image of a similar object consists of similar features), noise resistance (feature must be as robust as possible against the noise), affline invariance (the descriptor should not be changed by shape distortion that preserves shape features), reliability, occultation invariance, statistically independent. Shape descriptor is a collection of numbers used to represent a certain shape aspect. A description tries to quantify the shape in ways that are intuitive to humans. The descriptors are usually in the form of a vector. Simple geometric features can usually only distinguish shapes with considerable variances; as a result, they are frequently employed as filters to eliminate false positives or in combination with additional shape descriptors to distinguish shapes [41].

### 9.5.3 Texture Features

A variety of images can make use of the varied characterization of texture. Human visual systems are hypothesized to use texture for interpretation and detection. Normally, color is a pixel attribute, while texture can only be determined from a group of pixels. Several methods have been investigated to extract texture features. According to the domain in which the feature extraction is taken, they can be categorized into two groups: methods for extracting spatial texture features and spectral texture features [42].

#### 9.5.3.1 Spatial Method

By calculating pixel statistics or identifying local pixel patterns in the source image domain, texture characteristics are retrieved using this method.

#### 9.5.3.2 Spectral Method

Texture features can be identified by converting an image into frequency domain, and then the features are calculated from the transformed image. Some advantages and disadvantages are included in Table 9.3.

Lin and coworkers suggested a visual consistency-dependent method for feature extraction to identify particular features, like aspect ratio, rectangularity, vertical eccentricity, shape complexity, and horizontal structure, to define leaf lamina. The authors also used the inertia axis method to spin leaves, which must be done in a specific orientation. This is done to mimic how people typically observe objects. The results demonstrated that characteristics of the same plant exhibit excellent consistency with negligible variation in laminae, while aspect ratio, vertical eccentricity and form complexity exhibit the greatest variation in the laminae of different plants [43]. Patil and Manza collected geometric information from photographs,

TABLE 9.3 Advantages and Disadvantages of Spatial and Spectral Texture Feature Extraction

| Method | Advantages | Disadvantages |
| --- | --- | --- |
| **Spatial method** | Relevant, simple to interpret and can be retrieved without losing information from any shape | The frequency domain is prone to noise and distortions, and the feature is calculated from the altered image. |
| **Spectral method** | Dependable, with fewer computations required | There is no semantic meaning; hence, square image portions of adequate size are required. |

including the maximum diameter, width, length, aspect ratio and form factor of the leaf. Additionally, the researchers extracted from the leaf the morphological traits of smoothness, rectangularity, physiological breadth, thinness, perimeter ratio of physiological length, perimeter ratio of diameter and vein features [44–49].

## 9.6 DATA AUGMENTATION

A deep learning approach typically performs well when given a lot of data. In general, the algorithm will score higher the more data we feed it. As the volume of data increases, the deep learning model's performance gets better. However, gathering a lot of data entails its own set of challenges. A deep learning network cannot ever be fed with an enormous amount of data. It is a approach for altering already existing photos to produce large data size for the ML model stage of training. In the other words, it is a method for extending the dataset that may be used to train deep learning models [50]. Different types of image augmentation method are as follow.

1. **Flipping:** This method enables flipping the image either left to right or up to down to create the different images [51].

2. **Rotation:** Rotation of particular images does not affect its properties. So, in image augmentation, images are rotated at different angles to create multiple sets of a single image [52].

3. **Image Shifting:** By using image shifting, we can change the position of images and thus create a different set of the images from a single original image [53].

4. **Noise Addition:** This method adds the unnecessary noise in the original images and thus creates new images sets having noises. New sets of images created by this approach enable the machine learning model to train for removal of noises from images efficiently [53].

5. **Blurring of Images:** This technique blurs the original clear images to create totally new sets of blurred images. As we know, the image source in a model does not consists of the same source, and the quality of the input images cannot be fixed. It can be sometimes of good quality or sometimes of rough quality. The new subsets of images created by using the blurring approach make the model more robust while using the images of different quality. Figure 9.3 depicts the flowchart for the model of herbal image identification.

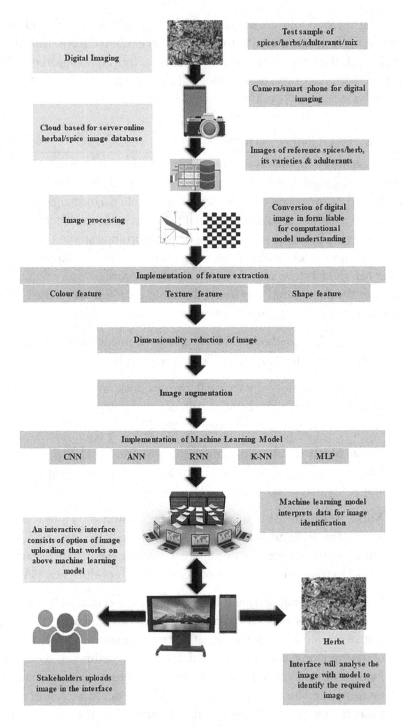

FIGURE 9.3 Model of herbal image identification.

## 9.7 CLASSIFICATION TECHNIQUES USING MACHINE LEARNING MODELS

After reducing various unwanted features from the image using DR techniques, the resultant image set can be increased using image augmentation techniques. Finally the different classification techniques based on the ML model were employed on the images to retrieve the desired features from them and make them compatible to obtain a fruitful result. Classification techniques based on the ML model uses a range of algorithms for classification and recognizes, understands and groups concepts, patterns and objects into predetermined classes according to established criteria, such as using training datasets. Predictive computations are used to assign data to predetermined groups or subpopulations using classification algorithms. Classification is the mapping of incoming data to a given class. These techniques will sort unsorted data into particular classes according to the training. Many criteria, such as Euclidean distance, constructing hyperplanes, nonlinear relationships and activation functions, among others, govern how classification algorithms work between input and output [54, 55]. Some of the common machine-learning-technique-based classification models have been described in a later section.

The model "sees about an image" when features are taken from photos, and the features selected are very problem and object specific. For past classification performance, manually extracting typical features was necessary, but it was also a time-consuming and expert task. Additionally, many features can't currently be correctly retrieved manually. As a result, it was a long sought-after a method that enabled the automatic identification of relevant features for a challenge without a specified explanation [56].

### 9.7.1 Artificial Neural Network (ANN)

An artificial neural network (ANN) is based on the judgment and architecture of the 1000 billion neurons that make up the human brain's biological neural network, which is renowned as an astounding parallel processor [57, 58]. As demonstrated in Figure 9.4, it works with nonlinear statistical information and then analyzes the nonlinear connection between dependent and independent in parallel. In order to identify a novel pattern, nonlinear statistical models, or ANNs, show a complex link between inputs and outputs. The major advantage of ANN is that it adapts from sample data sets. Random function approximation is the most frequent use of ANN. These kinds of technologies enable the development of solutions that efficiently

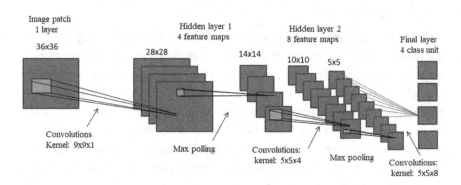

FIGURE 9.4    Basic representation of convolutional neural network.

specify the distribution. Instead of using the entire dataset, ANN can alternatively produce findings based on sample data and can be used to enhance current data analysis methods due of their powerful prediction capabilities [59, 60].

There are different layers present in the ANNs, which are explained as follows:

1. **Input Layers:** An ANN's input layer, which is the first layer, accepts data in the format of text, numbers, audio snippets, image pixels and other formats.

2. **Hidden Layers:** The ANN model's center contains the hidden layers. A solitary hidden layer, as in a perceptron, or several hidden layers are possible. These hidden layers use the supplied data to execute multiple kinds of mathematical computations and recognize patterns.

3. **Output Layers:** The result obtained through stringent computation conducted by the center of the frame is obtained in the output layer. Many factors and hyper-parameters can affect how well a neural network performs. These factors play a significant role in determining how well ANNs perform. They include factors like weights, biases, learning rate, batch size and others. Each node in the ANN is given a specified amount of weight. Every node in the network is given a weight. A transfer function is used to determine the bias and the input weighting factor. Based on the information that the nodes have fired, we receive

the final result. Additionally, we analyze the discrepancies among the expected and actual results using the error function and then alter the neural network's weights using back propagation [58–60].

### 9.7.2 Convolutional Neural Network (CNN)

A CNN is a form of deep neural network that employs filter to learn the many features of a picture as input. It can recognize the picture's main elements and tell one thing from another as a result [7, 61]. For example, the CNN gains knowledge from the characteristics that differentiate cats from dogs so that it can readily distinguish between the two when given the input of cats and dogs. CNNs are distinguished from other machine learning methods by their ability to preprocess input on their own. Consequently, you might not have to spend a lot of money on data preprocessing. The filters may help retain engineering during cold start, but as training progresses, they are able to adapt to the acquired features and develop their own filters. As a result, CNN is always changing in response to new inputs [62–64].

### 9.7.3 Recurrent Neural Networks (RNNs)

The RNN is particularly adept at handling time series and other sequential data. We cover some of the most popular recurrent designs being used, such as long short-term memory (LSTM) and gated recurrent units, as well as recurrent neural networks, as either a feed-forward network extension that enables varying (or even infinite-length) sequences to be analyzed [65]. RNNs are feed-forward deep neural networks that specialize in temporal modeling. RNNs are distinguished by their capacity to send information in time increments. RNNs feature an extra feature matrix for connections across time steps in their structure, which improves learning in the temporal domain and utilization of the input's sequential character. RNNs are trained to create, at each time step, output with predictions depending on existing input and knowledge from prior time steps. An RNN includes three stages of operation. It proceeds onward across the hidden layer in the first stage and generates a prediction. The loss function is used in the second step to compare the prediction to the true value. The loss function displays how well a model performs. The model is better if the loss function has a lower value. It then utilizes the error information in back-propagation to determine the gradient for every location in the final stage (node). The gradients are the amount by which the network's weights are adjusted at each point [66]. The basic representation of RNNs is presented in Figure 9.5.

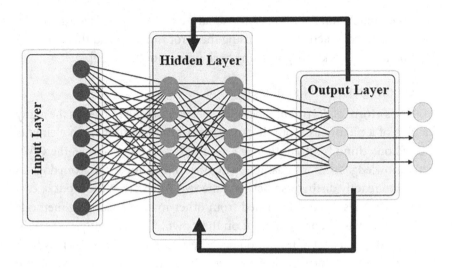

FIGURE 9.5   Basic representation of recurrent neural networks.

### 9.7.4 Nearest Neighbor (k-NN)

A non-parametric and slow learning method that records all accessible examples and distinguishes the new tested one using metrics like a distance function is generally considered a k-NN model (Figure 9.6). When there is little or no previous experience of the data, it is chosen as the best method. Speech, video recognition, healthcare, finance, handwriting identification, picture recognition and any sort of pattern classification, political science, and statistical estimations are all uses of k-NN. When the k-NN technique receives new data, it simply divides it into a category that is almost identical to the original data. The k-NN method merely retains the information during the training phase [67, 68].

### 9.7.5 Multilayer Perceptron (MLP)

An improvement to feed-forward neural networks is the multilayer perceptron (MLP). The three different sorts of layers are input, output and hidden layers. Every input data that must be handled is delivered to the input layer. A couple of examples of tasks that fall under the output layer's jurisdiction include forecasting and categorization. The actual computational mechanism of the MLP is made up of an infinite number of hidden layers positioned between the output and input layers [69]. Various reviews related to different models are compiled into Table 9.4.

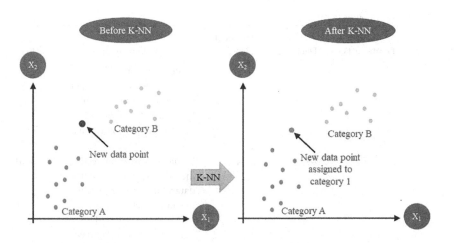

FIGURE 9.6   Basic representation of nearest neighbor (k-NN).

TABLE 9.4   Compilation of the Previous Work Related to Various Machine Learning Models

| S. No. | Plants Parts | Datasets | ML Model/ Classifier | Outcomes | Ref. |
|---|---|---|---|---|---|
| **Artificial Neural Network** | | | | | |
| 1. | Leaves | 63 | ANN and MATLAB | The system was discovered to have the lowest complexity when 8 input features were included since they required the least amount of input and computational effort. With respect to the 63 leaf photos in the dataset, the system's accuracy was 94.4%. | [77] |
| 2. | Leaves | Self-developed dataset | ANN | With an accuracy of 91.98%, the proposed system performed more accurately than the other approaches used in the study. Entropy was used as the primary criterion for classifying leaves. | [78] |
| 3. | Leaves | Self-developed dataset | ANN | The experimental findings of the suggested method have been found to be able to extract a more exact venation structure of the leaf data for pattern | [79] |

*(Continued)*

TABLE 9.4 *(Continued)*

| S. No. | Plants Parts | Datasets | ML Model/ Classifier | Outcomes | Ref. |
|---|---|---|---|---|---|
| | | | | recognition with 97.3% accuracy, while also reducing computing time as compared to the traditional neural approach, which reached an accuracy of 84.4%. | |
| 4. | Leaves | 1907 | ANN | The datasets used for testing included a medicinal herbs dataset of 6 species and the Flavia dataset of 32 species (1907 pictures, 50–60 leaves per species) (30 images each). Since k-NN and naïve Bayes classifiers are algorithms for lazy learners, SVM and PNN have comparable greater accuracy than these classifiers. | [80] |
| 5. | Leaves | Self-developed dataset | ANN | Accuracy was found to be 93.3% in identification of leaves. | [81] |
| 6. | Leaves | Self-developed dataset | ANN | An ANN model was created utilizing the morpho-colorimetric characteristics as inputs, and it classified the leaves of the 20 medicinal plants with an accuracy of 98.3%. | [82] |
| 7. | Leaves | Self-developed dataset | ANN | Python is used to create an ANN model with improved parameters, resulting in a 98.16% identification rate over the entire dataset. | [83] |
| 8. | Leaves | Self-developed dataset | ANN | Entropy was chosen as the primary characteristic for classifying leaves, and the resulting accuracy was 91.98%. | [78] |
| 9. | Leaves | Self-developed dataset | ANN | ANN had a 97.3% accuracy rate while processing the data faster than the direct neural network method, which had an accuracy of 84.4% for pattern identification on the leaf samples. | [79] |
| 10. | Leaves | Flavia | ANN & k-NN | Accuracy was found to be 93.3% and 85.9% for both ML models. | [84] |

| S. No. | Plants Parts | Datasets | ML Model/ Classifier | Outcomes | Ref. |
|---|---|---|---|---|---|
| **Convolutional Neural Network** | | | | | |
| 11. | Leaves | Self-developed dataset | CNN | With top-3 final scores on all other datasets and nearly perfect top-1 match results on the Flavia dataset, the dual-path CNN method outperforms a number of other CNN methods. | [85] |
| 12. | Weed and crop species | 10,413 | CNN | The system is able to classify 22 species with an accuracy of 86.2%. | [86] |
| 13. | Flowers and leaves | Self-developed dataset | CNN | In comparison to the traditional CNN plant image identification model, the results are based on successful area selection, which can more efficiently extract picture features and increase identification accuracy. | [87] |
| 14. | Leaves of Thai herbal plants | Self-developed datasets of >2500 images | CNN | Model was successful in identifying the Thai herbal plants with recall of 0.75 and precision of 0.8. | [88] |
| 15. | Flowers and leaves of herbal plants | 3 different datasets | CNN | Accuracy for identifying the herbal plants from 3 different datasets are found to be an average of 87.19%. | [62] |
| 16. | Leaves of Vietnamese herbal plants | VN-plant snapshot datasets | CNN | Accuracy for identifying the herbal plants is 88.26% when evaluated in different frameworks, VGG16, Resnet50, InceptionV3, DenseNet121. | [62] |
| 17. | Medicinal leaves | Self-developed datasets of >2500 images | CNN | The developed model with Gabor filter found accuracy of 98% in identification of medicinal plants. | [89] |
| 18. | Leaves of ayurvedic plant | Self-developed datasets of >2500 images | CNN | Developed model with SVM and softmax classifier achieved an accuracy of 96.7%. | [77] |

*(Continued)*

TABLE 9.4 *(Continued)*

| S. No. | Plants Parts | Datasets | ML Model/ Classifier | Outcomes | Ref. |
|---|---|---|---|---|---|
| 19. | Leaves of Bangladeshi medicinal plants | Self-developed datasets of 500 images | CNN | Accuracy of the developed model has been found to be 88.16%. | [90] |
| 20. | Leaves of indigenous plants of Kerela | Self-developed datasets of >64,000 images | CNN | Model accompanied with pretrained model of VGG16 and VGG19 achieved an accuracy of 97.8% and 97.6%. | [91] |
| **Nearest Neighbor (k-NN)** | | | | | |
| 21. | Leaves | 640 leaves datasets | k-NN | Initially the accuracy was 83.5%, which was further increased to 87.5% by using the color histogram technique. | [92] |
| 22. | Leaves | Swedish leaves datasets | k-NN | SPM and LLC have been utilized for extracting shape features of the leaves, and accuracy was found to be 96.6%. | [93] |
| 23. | Leaves | 1500 image datasets | k-NN | DHNG has been utilized for the pattern recognition of leaves, and accuracy was found to be 71.5%. | [94] |
| 24. | Leaves | 640 | k-NN | 640 leaf sample images of different sizes, shapes and orientations were tested in the experiment, and it was found that they outperformed k-NNC and NNC with accuracy rates of 97.5% and 79.7%. The disadvantage of the suggested strategy is that it consistently works only when deformations do not alter the lengths of the major and minor axis. | [95] |
| 25. | Leaves | 640 leaves datasets | k-NN | Initially the accuracy was 83.5% which was further increased to 87.5% by using the color histogram technique. | [20] |
| 26. | Leaves | Swedish leaves datasets | k-NN | SPM and LLC has been utilized for extracting shape features of the leaves, and accuracy was found to be 96.6%. | [93] |

| S. No. | Plants Parts | Datasets | ML Model/ Classifier | Outcomes | Ref. |
|---|---|---|---|---|---|
| 27. | Leaves | 1500 images datasets | k-NN | DHNG has been utilized for the pattern recognition of leaves, and accuracy was found to be 71.5%. | [94] |
| **Multilayer Perceptron (MLP)** | | | | | |
| 28. | Grape leaves | Self-developed dataset | MLP | Used for the detection of black rot, downey mildew diseases, and the accuracy was found to be 96.6 %. | [96] |
| 29. | Kalmegh and tulsi leaves | Self-developed dataset | MLP | Overall accuracy was found to be 80%. | [97] |

## 9.8 VALIDATION OF DEVELOPED MODEL

After applying all the steps mentioned in Figure 9.4, a machine-learning-based model for the identification of images can be formed which could be later utilized for the identification of required herbal and spice images. But for making a model robust, the validation of the model is one of the important steps and should be performed at the end to test the working suitability of the model. Accuracy, precision, true positive (TP), false positive (FP), true positive ratio (TPR), false positive ratio (FPR), sensitivity, specificity, miss rate, recall, F1 score and CPU elapsed time are some of the parameters employed for the validation of a developed machine learning model [70, 71].

- **Accuracy:** Accuracy is the proportion of trial data forecasts that were correct. It is simple to determine by dividing the total number of forecasts by the proportion of accurate estimations. It can be calculated as follows:

$$\text{Accuracy (\%)} = \frac{\text{Correct prediction}}{\text{Total no. of prediction}} \times 100$$

Accuracy above 70% is generally considered good for a machine learning model [72].

- **Precision:** The proportion of particular examples (true positives) among all the examples predicted belong to a certain class known as precision [73]. It can be calculated as follows:

$$\text{Precision} = \frac{\text{True positive}}{\text{True positive} + \text{False positive}}$$

- **TP:** True positive occurs when an observation related to a specific class is actually more common than you would have thought [74].

- **TN:** True negative happens when you predict that a piece of information doesn't really fit into a category, and it actually does not [74, 75].

- **Recall:** Recall is the proportion of examples anticipated to belong to a class relative to all of the examples that actually do [76].

## 9.9 TRANSFER LEARNING

To achieve the desired accuracy, a new machine learning model must be developed using a great deal of data. For achieving high accuracy, it is necessary to train the model on large datasets; otherwise, the developed model will not work well. Developing a new model for identification of herbs requires a large dataset that is quite not possible. To overcome this problem, the concept of transfer learning came into play. Transfer learning is an approach in which a pretrained model can be applied in a developing model. The model has already been pretrained in large datasets such as ImageNet and can be used for extracting the feature from images of the new model. As discussed, a CNN model has been largely employed for the identification of herbal images, so in this chapter further we have discussed the various CNN-model-based transfer learning models that can be employed for the identification of herbal plants [98]. Various CNN pretrained models are discussed next.

### 9.9.1 VGGNet

VGG-16, presented at ILSVRC2014, was the Visual Geometry Group's (VGG) first successful ImageNet architecture, which was followed by VGG-19 [98]. By substituting numerous small kernel-sized filters for a single big kernel-sized filter, these models improve upon AlexNet and for VGG-16 and VGG-19, creating 13 and 16 convolution layers, correspondingly.

### 9.9.2 CaffeNet

This CNN model resembles AlexNet a bit. In contrast to AlexNet, CaffeNet inserts the pooling layer well before the normalization procedure and does not employ data augmentation. CaffeNet therefore marginally enhances AlexNet's computational performance by doing data dimension reduction prior to normalization.

### 9.9.3 Inception

The GoogLeNet model, also known as Inception-V1, made an effort to increase VGGNet's effectiveness in terms of memory consumption and runtime without compromising accuracy [99]. This was accomplished by removing the VGGNet activation functions that were duplicated or zero due to their correlations. In order to approximate the sparse interconnections among the activation functions, GoogleLeNet developed and incorporated the Inception module. Three additional versions were released after Inception-V1 that substantially improved the architecture. Batch normalization was utilized by Inception-V2 for training [100]. To increase the computation cost of convolution layers, Inception-V3 suggested a factorization technique [101]. A uniformly simplified Inception-V3 design with much more Inception modules was released in Inception V-4 [102].

### 9.9.4 ResNet

Accuracy saturation and disappearing gradients may result from CNN models having too many layers. This issue is addressed by residual learning, which serves as the foundation of ResNet CNN [98]. At the conclusion of each convolution layer, CNN models that came before ResNet learned features at various levels of abstraction. ResNet does not learn features; instead, it learns residuals, which are the learned features from the input for each convolution layer. Identity shortcut connections, which include linking a layer's input to $x$ other layers, are used to do this [103]. ResNet variants like ResNet-34, ResNet-50 and ResNet-101 use a varied number of layers.

### 9.9.5 Xception

Extreme Inception, sometimes known as Xception, is a modified Inception-V3. This CNN model uses depth-wise separable convolution to separately train the picture's spatial and channel dimensions. Xception performs a little better on ImageNet while having approximately the same number of variables as InceptionV3 [104].

## 9.10 CONCLUSION AND FUTURE PROSPECTS

Manual identification of medicinal plants/herbal medicines involves a substantial amount of labor and is subject to human error. Automatic plant identification might be a solution to these issues, but developing such a system involves great resources, including a sizable database, in-depth understanding of plant morphology and expertise in computer programming. The majority of current research on autonomous plant identification systems tests its effectiveness using pre-existing datasets that were created in a confined space. Therefore, more research on images under different lighting circumstances and with complicated backgrounds needs to be done. In addition, a substantially sized dataset should also be used to provide better training. This would improve the accuracy of the established identification system. The development of the usage of medicinal herbs in the medical field may be influenced by greater accuracy, and improving the automated identification system would have a substantial impact on environmental preservation. The examination in this area of study will be significantly affected by the development of future technology.

A consumer system that enables users to recognize plants utilizing their mobile phones wherever and whenever they are could be one of the emerging developments for plant recognition systems. However, this technique will need a powerful decoder with the capacity to recognize any part of plant in a range of situations. Consequently, it is necessary to create a database that contains several plant species with a range of environmental conditions. In addition, future herbal plant recognition systems should be able to automatically derive the mathematical model of the plant features. Utilizing a 3-D scan for this reason will be especially helpful because it will record every physical measurement.

## REFERENCES

[1] Babu N, Shankar M, Babu N. Complementary and alternative medicine an overview. *Am J Oral Med Radiol*. 2016;3(3):134–145.

[2] Jaiswal YS, Williams LL. A glimpse of Ayurveda–the forgotten history and principles of Indian traditional medicine. *J Tradit Complement Med*. 2017;7(1):50–53.

[3] Che Soh A, Yusof UK, Radzi NFM, Ishak AJ, Hassan MK. Classification of aromatic herbs using artificial intelligent technique. *Pertanika J Sci Technol*. 2017;25.

[4] Altemimi A, Lakhssassi N, Baharlouei A, Watson DG, Lightfoot DA. Phytochemicals: Extraction, isolation, and identification of bioactive compounds from plant extracts. *Plants*. 2017;6(4):42.

[5] Sladojevic S, Arsenovic M, Anderla A, Culibrk D, Stefanovic D. Deep neural networks based recognition of plant diseases by leaf image classification. *Comput Intell Neurosci*. 2016;29;2016.

[6] Singh V, Misra AK. Detection of plant leaf diseases using image segmentation and soft computing techniques. *Inf Process Agric*. 2017;4(1):41–49.

[7] Wäldchen J, Mäder P. Machine learning for image based species identification. *Methods Ecol Evol*. 2018;9(11):2216–2225.

[8] Shavlik JW, Dietterich T, Dietterich TG. *Readings in machine learning*. Morgan Kaufmann; 1990;1–11.

[9] Došilović FK, Brčić M, Hlupić N. Explainable artificial intelligence: A survey. In: *20¹⁸ 41st International Convention on Information and Communication Technology, Electronics and Microelectronics*. IEEE; 2018;210–215.

[10] Laxmi GF, Herdiyeni Y, Arkeman Y. Identification of medicinal plant by fuzzy local binary pattem and multi objective genetic algorithm. In: *2017 International Conference on Computer, Control, Informatics and Its Applications*. IEEE; 2017;29–34.

[11] Culman MA, Gomez JA, Talavera J, Quiroz LA, Tobon LE, Aranda JM, et al. A novel application for identification of nutrient deficiencies in oil palm using the internet of things. In: *2017 5th IEEE International Conference on Mobile Cloud Computing, Services, and Engineering (MobileCloud)*. IEEE; 2017;169–172.

[12] Elhassouny A, Smarandache F. Smart mobile application to recognize tomato leaf diseases using convolutional neural networks. In: *2019 International Conference of Computer Science and Renewable Energies (ICCSRE)*. IEEE; 2019;1–4.

[13] Akiyama T, Kobayashi Y, Sasaki Y, Sasaki K, Kawaguchi T, Kishigami J. Mobile Leaf Identification System using CNN applied to plants in Hokkaido. In: *2019 I$^{EE}$E 8th Global Conference on Consumer Electronics (GCCE)*. IEEE; 2019;324–325.

[14] Tang Y, Chen M, Wang C, Luo L, Li J, Lian G, et al. Recognition and localization methods for vision-based fruit picking robots: A review. *Front Plant Sci.* 2020;11:510.

[15] Yang X, Guo T. Machine learning in plant disease research. *March.* 2017;31:1.

[16] Ferentinos KP. Deep learning models for plant disease detection and diagnosis. *Comput Electron Agric.* 2018;145:311–318.

[17] De Luna RG, Baldovino RG, Cotoco EA, De Ocampo ALP, Valenzuela IC, Culaba AB, et al. Identification of philippine herbal medicine plant leaf using artificial neural network. In: *2017 I$^{EE}$E 9th International Conference on Humanoid, Nanotechnology, Information Technology, Communication and Control, Environment and Management (HNICEM)*. IEEE; 2017;1–8.

[18] Joseph DS, Pawar PM, Pramanik R. Intelligent plant disease diagnosis using convolutional neural network: A review. *Multimed Tools Appl.* 2022;1–67.

[19] Putzu L, Di Ruberto C, Fenu G. A mobile application for leaf detection in complex background using saliency maps. In: *International Conference on Advanced Concepts for Intelligent Vision Systems*. Springer; 2016;570–581.

[20] Munisami T, Ramsurn M, Kishnah S, Pudaruth S. Plant leaf recognition using shape features and colour histogram with K-nearest neighbour classifiers. *Procedia Comput Sci.* 2015;58:740–747.

[21] Lee SH, Chan CS, Wilkin P, Remagnino P. Deep-plant: Plant identification with convolutional neural networks. In: *2015 IEEE International Conference on Image Processing (ICIP)*. IEEE; 2015;452–456.

[22] Mjolsness E, DeCoste D. Machine learning for science: State of the art and future prospects. *Science.* 2001;293(5537):2051–2055.

[23] Chin K, Hellebrekers T, Majidi C. Machine learning for soft robotic sensing and control. *Adv Intell Syst.* 2020;2(6):1900171.

[24] Sonka M, Hlavac V, Boyle R. *Image processing, analysis, and machine vision.* Cengage Learning; 2014.

[25] Fenrich R, Hull JJ. Concerns in creation of image databases. In: *Proc IWFHR-III*. Buffalo, New York; 1993;112–121.

[26] Mzoughi O, Yahiaoui I, Boujemaa N, Zagrouba E. Semantic-based automatic structuring of leaf images for advanced plant species identification. *Multimed Tools Appl*. 2016;75(3):1615–1646.

[27] Mzoughi O, Yahiaoui I, Boujemaa N, Zagrouba E. Semantic shape models for leaf species identification. In: *International Conference on Advanced Concepts for Intelligent Vision Systems*. Springer; 2015;661–671.

[28] Ma L-H, Zhao Z-Q, Wang J. ApLeafis: An android-based plant leaf identification system. In: *International Conference on Intelligent Computing*. Springer; 2013;106–111.

[29] Aptoula E, Yanikoglu B. Morphological features for leaf based plant recognition. In: *2013 IEEE International Conference on Image Processing*. IEEE; 2013;1496–1499.

[30] Rejeb Sfar A, Boujemaa N, Geman D. Confidence sets for fine-grained categorization and plant species identification. *Int J Comput Vis*. 2015;111(3):255–275.

[31] Yanikoglu B, Aptoula E, Tirkaz C. Automatic plant identification from photographs. *Mach Vis Appl*. 2014;25(6):1369–1383.

[32] Wang B, Brown D, Gao Y, La Salle J. March: Multiscale-arch-height description for mobile retrieval of leaf images. *Inf Sci (Ny)*. 2015;302:132–148.

[33] Wu SG, Bao FS, Xu EY, Wang Y-X, Chang Y-F, Xiang Q-L. A leaf recognition algorithm for plant classification using probabilistic neural network. In: *2007 IEEE International Symposium on Signal Processing and Information Technology*. IEEE; 2007;11–16.

[34] Hu R, Jia W, Ling H, Huang D. Multiscale distance matrix for fast plant leaf recognition. *IEEE Trans Image Process*. 2012;21(11):4667–4672.

[35] Wang X, Liang J, Guo F. Feature extraction algorithm based on dual-scale decomposition and local binary descriptors for plant leaf recognition. *Digit Signal Process*. 2014;34:101–107.

[36] Aakif A, Khan MF. Automatic classification of plants based on their leaves. *Biosyst Eng*. 2015;139:66–75.

[37] Kalyoncu C, Toygar Ö. Geometric leaf classification. *Comput Vis Image Underst*. 2015;133:102–109.

[38] Zhao C, Chan SSF, Cham W-K, Chu LM. Plant identification using leaf shapes—a pattern counting approach. *Pattern Recognit*. 2015;48(10):3203–3215.

[39] Robins A, Rountree J, Rountree N. Learning and teaching programming: A review and discussion. *Comput Sci Educ*. 2003;13(2):137–172.

[40] Satpute MR, Jagdale SM. Color, size, volume, shape and texture feature extraction techniques for fruits: A review. *Int Res J Eng Technol*. 2016;3:703–708.

[41] Meruliya T, Dhameliya P, Patel J, Panchal D, Kadam P, Naik S. Image processing for fruit shape and texture feature extraction-review. *Int J Comput Appl*. 2015;129(8):30–33.

[42] Patel A, Kadam P, Naik S. Color, size and shape feature extraction techniques for fruits: A technical review. *Int J Comput Appl.* 2015;130(16).

[43] Lin F-Y, Zheng C-H, Wang X-F, Man Q-K. Multiple classification of plant leaves based on Gabor transform and LBP operator. In: *International Conference on Intelligent Computing.* Springer; 2008;432–439.

[44] Patil VR, Manza RR. A method of feature extraction from leaf architecture. *Int J Adv Res Comput Sci Softw Eng.* 2015;5(7):1025–1029.

[45] Bagal VC, Manza RR. Feature extraction of plant species from leaf architecture. In: *2016 International Conference on Electrical, Electronics, and Optimization Techniques (ICEEOT).* IEEE; 2016;4079–4081.

[46] Vijayalakshmi B. A new shape feature extraction method for leaf image retrieval. In: *Proceedings of the Fourth International Conference on Signal and Image Processing 2012 (ICSIP 2012).* Springer; 2013;235–245.

[47] Fotopoulou F, Laskaris N, Economou G, Fotopoulos S. Advanced leaf image retrieval via multidimensional embedding sequence similarity (MESS) method. *Pattern Anal Appl.* 2013;16(3):381–392.

[48] Shabanzade M, Zahedi M, Aghvami SA. Combination of local descriptors and global features for leaf recognition. *Signal Image Process.* 2011;2(3):23.

[49] Wang H, Tian D, Li C, Tian Y, Zhou H. Plant leaf tooth feature extraction. *PLoS One.* 2019;14(2):e0204714.

[50] Shorten C, Khoshgoftaar TM. A survey on image data augmentation for deep learning. *J Big Data.* 2019;6(1):1–48.

[51] Chlap P, Min H, Vandenberg N, Dowling J, Holloway L, Haworth A. A review of medical image data augmentation techniques for deep learning applications. *J Med Imaging Radiat Oncol.* 2021;65(5):545–563.

[52] Mikołajczyk A, Grochowski M. Data augmentation for improving deep learning in image classification problem. In: *2018 International Interdisciplinary PhD Workshop (IIPhDW).* IEEE; 2018;117–122.

[53] Shijie J, Ping W, Peiyi J, Siping H. Research on data augmentation for image classification based on convolution neural networks. In: *2017 Chinese Automation Congress (CAC).* IEEE; 2017;4165–4170.

[54] Omondiagbe DA, Veeramani S, Sidhu AS. Machine learning classification techniques for breast cancer diagnosis. In: *IOP Conference Series: Materials Science and Engineering.* IOP Publishing; 2019;012033.

[55] Kesavaraj G, Sukumaran S. A study on classification techniques in data mining. In: *2013 Fourth International Conference on Computing, Communications and Networking Technologies (ICCCNT).* IEEE; 2013;1–7.

[56] Soofi AA, Awan A. Classification techniques in machine learning: Applications and issues. *J Basic Appl Sci.* 2017;13:459–465.

[57] Bambil D, Pistori H, Bao F, Weber V, Alves FM, Gonçalves EG, et al. Plant species identification using color learning resources, shape, texture, through machine learning and artificial neural networks. *Environ Syst Decis.* 2020;40(4):480–484.

[58] Sharifzadeh M, Sikinioti-Lock A, Shah N. Machine-learning methods for integrated renewable power generation: A comparative study of artificial

neural networks, support vector regression, and Gaussian process regression. *Renew Sustain Energy Rev.* 2019;108:513–538.

[59] Chen M, Challita U, Saad W, Yin C, Debbah M. Artificial neural networks-based machine learning for wireless networks: A tutorial. *IEEE Commun Surv Tutorials.* 2019;21(4):3039–3071.

[60] Prieto A, Atencia M, Sandoval F. Advances in artificial neural networks and machine learning. *Neurocomputing.* Elsevier; 2013;121:1–4.

[61] Lu J, Tan L, Jiang H. Review on convolutional neural network (CNN) applied to plant leaf disease classification. *Agriculture.* 2021;11(8):707.

[62] Bao HY, Wen RJ, Li XY, Zhao C, Chen ZN. A brief overview of traditional Chinese medicine prescription powered by artificial intelligence. *TMR Mod Herb Med.* 2021;4(2):13.

[63] Roslan NAM, Diah NM, Ibrahim Z, Hanum HM, Ismail M. Automatic plant recognition: A survey of relevant algorithms. In: *2022 IE$^{EE}$ 18th International Colloquium on Signal Processing & Applications (CSPA).* IEEE; 2022;5–9.

[64] Taori T, Gupta S, Bhagat S, Gajre S, Manthalkar R. Cross-task cognitive load classification with identity mapping-based distributed CNN and attention-based RNN using Gabor decomposed data images. *IETE J Res.* 2022;1–17.

[65] Medsker LR, Jain LC. Recurrent neural networks. *Des Appl.* 2001;5:64–67.

[66] Joshua Thomas J, Pillai N. A deep learning framework on generation of image descriptions with bidirectional recurrent neural networks. In: *International Conference on Intelligent Computing & Optimization.* Springer; 2018;219–230.

[67] Auleria M, Arrahmah AI, Saputra DE. A review on KN earest neighbour based classification for object recognition. In: *2021 International Conference on Data Science and Its Applications (ICoDSA).* IEEE; 2021;274–280.

[68] Amrutha K, Prabu P. ML Based sign language recognition system. In: *2021 International Conference on Innovative Trends in Information Technology (ICITIIT).* IEEE; 2021;1–6.

[69] Boughrara H, Chtourou M, Amar C Ben. MLP neural network based face recognition system using constructive training algorithm. In: *2012 International Conference on Multimedia Computing and Systems.* IEEE; 2012;233–238.

[70] Son J, Shin JY, Kim HD, Jung K-H, Park KH, Park SJ. Development and validation of deep learning models for screening multiple abnormal findings in retinal fundus images. *Ophthalmology.* 2020;127(1):85–94.

[71] Yang J, Zhang K, Fan H, Huang Z, Xiang Y, Yang J, et al. Development and validation of deep learning algorithms for scoliosis screening using back images. *Commun Biol.* 2019;2(1):1–8.

[72] Yue Z, Ma L, Zhang R. Comparison and validation of deep learning models for the diagnosis of pneumonia. *Comput Intell Neurosci.* 2020;(2020);1–8.

[73] Madani A, Arnaout R, Mofrad M, Arnaout R. Fast and accurate view classification of echocardiograms using deep learning. *NPJ Digit Med.* 2018;1(1):1–8.

[74] Dvoršak G, Dwivedi A, Štruc V, Peer P, Emeršič Ž. Kinship verification from ear images: An explorative study with deep learning models. In: *2022 International Workshop on Biometrics and Forensics (IWBF)*. IEEE; 2022;1–6.

[75] Yamashita R, Kapoor T, Alam MN, Galimzianova A, Syed SA, Ugur Akdogan M, et al. Toward reduction in false-positive thyroid nodule biopsies with a deep learning–based risk stratification system using US cine-clip images. *Radiol Artif Intell*. 2022;4(3):e210174.

[76] Geetharamani G, Pandian A. Identification of plant leaf diseases using a nine-layer deep convolutional neural network. *Comput Electr Eng*. 2019;76:323–338.

[77] Dileep MR, Pournami PN. AyurLeaf: A deep learning approach for classification of medicinal plants. In: *TENCON 2019–2019 IEEE Region 10 Conference (TENCON)*. IEEE; 2019;321–325.

[78] Wable PB, Chilveri P. Neural network based leaf recognition. In: *Proceedings of the 2016 International Conference on Automatic Control and Dynamic Optimization Techniques (ICACDOT)*. Pune; 2016;645–648.

[79] Fu H, Chi Z. Combined thresholding and neural network approach for vein pattern extraction from leaf images. *IEE Proc-Vision, Image Signal Process*. 2006;153(6):881–892.

[80] Harish BS, Hedge A, Venkatesh O, Spoorthy D, Sushma D. Classification of plant leaves using Morphological features and Zernike moments. In: *Proceedings of the 2013 International Conference on Advances in Computing, Communications and Informatics (ICACCI)*. Mysore; 2013;1827–1831.

[81] Janani R, Gopal A. Identification of selected medicinal plant leaves using image features and ANN. In: *2013 International Conference on Advanced Electronic Systems (ICAES)*. 2013;238–242.

[82] Anami B, Nandyal S, Govardhan D. A combined color, texture and edge features based approach for identification and classification of Indian medicinal plants. *Int J Comput Appl*. 2010;10;6.

[83] Luna RG de, Baldovino RG, Cotoco EA, Ocampo ALP de, Valenzuela IC, Culaba AB, et al. Identification of philippine herbal medicine plant leaf using artificial neural network. In: *2017 I$^{EE}$E 9th International Conference on Humanoid, Nanotechnology, Information Technology, Communication and Control, Environment and Management (HNICEM)*. 2017;1–8.

[84] Satti V. An automatic leaf recognition system for plant identification using machine vision technology. *Int J Eng Sci Technol*. 2013 Apr 1;5(4):874.

[85] Shah MP, Singha S, Awate SP. Leaf classification using marginalized shape context and shape+ texture dual-path deep convolutional neural network. In: *2017 IEEE International Conference on Image Processing (ICIP)*. IEEE; 2017;860–864.

[86] Dyrmann M, Karstoft H, Midtiby HS. Plant species classification using deep convolutional neural network. *Biosyst Eng*. 2016;151:72–80.

[87] Xiaoyu S, Liting J, Yang Z, Yue S, Tong L. Plant image recognition with complex background based on effective region screening. *Laser Optoelectron Prog*. 2020;57(4).

[88] Mookdarsanit L, Mookdarsanit P. Thai herb identification with medicinal properties using convolutional neural network. *Suan Sunandha Sci Technol J.* 2019;6(2):34–40.

[89] Amulya K, Deepika K, Kamakshi P. An optimized hyper parameter-based CNN approach for predicting medicinal or non-medicinal leaves. *Adv Eng Softw.* 2022;172:103181.

[90] Bhuiyan M, Abdullahil-Oaphy M, Khanam RS, Islam M. MediNET: A deep learning approach to recognize Bangladeshi ordinary medicinal plants using CNN. In: *Soft computing techniques and applications.* Springer; 2021;371–380.

[91] Paulson A, Ravishankar S. AI based indigenous medicinal plant identification. In: 2020 *Advanced Computing And Communication Technologies For High Performance Applications (ACCTHPA).* IEEE; 2020;57–63.

[92] Larese MG, Namías R, Craviotto RM, Arango MR, Gallo C, Granitto PM. Automatic classification of legumes using leaf vein image features. *Pattern Recognit.* 2014;47(1):158–168.

[93] Wang X, Feng B, Bai X, Liu W, Latecki LJ. Bag of contour fragments for robust shape classification. *Pattern Recognit.* 2014;47(6):2116–2125.

[94] Amin AHM, Khan AI. One-shot classification of 2-D leaf shapes using distributed hierarchical graph neuron (DHGN) scheme with k-NN classifier. *Procedia Comput Sci.* 2013;24:84–96.

[95] Chaki J, Parekh R, Bhattacharya S. Plant leaf recognition using texture and shape features with neural classifiers. *Pattern Recognit Lett.* 2015; 58:61–68.

[96] Waghmare H, Kokare R, Dandawate Y. Detection and classification of diseases of grape plant using opposite colour local binary pattern feature and machine learning for automated decision support system. In: *2016 3rd International Conference On Signal Processing and Integrated Networks (SPIN).* IEEE; 2016;513–518.

[97] Mukherjee G, Chatterjee A, Tudu B. Morphological feature based maturity level identification of Kalmegh and Tulsi leaves. In: *2017 Third International Conference on Research in Computational Intelligence and Communication Networks (ICRCICN).* IEEE; 2017;1–5.

[98] Kensert A, Harrison PJ, Spjuth O. Transfer learning with deep convolutional neural networks for classifying cellular morphological changes. *SLAS Discov Adv Life Sci R&D.* 2019;24(4):466–475.

[99] Shi L, Zhang Y, Cheng J, Lu H. Two-stream adaptive graph convolutional networks for skeleton-based action recognition. In: *Proceedings of the IEEE/CVF Conference on Computer Vision and Pattern Recognition.* 2019;12026–12035.

[100] Ioffe S, Szegedy C. Batch normalization: Accelerating deep network training by reducing internal covariate shift. In: *International Conference on Machine Learning.* PMLR; 2015;448–456.

[101] Szegedy C, Vanhoucke V, Ioffe S, Shlens J, Wojna Z. Rethinking the inception architecture for computer vision. In: *Proceedings of the IEEE Conference on Computer Vision and Pattern Recognition.* 2016;2818–2826.

[102] Szegedy C, Ioffe S, Vanhoucke V, Alemi AA. Inception-v4, inception-resnet and the impact of residual connections on learning. In: *Thirty-first AAAI Conference on Artificial Intelligence*. 2017.

[103] He K, Zhang X, Ren S, Sun J. Deep residual learning for image recognition. *IEEE*. 2016;770–778.

[104] Chollet F. Xception: Deep learning with depthwise separable convolutions. In: *Proceedings of the IEEE Conference on Computer Vision and Pattern Recognition*. 2017;1251–1258

# CNN-Based Fire Prediction Using Fractional Order Optical Flow and Smoke Features

Muzammil Khan, Pushpendra Kumar
and Nitish Kumar Mahala

*Department of Mathematics, Bioinformatics and
Computer Applications, Maulana Azad National
Institute of Technology Bhopal, India*

## 10.1 INTRODUCTION

Fires are frequently abrupt, impactful and widespread public and forest areas and are difficult to extinguish. Therefore, to protect buildings, offices, forests or workplaces from fire, early detection becomes very important [1, 2]. The early detection of fire can be done with the help of smoke because it is a starting stage of fire before the appearance of flames, and it is highly visible from long distances through digital cameras installed in many public locations [3]. However, smoke is small at the beginning and has different colors, shapes and texturess compared to fire. Hence, the detection of smoke is a crucial step in the early prevention of fire [4].

With recent rapid advancements in digital video camera technology, the video cameras have become highly affordable and economical [5].

DOI: 10.1201/9781003364856-10

These video cameras are either mounted at hilltops or on walls or ceilings of buildings, and they continuously record videos in the form of image sequences. Since manually processing this huge amount of video data is extremely tedious, an automatic approach to classify such events is an inevitable requirement of the time. Computer vision and deep learning algorithms together have constituted one sort of sophisticated technology that is becoming more prevalent in various areas of image processing, such as face recognition, image retrieval, surveillance, object detection and classification [6–10]. Detection of fire signatures in terms of smoke in videos is one of its fruitful applications [11].

A considerable amount of work in the detection of smoke in videos is available in the literature. Generally, smoke detection framework can be categorized into two groups: (1) the traditional computer-vision-based approach and (2) the deep-learning-based approach [12]. Computer-vision-based approaches rely on mathematical formulation, while deep learning approaches are based on training [13]. In [14], Hanh et al. performed direct fire detection using aerial forest videos in which the fire regions are detected with the help of RGB, YCbCr and HSI color spaces. Xu et al. [15] proposed a framework based on the deep domain adaptation technique, which utilizes synthetic data in smoke characterization using a convolution neural network (CNN). Moreover, Muhammad et al. [16] discussed a fine-tuned GoogleNet architecture with low computing complexity. However, the detection of fire and smoke in natural videos faces a basic hurdle of recognition in dynamic texture. For this purpose, pretrained CNN models with SVM or random forest classifiers were employed in [17]. Luo et al. [18] identified the suspicious region based on a dark channel obtained from the dynamic update of background. Pundir et al. [11] used the local extrema co-occurrence pattern to characterize the foreground regions, intensity and hue of smoke in an HSV color space. Ahn et al. [19] utilized CNNs to develop a computer-vision-based early fire detection model (EFDM) by using indoor CCTV videos. In their experiments, they derived a fire detection speed from EFDM, faster by 307 s compared to general fire detectors. All such deep learning techniques employ image (video) datasets.

In vision-based techniques, object motion is generally extracted with the aid of optical flow [13]. The optical flow field is estimated by assuming that the same object in different image frames does not show any alteration in its intensity values [20–22]. Optical flow-based approaches are used to find the value of motion velocities at the pixel position [23]. In [1], optical flow was determined for classifying moving blobs with an adaptive background subtraction algorithm. The dual deep learning framework presented in [3] employed optical flow calculation for characterizing the motion based on features. In [2], Mueller et al., developed two methods for optical flow estimation, which estimate the dynamic texture of fire and saturated flames. Their methods provide feature vectors for the neural network in the classification task. Wu et al. [24] performed a local binary pattern with a dense optical flow estimator in video smoke detection, where color maps were converted to HSV color space with specified values of HSV parameters. All these techniques rely on integer order derivative-based variational models for the extraction of dynamic features of fire and smoke through optical flow. However, integer order derivatives are known to work with local and smooth functions, whereas fire and smoke manifest large and discontinuous variations in the features such as texture, color, shapes, etc. [7, 25, 26]. Therefore, in carrying the early prediction of fire, we shall perform smoke detection by evaluating its dynamic features using the fractional order optical-flow-based on a nonlinear variational model, which generalizes the traditional integer order derivatives-based variational models. Fractional order derivatives deal with differentiation of arbitrary order and provide a long-term memory, which allows nonlocal variations in the functions to be calculated [23, 27]. Literature has several definitions of these derivatives, among which the quite renowned are Riemann–Liouville, Marchaud, Grünwald–Letnikov fractional derivatives [28, 29].

This chapter proposed a novel CNN-based framework for fire prediction using fractional order optical flow and smoke features. The smoke is detected through its dynamic and static features. The static features are estimated in terms of smoke color content, while the dynamic features are determined as fractional order optical flow by using a generalized nonlinear fractional variational model. The optical flow is represented with the help of color maps and used to find the active region of the images (video). Now, using static features and smoke motion sensitive channel of color map, a binary mask is developed. This binary mask is employed in extracting the active smoke region from color map. The segmented color maps and the reference images are simultaneously utilized for the training and testing of a novel designed CNN architecture for fire prediction. This architecture is developed with the help of the VGG16 and DenseNet121 models. For a thorough assessment, the results are evaluated in terms of different metrics such as classification accuracy (Acc), recall (R), precision (P), F1-score (F1), hamming loss (H–loss) and AUC (area under the curve). Moreover, a dataset of optical flow color maps is generated using 16 fire-smoke videos and 19 normal (non-smoke) videos. The performance of the proposed framework is compared against various existing models through learning and ROC curves.

## 10.2 METHODOLOGY

The complete methodology of the proposed framework is depicted in Figure 10.1. The video dataset used in this chapter is collected from [30, 31]. This dataset is composed of 16 smoke videos (346 frames) and 19 normal videos (250 frames). These videos represent several indoor and outdoor scenes such as rooms, forests and roads under various conditions of cloud, illumination changes and fog etc. Now, from each of the videos, two temporally correlated image frames are taken and resized to 384×384. These resized frames are processed using a nonlinear fractional-order-based variational model. This process produces a fractional order optical flow field corresponding to each pair of image frames. This flow field is a vector field; therefore, it is converted into a color map using the color wheel as described by [32]. This color map is an RGB image having the same dimensions as compared to the reference images. Thus a total of 324 color maps for smoke and 228 color maps for normal videos are obtained here. Further, using these color maps along with the smoke color information obtained from the corresponding reference images, a binary mask is constructed for each pair of images. This binary mask segments the smoke active region from the rest of the part in the corresponding color maps. Finally, the dataset, which contains total 324 and 228 segmented color maps for smoke and normal videos, respectively, along with their corresponding reference images, is employed in the training and testing of the proposed CNN architecture.

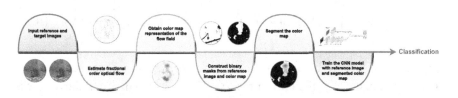

FIGURE 10.1   Proposed framework for fire-smoke motion detection.

## 10.3 ESTIMATION OF FRACTIONAL ORDER OPTICAL FLOW

### 10.3.1 Formulation of Nonlinear Fractional Order Variational Optical Flow Model

At any pixel position, let intensity values be $\mathcal{J}(\mathcal{X},\mathcal{Y},\mathcal{T})$ and $\mathcal{J}(\mathcal{X}+\delta\mathcal{X},\mathcal{Y}+\delta\mathcal{Y},\mathcal{T}+\delta\mathcal{T})$ at spatiotemporal coordinates $(\mathcal{X},\mathcal{Y},\mathcal{T})$ and $(\mathcal{X}+\delta\mathcal{X},\mathcal{Y}+\delta\mathcal{Y},\mathcal{T}+\delta\mathcal{T})$, respectively. By employing the data conservation assumption (BCA) [20], we obtain

$$\mathcal{J}(\mathcal{X}+\delta\mathcal{X},\mathcal{Y}+\delta\mathcal{Y},\mathcal{T}+\delta\mathcal{T})=\mathcal{J}(\mathcal{X},\mathcal{Y},\mathcal{T}) \tag{10.1}$$

where, $\mathcal{J}:\Omega\subset\mathbb{R}^3\rightarrow\mathbb{R}$ is a volume representing a rectangular image sequence. Therefore, using Taylor series expansion in Eq. (10.1), we have

$$(\nabla\mathcal{J})^T w + \mathcal{J}_\mathcal{T} = 0 \tag{10.2}$$

where $\nabla\mathcal{J}=(\mathcal{J}_\mathcal{X},\mathcal{J}_\mathcal{Y})^T$ stands for the intensity gradient in the spatial region, $w=(\mu,v)^T$ is the desired optical flow field with $\mu(\mathcal{X},\mathcal{Y})$ and $v(\mathcal{X},\mathcal{Y})$ as its $\mathcal{X}$ and $\mathcal{Y}$ flow components. Here, $\mathcal{J}_\mathcal{T}$ denotes the intensity temporal derivative. The problem of optical flow estimation using Eq. (10.2) is referred to as an ill-posed problem. To convert this problem into a well posed one, it needs to be regularized by introducing an additional constraint called the smoothness constraint [20]. This constraint is laid down on the assumption that all the neighboring pixels of any pixel in an image plane move coherently. The general form of smoothness terms is as follows:

$$F(\mu,v,\nabla\mu,\nabla v)=F_1(\mu,v)+F_2(\nabla\mu,\nabla v) \tag{10.3}$$

where $F_1$ and $F_2$ are scalar valued functions that are convex in nature. Here, $F_2(\nabla\mu,\nabla v)$ is based on the pixel flow rate. Thus, in general, optical flow is estimated with the help of following variational functional [20, 33]

$$E(w)=\int_\Omega\left[\left(\nabla\mathcal{J}^T w + \mathcal{J}_\mathcal{T}\right)^2 + F_1(\mu,v)+F_2(\nabla\mu,\nabla v)\right]d\mathcal{X} \tag{10.4}$$

where $X=(\mathcal{X},\mathcal{Y})$. The discontinuous information on images such as texture and edges are efficiently preserved by fractional order derivatives. Moreover, fractional order derivatives can be evaluated corresponding to an optimal choice of fractional order $\alpha$ for which the solutions are stable

[26, 34, 35]. Therefore, in the presented model $F_2(\nabla\mu,\nabla v)$ is replaced by a fractional-order-derivative-based term $F_2(D_+^\alpha\mu, D_+^\alpha v)$.

*10.3.1.1 Nonlinear Fractional Order Variational Model*

This chapter proposes the following nonlinear fractional order variational model by embedding the Charbonnier norm [36] and Marchaud fractional [37] derivative to make the estimated optical flow accurate and robust.

$$E(w) = \int_\Omega \left[ \psi\left(\nabla\mathcal{J}^T w + \mathcal{J}_T\right) + F_1(\mu,v) + F_2\left(D_+^\alpha\mu, D_+^\alpha v\right) \right] d\mathbf{X} \quad (10.5)$$

where $\psi(z) = \sigma\sqrt{1+\left(\dfrac{z}{\sigma}\right)^2}$ describes Charbonnier norm in $z$, and $\sigma$ denotes a small positive parameter selected as per Bruhn et al. [36]. The functions $F_1$ and $F_2$ are given by $F_1(\mu,v) = \beta^2 w^T w$ and $F_2\left(D_+^\alpha\mu, D_+^\alpha v\right) = \lambda e^T\left(D_+^\alpha w^T \odot D_+^\alpha w^T\right)e$, where $\beta, \lambda \in \mathbb{R}^+$ and $D_+^\alpha \mathcal{Z} = \left(D_\mathcal{X}^\alpha \mathcal{Z}, D_\mathcal{Y}^\alpha \mathcal{Z}\right)^T$. Here, $D_\mathcal{X}^\alpha \mathcal{Z}$ and $D_\mathcal{Y}^\alpha \mathcal{Z}$ denote the Marchaud differentiation of $\mathcal{Z}$ related with $\mathcal{X}$ and $\mathcal{Y}$, respectively, for $\alpha \in (0,1)$. The symbol $\odot$ denotes the Hadamard product, and $e \in \mathbb{R}^{2\times 1}$ is the column vector with all entries as 1. It is observed that as $\sigma \to 0$, model (5) tends to demonstrate an $L_1$-norm based model, and whenever $\alpha \in \mathbb{Z}^+$, the presented model describes an integer-order-based model. In addition, the use of Charbonnier norm and Marchaud derivative in the presented work is motivated by the following:

- Charbonnier norm is a well-known robust statistic that is less sensitive to outliers than quadratic approaches [36].

- Since the Charbonnier norm is non-quadratic in nature, nonlinear models are capable of producing satisfactory results in the presence of flow discontinuities [36].

- Its convex nature ensures a unique solution for the minimization problem. This makes it superior to the non-convex Lorentzian norm [38].

- The Charbonnier norm can be scaled to the $L_1$-norm through the use of $\sigma$ [36].

- The Marchaud derivative is useful as it can be used also with those functions that are not continuous (such as images).

For performing the estimation of optical flow, the functional Eq. (10.5) needs to be minimized. Let $\mu \equiv \mu(\mathcal{X}, \mathcal{Y})$ and $v \equiv v(\mathcal{X}, \mathcal{Y})$ be two arbitrary functions such that the deviations $w$ from the desired optical flow solution $w^*$ can be written as

$$w = w^* + \epsilon \, \Phi \tag{10.6}$$

where $\epsilon$ represents a real variable, and $\Phi = (\eta, \phi)^T$. Let us describe the Marchaud differentiation of Eq. (10.6) of order $\alpha$ as follows:

$$D_+^{\alpha} w^T = D_+^{\alpha} w^{*T} + \epsilon \, D_+^{\alpha} \Phi^T \tag{10.7}$$

Substituting the right-hand sides of Eqs. (10.6) and (10.7) into the expression (10.5) and employing the definition of $\psi$, the following variable scalar valued function is obtained:

$$
E(\epsilon) = \int_{\Omega} \left[ \sigma \sqrt{1 + \left( \frac{\nabla \mathcal{J}^T \left( w^* + \epsilon \, \Phi \right) + \mathcal{J}_T}{\sigma} \right)^2} \right.
$$
$$
\left. + \beta^2 \left( w^* + \epsilon \, \Phi \right)^T \left( w^* + \epsilon \, \Phi \right) + \lambda e^T \vphantom{\int} \right.
$$
$$
\left. \left[ \left( D_+^{\alpha} w^{*T} + \epsilon \, D_+^{\alpha} \Phi^T \right) \odot \left( D_+^{\alpha} w^{*T} + \epsilon \, D_+^{\alpha} \Phi^T \right) \right] e \right] dX \tag{10.8}
$$

This function gives the required solution when $\epsilon = 0$; therefore, the derivative of Eq. (10.8) with respect to $\epsilon$ vanishes for $\epsilon = 0$ [39].

$$
0 = \int_{\Omega} \left[ \left\{ \frac{\left( \nabla \mathcal{J}^T w^* + \mathcal{J}_T \right) \left( \nabla \mathcal{J}^T \Phi \right)}{\psi \left( \nabla \mathcal{J}^T w^* + \mathcal{J}_T \right)} \right\} \right.
$$
$$
\left. + 2\beta^2 w^{*T} \Phi + 2\lambda \left\{ e^T \left( D_+^{\alpha} w^{*T} \odot D_+^{\alpha} \Phi^T \right) e \right\} \right] dX \tag{10.9}
$$

on applying the Fubini theorem [40], the theorem in [23] and the Marchaud derivative [37] on Eq. (10.9), we obtain

$$\int_{\Omega} e^T \left( D_+^{\alpha} w^{*T} \odot D_+^{\alpha} \Phi^T \right) e \, dX = \int_{\Omega} \left[ \left\{ \left( D_-^{\alpha} D_+^{\alpha} \right)^T e \right\} w^* \odot \Phi \right] dX \tag{10.10}$$

Thus, substituting Eq. (10.10) for its right-hand side into Eq. (10.9) provides the following expression:

$$0 = \int_{\Omega} \left[ \left\{ \frac{\left(\nabla \mathcal{J}^T w^* + \mathcal{J}_T\right)\left(\nabla \mathcal{J}\right)}{\psi\left(\nabla \mathcal{J}^T w^* + \mathcal{J}_T\right)} + 2\beta^2 w^* + 2\lambda \right. \right.$$
$$\left. \left. \left\{ \left(D_-^{\alpha} D_+^{\alpha}\right)^T e \right\} w^* \right\} \odot \Phi \right] dX \qquad (10.11)$$

where $D_-^{\alpha} D_+^{\alpha} = \left(D_{-x}^{\alpha} D_x^{\alpha}, D_{-y}^{\alpha} D_y^{\alpha}\right)^T$ and $D_{-x}^{\alpha}$ and $D_{-y}^{\alpha}$ stand for the left Marchaud derivative with respect to $\mathcal{X}$ and $\mathcal{Y}$, respectively. Hence a system of Euler–Lagrange equations is obtained from Eq. (10.11) for each pixel in the image frame in accordance with the concept of the calculus of variation [41]

$$\frac{\left(\nabla \mathcal{J}^T w^* + \mathcal{J}_T\right)\left(\nabla \mathcal{J}\right)}{\psi\left(\nabla \mathcal{J}^T w^* + \mathcal{J}_T\right)} + 2\beta^2 w^* + 2\lambda \left\{ \left(D_-^{\alpha} D_+^{\alpha}\right)^T e \right\} w^* = O_{2\times 1} \qquad (10.12)$$

where $o_{2\times 1} \in \mathbb{R}^{2\times 1}$ is a zero vector and $w = (\mu, v)^T$.

## 10.3.2 Numerical Solution

### 10.3.2.1 Derivative Discretization Scheme

The estimated optical flow components and their corresponding reference image are of the same size $m \times n$. Therefore, the discretization of $\mu$ and $v$ is described:

$$w \equiv w(i, j) = w(i\Delta h, j\Delta h)$$

where a pixel position is specified by the index pair $(i, j)$, and $\Delta h$ represents the side length of a pixel in the image frame, which is generally equal to 1. Now, for numerical implementation purposes, the Marchaud derivative discretization is performed with the help of the Grünwald–Letnikov derivative [29]:

$$D_+^{\alpha} w^T = \sum_{k=0}^{\infty} \omega_k^{(\alpha)} E_{\mathcal{X}}^{-k} w^T \qquad (10.13)$$

where $E_{\mathcal{X}}^{-k} = \left( E_{\mathcal{X}}^{-k}, E_{\mathcal{Y}}^{-k} \right)^T$ and $E_{\mathcal{X}}^{-k}, E_{\mathcal{Y}}^{-k}$ are the operators representing a shift of $-k$ steps from $(i,j)$ in $\mathcal{X}$ and $\mathcal{Y}$ directions, respectively. The term $\omega_k^{(\alpha)} = (-1)^k \binom{\alpha}{k}$ represents a binomial coefficient obtained from expanding $(1-z)^k$ and is evaluated using the following recursion formula:

$$\omega_0^{(\alpha)} = 1, \quad \omega_k^{(\alpha)} = \left( 1 - \frac{\alpha+1}{k} \right) \omega_{k-1}^{(\alpha)} \tag{10.14}$$

where $k = 1,2,3,\ldots$, employing the Grünwald–Letnikov derivative definition [29] in Eq. (10.13), this gives

$$D_-^\alpha D_+^\alpha w^T = -\sum_{k=-\infty}^{0} \omega_{|k|}^{(\alpha)} E_{\mathcal{X}}^{-k} w^T - \sum_{k=0}^{\infty} \omega_k^{(\alpha)} E_{\mathcal{X}}^{-k} w^T \tag{10.15}$$

Since $\sum_{k=0}^{\infty} \omega_k^\alpha = 0$, Eq. (10.15) is rearranged as

$$D_-^\alpha D_+^\alpha w^T = -\sum_{k=-\infty}^{0} \omega_{|k|}^{(\alpha)} \nabla \left( E_{\mathcal{X}}^{-k} w^T \right) - \sum_{k=0}^{\infty} \omega_k^{(\alpha)} \nabla \left( E_{\mathcal{X}}^{-k} w^T \right) \tag{10.16}$$

where $\nabla \left( E_{\mathcal{X}}^{-k} w^T \right) = E_{\mathcal{X}}^{-k} w^T - (Rw)^T$, and $R$ represents an operator that, when acted on $a \in \mathbb{R}^n$, provides $\left[ aa\ldots a \right] \in \mathbb{R}^{n \times n}$. Further, taking pre-multiplication by $e^T$ on both sides of Eq. (10.16), we obtain

$$e^T D_-^\alpha D_+^\alpha w^T = -\sum_{k=-\infty}^{0} \omega_{|k|}^{(\alpha)} e^T \nabla \left( E_{\mathcal{X}}^{-k} w^T \right) - \sum_{k=0}^{\infty} \omega_k^{(\alpha)} e^T \nabla \left( E_{\mathcal{X}}^{-k} w^T \right) \tag{10.17}$$

Since the presented algorithm is purposed to be employed in the field of image processing, Eq. (10.17) is approximated as

$$e^T D_-^\alpha D_+^\alpha w^T \approx -\sum_{k=-W}^{0} \omega_{|k|}^{(\alpha)} e^T \nabla \left( E_{\mathcal{X}}^{-k} w^T \right) - \sum_{k=0}^{W} \omega_k^{(\alpha)} e^T \nabla \left( E_{\mathcal{X}}^{-k} w^T \right) \tag{10.18}$$

where the window mask size is specified as $W$. Next, Eq. (10.18) is rewritten to obtain the following expression:

$$\left\{ \left( D_-^\alpha D_+^\alpha \right)^T e \right\} w \approx \sum_{(\bar{\imath},\bar{\jmath}) \in \wp(i,j)} \omega_{p_{ij}}^{(\alpha)} \left\{ w(i,j) - w(\bar{\imath},\bar{\jmath}) \right\} \tag{10.19}$$

where all the neighboring pixels of the pixel at $(i, j)$ position that lie along the $X$ and $Y$ directions through $(i, j)$ are contained in the set $\wp$ and $p_{ij} = \max\left[\left|\bar{\imath} - i\right|, \left|\bar{\jmath} - j\right|\right]$.

### 10.3.2.2 Numerical Scheme

The following discussion demonstrates a system of discretized equations for the two optical flow components that are derived with the help of expression (10.19) and system Eq. (10.12):

$$\begin{bmatrix} \dfrac{1}{\psi\left(\nabla \mathcal{J}^T w + \mathcal{J}_T\right)} \mathcal{J}_{xx} + K & \dfrac{1}{\psi\left(\nabla \mathcal{J}^T w + \mathcal{J}_T\right)} \mathcal{J}_{xy} \\[4mm] \dfrac{1}{\psi\left(\nabla \mathcal{J}^T w + \mathcal{J}_T\right)} \mathcal{J}_{xy} & \dfrac{1}{\psi\left(\nabla \mathcal{J}^T w + \mathcal{J}_T\right)} \mathcal{J}_{yy} + K \end{bmatrix} \quad (10.20)$$

$$w = 2\lambda \sum_{(\bar{\imath},\bar{\jmath})\in\wp(i,j)} \omega_{p_{ij}}^{(\alpha)} \bar{w} - \dfrac{1}{\psi\left(\nabla \mathcal{J}^T w\right)} \mathcal{J}^T$$

For the sake of convenience, we abbreviate various terms in Eq. (10.20):

$$\begin{aligned} \mathcal{J}_{xx} &= \mathcal{J}_x^2, & \mathcal{J}^T &= \left(\mathcal{J}_x \mathcal{J}_T, \mathcal{J}_y \mathcal{J}_T\right)^T \\ \mathcal{J}_{yy} &= \mathcal{J}_y^2, & w &= \left(\mu\left(\bar{\imath},\bar{\jmath}\right), v\left(\bar{\imath},\bar{\jmath}\right)\right), \\ \mathcal{J}_{xy} &= \mathcal{J}_x \mathcal{J}_y, & K &= 2\beta^2 + 2\lambda \sum_{(\bar{\imath},\bar{\jmath})\in\wp(i,j)} \omega_{p_{ij}}^{(\alpha)} \end{aligned}$$

Finally, optical flow $w$ is estimated at each pixel using the following system of iteration equations:

$$w^{(n+1)} = \mathfrak{T}^{(n)}\left[ 2\lambda \sum_{(\bar{\imath},\bar{\jmath})\in\wp(i,j)} \omega_{p_{ij}}^{(\alpha)} \bar{w}^{(n)} - \dfrac{1}{\psi\left(\nabla \mathcal{J}^T w^{(n)} + \mathcal{J}_T\right)} \right.$$

$$\left. \left(\mathcal{J}_{xy} w_{ud}^{(n)} + \mathcal{J}^T\right) \right] \quad (10.21)$$

where $w_{ud} = (v(i,j), \mu(i,j))^T$, $\mathfrak{T}^{(n)} = \left(\mathfrak{T}_\mu^{(n)}, \mathfrak{T}_v^{(n)}\right)^T$,

$$\mathfrak{T}_\mu^{(n)} = \left( \frac{1}{\psi\left(\nabla \mathcal{J}^T w^{(n)} + \mathcal{J}_T\right)} \mathcal{J}_{xx} + 2\beta^2 + 2\lambda \sum_{(\bar{\imath},\bar{\jmath}) \in \wp(i,j)} \omega_{p_{ij}}^{(\alpha)} \right)^{-1}$$

and $\mathfrak{T}_v^{(n)} = \left( \dfrac{1}{\psi\left(\nabla \mathcal{J}^T w^{(n)} + \mathcal{J}_T\right)} \mathcal{J}_{yy} + 2\beta^2 + 2\lambda \sum_{(\bar{\imath},\bar{\jmath}) \in \wp(i,j)} \omega_{p_{ij}}^{(\alpha)} \right)^{-1}$. An outer

fixed point iteration technique is utilized in converting this nonlinear system into a linear system of equations. Further, Gauss–Seidel method [42, 43] is employed for solving the resulting linear system. The pseudocode of the fractional order optical flow estimation algorithm is given as Algorithm 1 and illustrated in Figure 10.2.

---

**Algorithm 1:** Fractional order optical flow estimation algorithm

---

**Input:** $\mathcal{J}_1, \mathcal{J}_2$ (reference and target image frames), $\alpha$, $\beta$, $\lambda$, $W$, $N_{warp}$, $N_{pyr}$ and $N_{it}$
**Output:** Optical flow field $w = (\mu, \nu)$
Set up image pyramids $\mathcal{J}_1^{pyr(k)}$ and $\mathcal{J}_2^{pyr(k)}$
**for** $k = N_{pyr}-1$ *to* $0$ **do**
   $\mathcal{J}_1 = \mathcal{J}_1^{pyr(k)}$, $\mathcal{J}_2 = \mathcal{J}_2^{pyr(k)}$;
   **if** $k == N_{pyr}-1$ **then**
    | Set $w = 0$;
   **else**
    └ Upsample $\mu$, $\nu$ to the current level;
   **if** $k \neq N_{pyr}-1$ **then**
    └ Update $\mathcal{J}_1 = warping(\mathcal{J}_1, w)$;
   Initialize $\delta w$ to zero with $size == size(\mathcal{J}_1)$;
   **for** $w = 1$ *to* $N_{warp}$ **do**
      Compute $\mathcal{J}_x$, $\mathcal{J}_y$ and $\mathcal{J}_T$, using $\mathcal{J}_1$ and $\mathcal{J}_2$;
      **for** $it = 1$ *to* $N_{it}$ **do**
        | Compute fractional order derivatives of order $0 < \alpha < 1$ of $\delta w$;
        └ Update $\delta w$ using Eq. 21;
      Update $w = w + \delta w$;
      Update $\mathcal{J}_1 = warping(\mathcal{J}_1, \delta w)$;
      └ Initialize $\delta w$ to zero;

---

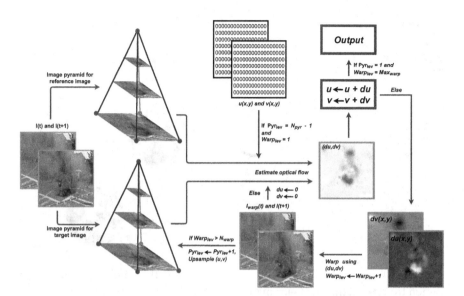

FIGURE 10.2   Proposed algorithm for fractional order optical flow estimation.

## 10.4 EXTRACTION OF SMOKE MOTION ACTIVE REGION FROM COLOR MAP

Figure 10.3 illustrates the algorithm for the extraction of a smoke motion active region from a color map. The reference and target images are processed using the fractional order optical flow estimation algorithm. This algorithm produces their corresponding fractional order optical flow field as a vector plot. In vector plot representation, each vector represents the pixel flow (motion) with respect to the reference images. To utilize this flow field in the training and testing of a CNN architecture, the vector plots are converted into color maps as described in [32]. These color maps contain the same dimensions as compared to the reference images. In color maps, different colors delineate various flow directions, and color saturation shows flow magnitudes. However, the blue channel of the color maps reflects more sensitivity toward upward motion. In general, smoke shows a tendency to diffuse in an upward direction [44], therefore the blue channel is extracted from the color maps. Hence a dynamic binary mask is developed using the blue channel. Since smoke also demonstrates black, gray and nearly white colors due to the variety of fuel and air supply [45], a static binary mask is also constructed based on the color information. Finally, these dynamic and static binary masks are fused to generate the

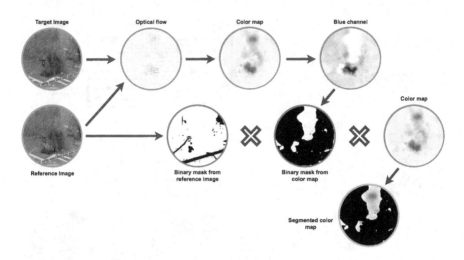

FIGURE 10.3 Proposed algorithm for segmenting the smoke motion active region from the estimated color map.

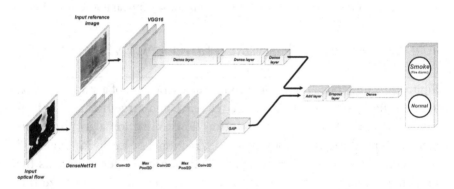

FIGURE 10.4 Design of the proposed CNN architecture for fire prediction using smoke.

resulting mask for segmenting the corresponding color map. Further, the architecture of the proposed CNN model for smoke detection is illustrated in Figure 10.4.

## 10.5 EXPERIMENTS, RESULTS AND DISCUSSION

### 10.5.1 Performance Evaluation Metrics

In binary classification, the discriminatory performance of a model is best described with the help of a confusion matrix [46]. This is a matrix of size $2 \times 2$, in which rows and columns represent the actual and predicted data, respectively. Here, the first row contains $t_p$ and $f_n$, while the second row contains $f_p$ and $t_n$. The evaluation metrics utilized in the performance analysis of the CNN model are often derived from the confusion matrix. This chapter considers the following metrics based on the requirement of the proposed work.

1. **Accuracy (Acc):** Acc provides the proportion of correct predictions in the set of all predictions [47]. It is defined as

$$CA = \frac{t_p + t_n}{t_p + f_p + f_n + t_n}$$

This metric generally fails to provide a good description of discrimination, if one class has a very few samples while the other one has a very large number of samples.

2. **Recall (R):** This gives the ratio of correctly classified positive samples over the set of all positive samples [46]. It is also known as sensitivity and is given as

$$R = \frac{t_p}{t_p + f_n}$$

It cannot be used to classify an overall proportion of true positives in the set of all the correctly predicted samples.

3. **Precision (P):** It calculates the proportion of correctly classified positives in the set of all positively classified samples [46]. It is also called "positive predictive value" (PPV). It is written as

$$P = \frac{t_p}{t_p + f_p}$$

It does not provide any information regarding the true positive proportion in the class of positives.

4. **F1-Score (F1):** It is defined as the harmonic mean of R and P [48]. The value of F1 can be small or large according to whether R and P are both small or large. It is denoted as

$$F1 = \frac{t_p}{t_p + \frac{1}{2}(f_n + f_p)}$$

5. **Hamming Loss (H-Loss):** This provides the proportion of false classified samples in the set of all predicted samples [49]. It is defined as

$$H\text{-}loss = \frac{f_p + f_n}{t_p + f_p + f_n + t_n}$$

In addition to these metrics, the performance of the model is also tested using the AUC (area under curve). This AUC gives the area under the ROC curve [50]. Hence larger values of this area correspond to higher true positive rate (TPR). However, an AUC value greater than 50% is generally considered acceptable.

## 10.5.2 Experimental Discussion

The experiments were performed using the Google Colab and MATLAB® software [51] on a Windows 11 platform with 16 GB RAM. They were carried out over a dataset consisting of 324 and 228 reference images and their corresponding color maps for smoke and normal videos, respectively. In order to analyze the performance of the proposed framework, various metrics have been utilized. Also, the proposed framework is comprehensively compared against different existing models, which are discussed in tabular form, learning and ROC curves.

The first experiment discusses the estimated fractional order optical flow fields obtained by implementing the proposed variational model. The parameter values are set to $\sigma = 0.4$, $\beta = 0.1$, $\lambda = 200$, and $\alpha = 0.7$. The image frames (video) collected from [30, 31] are of different sizes; therefore, in optical flow estimation, these have been resized in 384×384 size. The few sample reference images for smoke and non-smoke videos, along with their corresponding optical flow fields, are demonstrated in Figure 10.5. The first and second rows in Figure 10.5 illustrate the reference images and corresponding optical flow fields for smoke videos, respectively, while the third and fourth rows represent the reference images and optical flow fields for non-smoke (normal) videos, respectively. Since smoke has a tendency to diffuse in the upward direction and a particular optical flow channel is more sensitive to upward motion, this characteristic of color map channels is clearly visible in the corresponding color maps of smoke. In the case of non-smoke, objects generally do not tend to move upward, which can be seen from their optical flows in Figure 10.5. Moreover, the estimated fractional order optical flow is highly insensitive toward the outliers such as illumination change present in the scenes. This shows the significance

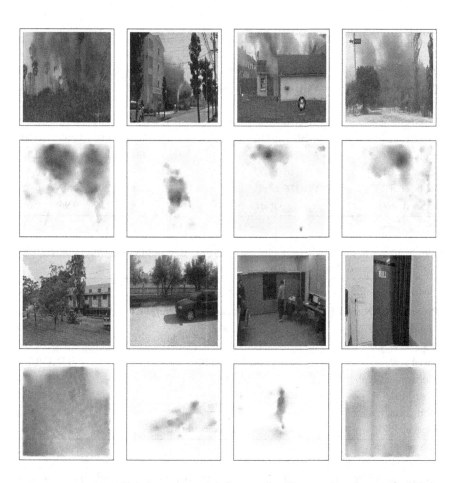

FIGURE 10.5 Sample reference smoke-fire images (first row) and corresponding optical flow fields (second row), non-smoke images (third row), and corresponding optical flow fields (fourth row).

of the nonlinear character of the presented variational model and makes the color maps a helpful tool in classifying smoke and normal scenes. The obtained color maps manifest that the estimated flow fields are dense and preserve motion edge. Finally, the generated datasets is used in the training and testing of the proposed CNN model.

The second experiment comprehensively compares the proposed CNN framework against various existing models in terms of different metrics and the number of parameters in Tables 10.1–10.2. The training and testing of all the existing models in Tables 10.1–10.2 have been conducted over

TABLE 10.1    Results Comparison between the Proposed and Existing Algorithms

| Model | CNN Architecture | Acc | R | P | F1 | H-loss |
|---|---|---|---|---|---|---|
| **Proposed model** | **VGG16 and DenseNet121** | **1.00** | **1.00** | **1.00** | **1.00** | **0.00** |
| Majid et al. [52] | ResNet50 | 0.82 | 0.71 | 1.00 | 0.83 | 0.18 |
| Majid et al. [52] | VGG16 | 0.64 | 1.00 | 0.64 | 0.78 | 0.36 |
| Saeed et al. [53] | Adaboost-LBP | 1.00 | 1.00 | 1.00 | 1.00 | 0.00 |
| Muhammad et al. [54] | AlexNet | 0.64 | 1.00 | 0.64 | 0.78 | 0.36 |
| Khan et al. [55] | VGG16 | 0.64 | 1.00 | 0.64 | 0.78 | 0.36 |
| Wang et al. [56] | VGG16 | 0.98 | 1.00 | 0.98 | 0.99 | 0.02 |
| He et al. [57] | Residual learning | 0.95 | 0.95 | 0.97 | 0.96 | 0.05 |

TABLE 10.2    Results Comparison between the Proposed and Existing Algorithms in Terms of Number of Trainable Parameters

| Model | CNN Architecture | Parameters |
|---|---|---|
| **Proposed CNN model** | **VGG16 and DenseNet121** | **10,553,346** |
| Majid et al. [52] | ResNet50 | 70,786 |
| Majid et al. [52] | VGG16 | 70,786 |
| Saeed et al. [53] | Adaboost-LBP | 171,110,274 |
| Muhammad et al. [54] | AlexNet | 171,110,274 |
| Khan et al. [55] | VGG16 | 72,142,146 |
| Wang et al. [56] | VGG16 | 8,237,442 |
| He at al. [57] | Residual learning | 4,194,690 |

the same reference image dataset. The proposed model used color maps as well as an image dataset. For comparing the proposed CNN model with Majid et al. [52], the attention layers of their model have been removed. These comparisons show that the propounded algorithm demonstrates better performance than the other existing models. It is observed that Table 10.1 depicts a satisfactory accuracy score of 1.00 for the proposed framework, while the model of Saeed et al. [53] also provides an accuracy score of 1.00 but requires more than 17 times the number of parameters as compared to the proposed model. This validates the applicability of the proposed framework.

In the last experiment, the performance of the proposed CNN model against various existing models is illustrated in Figures 10.6–10.8 in terms of learning and ROC curves. It can be seen that in case of learning curves for the proposed CNN model, the training and validation curves converge and coincide after only 4 epochs, while the other models either take more

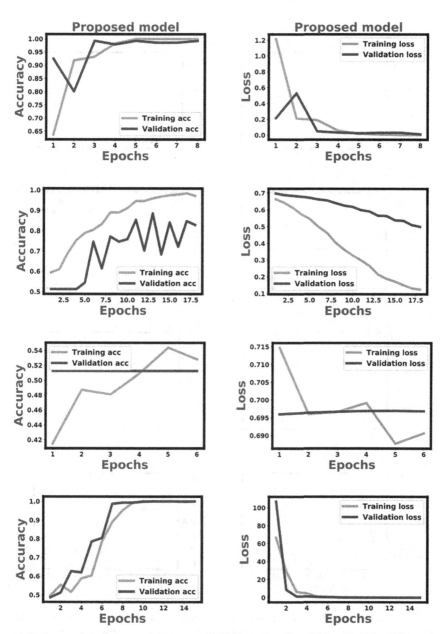

FIGURE 10.6 Learning curves in terms of accuracy and loss: Proposed framework (first row), Majid et al. [52] with ResNet50 (second row), Majid et al. [52] with VGG16 (third row), Saeed et al. [53] (fourth row).

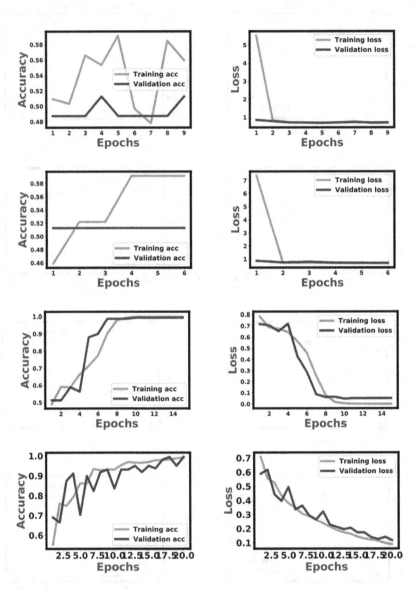

FIGURE 10.7   Learning curves in terms of accuracy and loss: Muhammad et al. [54] (first row), Khan et al. [55] (second row), Wang et al. [56] (third row), He et al. [57] (fourth row).

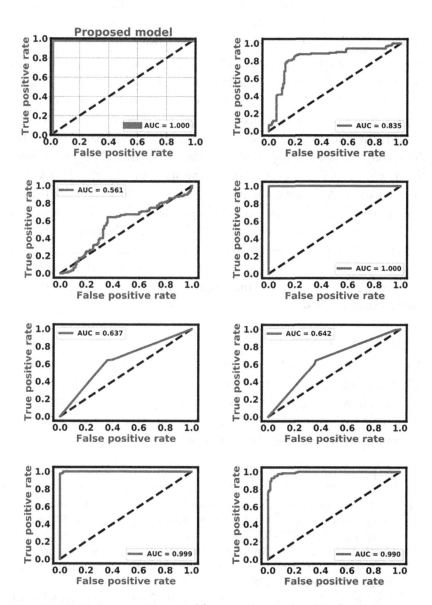

FIGURE 10.8 ROC curves: Proposed framework, Majid et al. [52] with ResNet50, Majid et al. [52] with VGG16 (third row), Saeed et al. [53], Muhammad et al. [54], Khan et al. [55], Wang et al. [56], He et al. [57].

epochs or do not converge. Also, the AUC score of the given model is 1, which provides a verification of an acceptable classification performance.

## 10.6 CONCLUSION AND FUTURE WORK

This chapter proposed a novel CNN-based framework for fire prediction using the fractional order optical flow and the dynamic as well as static features of smoke. The dataset used for experiments contain a total of 16 fire-smoke and 19 non-smoke videos. The dynamic features are estimated as optical flow fields by making use of a variational model based on fraction derivative. The obtained optical flow fields are dense, robust and preserve the moving edges of smoke patterns. The static information is described in terms of smoke color content, which is used in forming a color-based binary mask. Utilizing these binary masks, the smoke active region is successfully segmented from color maps. The proposed CNN architecture has been trained and tested on color maps as well as image dataset. The estimated results are quite better than other existing models. The future scope involves the generalization of the proposed work in determining the fire-smoke fraction in a scene.

## ACKNOWLEDGMENTS

Pushpendra Kumar and Nitish Kumar Mahala acknowledge the support of NBHM, Mumbai for grant no. 02011/24/2021 NBHM (R.P)/R&D-II/8669. Pushpendra Kumar also acknowledges the support of SERB, New Delhi for grant no. EEQ/2020/000154. The author Muzammil Khan thankfully acknowledges MHRD, New Delhi, Government of India.

## REFERENCES

[1] Sergey V Ablameyko, N Brovko, and R Bogush. Smoke detection in video based on motion and contrast. *Journal of Computer Science and Cybernatics*, 28(3):195–205, 2012.

[2] Martin Mueller, Peter Karasev, Ivan Kolesov, and Allen Tannenbaum. Optical flow estimation for flame detection in videos. *IEEE Transactions on Image Processing*, 22(7):2786–2797, 2013.

[3] Arun Singh Pundir and Balasubramanian Raman. Dual deep learning model for image based smoke detection. *Fire Technology*, 55(6):2419–2442, 2019.

[4] Viet Thang Nguyen, Cong Hoang Quach, and Minh Trien Pham. Video smoke detection for surveillance cameras based on deep learning in indoor environment. In *International Conference on Recent Advances in Signal Processing, Telecommunications & Computing*, 82–86, 2020.

[5] James Pincott, Paige Wenbin Tien, Shuangyu Wei, and John Kaiser Calautit. Development and evaluation of a vision-based transfer learning approach for indoor fire and smoke detection. *Building Services Engineering Research and Technology*, 2022. http://dx.doi.org/10.1177/01436244221089445.

[6] Shubhangi Chaturvedi, Pritee Khanna, and Aparajita Ojha. A survey on vision-based outdoor smoke detection techniques for environmental safety. *ISPRS Journal of Photogrammetry and Remote Sensing*, 185:158–187, 2022.

[7] Pushpendra Kumar, Muzammil Khan, and Shreya Gupta. Development of an IR video surveillance system based on fractional order TV-model. In *International Conference on Control, Automation, Power and Signal Processing*, 1–7, 2021.

[8] Pushpendra Kumar. Development of a thermal-visible video surveillance system based on fractional order tv-model. *Journal of Physics: Conference Series*, 1950:012026, 2021. IOP Publishing.

[9] Zhigang Tu, Wei Xie, Dejun Zhang, Ronald Poppe, Remco C Veltkamp, Baoxin Li, and Junsong Yuan. A survey of variational and CNN-based optical flow techniques. *Signal Processing: Image Communication*, 72:9–24, 2019.

[10] Snehlata Shakya and Sanjeev Kumar. Characterising and predicting the movement of clouds using fractional-order optical flow. *IET Image Processing*, 13(8):1375–1381, 2019.

[11] Arun Singh Pundir and Balasubramanian Raman. Deep belief network for smoke detection. *Fire technology*, 53(6):1943–1960, 2017.

[12] Gaohua Lin, Yongming Zhang, Qixing Zhang, Yang Jia, Gao Xu, and Jinjun Wang. Smoke detection in video sequences based on dynamic texture using volume local binary patterns. *KSII Transactions on Internet and Information Systems*, 11(11):5522–5536, 2017.

[13] Simon Baker, Daniel Scharstein, JP Lewis, Stefan Roth, Michael J Black, and Richard Szeliski. A database and evaluation methodology for optical flow. *International Journal of Computer Vision*, 92(1):1–31, 2011.

[14] Hanh Dang-Ngoc and Hieu Nguyen-Trung. Aerial forest fire surveillance-evaluation of forest fire detection model using aerial videos. In *International Conference on Advanced Technologies for Communications*, 142–148, 2019.

[15] Gao Xu, Yongming Zhang, Qixing Zhang, Gaohua Lin, and Jinjun Wang. Deep domain adaptation based video smoke detection using synthetic smoke images. *Fire Safety Journal*, 93:53–59, 2017.

[16] Khan Muhammad, Jamil Ahmad, Irfan Mehmood, Seungmin Rho, and Sung Wook Baik. Convolutional neural networks based fire detection in surveil-lance videos. *IEEE Access*, 6:18174–18183, 2018.

[17] Rishabh Bansal, Arun Singh Pundir, and Balasubramanian Raman. Dynamic texture using deep learning. In *Region 10 Conference*, 2609–2614, 2017.

[18] Yanmin Luo, Liang Zhao, Peizhong Liu, and Detian Huang. Fire smoke detection algorithm based on motion characteristic and convolutional neural networks. *Multimedia Tools and Applications*, 77(12):15075–15092, 2018.

[19] Yusun Ahn, Haneul Choi, and Byungseon Sean Kim. Development of early fire detection model for buildings using computer vision-based CCTV. *Journal of Building Engineering*, 65:105647, 2023.

[20] Berthold KP Horn and Brian G Schunck. Determining optical flow. *Artificial Intelligence*, 17(1–3):185–203, 1981.

[21] Muzammil Khan and Pushpendra Kumar. A level set based fractional order variational model for motion estimation in application oriented spectrum. *Expert Systems with Applications*, 219:119628, 2023.

[22] Sana Rao and Hanzi Wang. Optical flow estimation via weighted guided filtering with non-local steering kernel. *The Visual Computer*, 39(3):835–845, 2023.

[23] Muzammil Khan and Pushpendra Kumar. A nonlinear modeling of fractional order based variational model in optical flow estimation. *Optik*, 261:169136, 2022.

[24] Yuanlu Wu, Minghao Chen, Yan Wo, and Guoqiang Han. Video smoke detection base on dense optical flow and convolutional neural network. *Multimedia Tools and Applications*, 80(28):35887–35901, 2021.

[25] Daniel YT Chino, Letricia PS Avalhais, Jose F Rodrigues, and Agma JM Traina. Bowfire: Detection of fire in still images by integrating pixel color and texture analysis. In *Conference on Graphics, Patterns and Images*, 95–102, 2015.

[26] Kenneth S Miller and Bertram Ross. *An introduction to the fractional calculus and fractional differential equations*. Wiley, 1993.

[27] Pushpendra Kumar and Muzammil Khan. Early prediction of covid-19 suspects based on fractional order optical flow. In *International Conference on Information Systems and Computer Networks*, 1–7, 2021.

[28] Bernhard Riemann. Versuch einer allgemeinen auffassung der integration und differentiation. *Gesammelte Werke*, 62, 1876.

[29] Fausto Ferrari. Weyl and marchaud derivatives: A forgotten history. *Mathematics*, 6(1):6, 2018.

[30] Fire segmentation image dataset. https://www.kaggle.com/datasets/diversisai/fire- segmentation-image-dataset.

[31] Forest-fire dataset. https://www.kaggle.com/datasets/kutaykutlu/forest-fire.

[32] Colors. http://members.shaw.ca/quadibloc/other/colint.htm.

[33] Muzammil Khan and Pushpendra Kumar. A vision based fractional order TV- model for underwater motion estimation. In *IEEE Bombay Section Signature Conference*, 1–6, 2021.

[34] Dali Chen, Hu Sheng, et al. Fractional order variational optical flow model for motion estimation. *Philosophical Transactions of the Royal Society A: Mathematical, Physical and Engineering Sciences*, 371(1990):201 20148, 2013.

[35] Pushpendra Kumar and Muzammil Khan. Charbonnier-Marchaud based fractional variational model for motion estimation in multispectral vision system. *Journal of Physics: Conference Series*, 2327:012031, 2022. IOP Publishing.

[36] Andrés Bruhn, Joachim Weickert, and Christoph Schnörr. Lucas/kanade meets horn/schunck: Combining local and global optic flow methods. *International Journal of Computer Vision*, 61(3):211–231, 2005.

[37] A Marchaud. *Sur les d´eriv´ees et sur les diff´erences des fonctions de variables r´eelles*. PhD thesis, Impr. Gauthier-Villars, 1927.

[38] Deqing Sun, Stefan Roth, and Michael J Black. Secrets of optical flow estimation and their principles. In *IEEE Computer Society Conference on Computer Vision and Pattern Recognition*, 2432–2439, 2010.

[39] TM Apostol. *Calculus, volume-I, one-variable calculus, with an introduction to linear algebra* (vol. 1). John Wiley & Sons, 2007.

[40] Guido Fubini. Sugli integrali multipli. *Rend. Acc. Naz. Lincei*, 16:608–614, 1907.

[41] SV Fomin and M Gelfand. *Calculus of variations*. Dover Publications, 2012.

[42] Mahinder Kumar Jain. *Numerical methods for scientific and engineering computation*. New Age International, 2003.

[43] Richard Hamming. *Numerical methods for scientists and engineers*. Courier Corporation, 2012.

[44] Shi Jie, Wang Wei, Gao Yuanqi, and Yu Nanpeng. Optimal placement and intelligent smoke detection algorithm for wildfire-monitoring cameras. *IEEE Access*, 8:72326–72339, 2020.

[45] Wang Yue, Wee Chua Teck, Chang Richard, and Trung Pham Nam. Real-time smoke detection using texture and color features. In *International Conference on Pattern Recognition*, 2012.

[46] Mohammad Hossin and Md Nasir Sulaiman. A review on evaluation metrics for data classification evaluations. *International Journal of Data Mining & Knowledge Management Process*, 5(2):1, 2015.

[47] Charles E Metz. Basic principles of ROC analysis. *Seminars in Nuclear Medicine*, 8:283–298, 1978. Elsevier.

[48] Abdel Aziz Taha and Allan Hanbury. Metrics for evaluating 3D medical image segmentation: Analysis, selection, and tool. *BMC Medical Imaging*, 15(1):1–28, 2015.

[49] Sebastien Destercke. Multilabel prediction with probability sets: The hamming loss case. In *International Conference on Information Processing and Management of Uncertainty in Knowledge-Based Systems*. Springer, 496–505, 2014.

[50] Sarang Narkhede. Understanding AUC-ROC curve. *Towards Data Science*, 26(1):220–227, 2018.

[51] Janez Demšar, Tomaž Curk, Aleš Erjavec, Črt Gorup, Tomaž Hočevar, Mitar Milutinovič, Martin Možina, Matija Polajnar, Marco Toplak, Anže Starič, et al. Orange: Data mining toolbox in python. *The Journal of Machine Learning Research*, 14(1): 2349–2353, 2013.

[52] Saima Majid, Fayadh Alenezi, Sarfaraz Masood, Musheer Ahmad, Emine Selda Gündüz, and Kemal Polat. Attention based CNN model for fire detection and localization in real-world images. *Expert Systems with Applications*, 189:116114, 2022.

[53] Faisal Saeed, Anand Paul, P Karthigaikumar, and Anand Nayyar. Convolutional neural network based early fire detection. *Multimedia Tools and Applications*, 79(13):9083–9099, 2020.

[54] Khan Muhammad, Jamil Ahmad, and Sung Wook Baik. Early fire detection using convolutional neural networks during surveillance for effective disaster management. *Neurocomputing*, 288:30–42, 2018.

[55] Salman Khan, Khan Muhammad, Shahid Mumtaz, Sung Wook Baik, and Victor Hugo C de Albuquerque. Energy-efficient deep CNN for smoke detection in foggy IoT environment. *IEEE Internet of Things Journal*, 6(6):9237–9245, 2019.

[56] Zilong Wang, Tianhang Zhang, Xiqiang Wu, and Xinyan Huang. Predicting transient building fire based on external smoke images and deep learning. *Journal of Building Engineering*, 47:103823, 2022.

[57] Kaiming He, Xiangyu Zhang, Shaoqing Ren, and Jian Sun. Deep residual learning for image recognition. *IEEE Conference on Computer Vision and Pattern Recognition*, 770–778, 2016.

# CHAPTER 11

# Early Prediction of Cardiac Diseases Using Ensemble Learning Techniques

## *A Machine Learning Technique to Deal with Heart Disease Problems*

Rima Sen and A. Manimaran

*Department of Mathematics, School of Advanced Sciences, VIT-AP University, India*

## 11.1 INTRODUCTION

Cardiovascular diseases have lately become the leading cause of death worldwide. Several advanced techniques and even different statistical prediction methods are increasingly being utilized for cardiovascular disease prediction. The results of such a diagnostic approach, while using the current algorithms, are insufficient in identifying heart disease patients. They also confront a huge hurdle in terms of service quality [1–3]. Accurately detecting sickness and efficiently treating patients are both critical aspects of service quality. Inadequate diagnosis can lead to unfavorable outcomes [4, 5]. Age, gender, smoking, obesity, physical inactivity, poor diet, family history, cholesterol, high blood pressure and alcohol use are all risk factors for a heart disorder, as are inherited risk

DOI: 10.1201/9781003364856-11

factors [6], including high blood pressure and diabetes. Some risk factors can be prevented. Aside from those aforementioned variables, lifestyle choices such as eating habits, obesity and physical inactivity are also substantial risk factors [7–9]. Coronary heart disease, angina pectoris, congestive heart failure, cardiomyopathy, congenital heart disease, arrhythmias and myocarditis are all examples of heart illnesses [10]. Manually calculating the chances of developing heart disease based on risk factors is too challenging. To deal with such medical emergencies in the healthcare industry, a prediction system based on ensemble learning techniques has been developed. Learning techniques prove to be effective in assisting decision making and predictions from the large quantity of data produced by the healthcare industry [11–13]. Hence, this paper uses a machine learning approach known as a classification to forecast heart disease risk from risk variables by examining patient data and classifying the presence of heart disease. It includes an ensemble technique of several supervised algorithms [14, 15] such as Naïve Bayes [16] and Decision Tree [17], Support Vector Machine [18], and Random Forest [19] model to enhance the accuracy of forecasting heart disease risk addressing the challenges in the healthcare sector.

### 11.1.1 Problem Statement

The major challenge in cardiac disease is its identification. Several tools can forecast heart disease, but they are either too expensive or ineffective in quantifying the risk of heart disease in humans. Early detection of cardiac diseases can decrease the mortality rate and overall consequences of heart disorders. However, it is not possible to precisely monitor patients every day in all circumstances, and a doctor's 24-hour consultation is not available since it needs more intelligence, time and skill [20]. Due to the availability of a humongous amount of data, various machine learning algorithms can be used to analyze the data for hidden trends in data. Hidden patterns in medical data can be utilized for health diagnosis too [21, 22]. In this research, the ensemble learning technique based on majority voting (max voting) is performed on the medical dataset to enhance the performance as well as the accuracy measure. The Cleveland dataset [23] is considered to train the model as well as to obtain a favorable result after testing it.

The problem statement framework is shown in Figure 11.1.

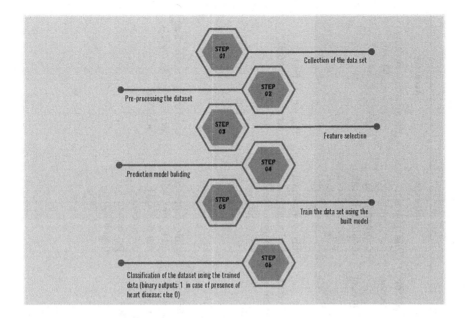

FIGURE 11.1    Problem statement framework.

## 11.2  RELATED WORK

Several studies have been developed for predicting heart disease using automated technologies [24]. Although those algorithms are beneficial in the healthcare field, they have a few drawbacks. In this paper, a few of those implementations are discussed, along with their limitations, to emphasize the importance of the proposed learning technique. See Table 11.1.

## 11.3  METHODOLOGY

### 11.3.1  Dataset Description

In this research, a dataset from Kaggle named Cleveland dataset [23], which consists of 298 instances and 14 attributes, is used. A brief description of the features of the dataset is discussed in Table 11.2.

This dataset includes patients ranging in age from 29 to 79. Male patients have a gender value of 1, while female patients have a gender value of 0. Four different forms of chest discomfort (CP) are considered heart disease. Symptoms of heart-disease-reduced blood flow cause type 1 angina. Because of constricted coronary arteries, blood flow to the heart muscles

TABLE 11.1 Related Work

| Sl. No. | Authors | Year | Methods Used | Advantages | Limitations | Accuracy |
|---|---|---|---|---|---|---|
| 1 | Saxena et al. | 2016 | Saxena et al. [25] proposed a new method using hill climbing and decision tree algorithms based on the Cleveland dataset. The knowledge extraction in this model was done utilizing evolutionary learning. | The model utilizes the knowledge extraction method and evolutionary learning technique to accelerate the model performance. | This approach performs poorly in comparison to existing algorithms in terms of accuracy. | The accuracy measure for this model was 86.7%. |
| 2 | Kannan et al. | 2019 | Utilizing the UCI Cleveland dataset, Kannan et al. [26] have presented numerous machine-learning techniques, including Logistic Regression, Support Vector Machine, and Random Forest Stochastic Gradient Boosting. | Machine learning approaches solved the problem statement efficiently. | This approach takes a bit longer to compute than other techniques. | This paper's best accuracy was 86.51%. |
| 3 | Thirumalai et al. | 2019 | Thirumalai et al. [27] proposed a hybrid machine learning algorithm using several methods such as a Decision Tree, Naïve Bayes, k-Nearest Neighbor, and Genetic algorithm to classify the presence and absence of heart disease. | The genetic algorithm, along with the learning techniques, increased the accuracy of the model. | While compared to other approaches, this method has considerable performance degradation. | Utilizing the method, an accuracy of 88.7% was achieved. |

| # | Author | Year | Description | | | |
|---|--------|------|-------------|---|---|---|
| 4 | Bhunia et al. | 2019 | Bhunia et al. [28] used eight algorithms, including the Logistic Model, Decision Tree, Random Forest classifier, J48 algorithm, Naïve Bayes, Support Vector Machine, and k-Nearest Neighbor to detect heart diseases. | A good approach to use in heart disease detection. | This approach does not produce a decent accuracy score for more complex models. | The best accuracy in this research is 56.76%, and the total computational time to train the dataset is 0.04 s. |
| 5 | Latifah et al. | 2020 | Latifah et al. [29] presented a comparison of two machine learning models for heart disease classification: Logistic Regression and Random Forest using the Framingham dataset, which had 3656 records. | The comparison study in this paper helps to choose the best suited method among those algorithms. | This method suffers from a significant accuracy degradation in comparison to the other algorithms. | The model attained an accuracy of 85.04% while using Logistic Regression for classification and 84.4% for using a Random Forest classifier. |
| 6 | Khan et al. | 2020 | Khan et al. [30] have conducted exploratory research among several machine learning techniques for heart disease classification, including Logistic Regression, Random Forest, k-Nearest Neighbor, and Naïve Bayes classifier. An analysis is based on the UCI Cleveland database. | Several learning techniques help the model efficiently. | While compared to other approaches, this method has a poorer accuracy score. | The Logistic Regression model results in an 85.71% accuracy. |

*(Continued)*

TABLE 11.1 *(Continued)*

| Sl. No. | Authors | Year | Methods Used | Advantages | Limitations | Accuracy |
|---------|---------|------|--------------|------------|-------------|----------|
| 7 | Iong et al. | 2021 | Iong et al. in [31] have proposed a pooled area curve technique for the early prediction of coronary artery disease. This proposed approach has a positive outcome of the medical image that is surrounded by weak pixels. | Pooled area technique is an efficient way of coronary artery disease detection using medical images. | This method will underperform if the number of properties for each data value outstrips the number of training data specimens. | It was also mentioned that among all those supervised models, SVM has the deepest impact on the early prediction of coronary artery disease, with the highest accuracy of 90.10%. |
| 8 | Thomas et al. | 2021 | Thomas et al. in [32] have suggested a hybrid system for decision making in the early prediction of heart disease. This hybrid system is a combination of Genetic Algorithm and recursive feature elimination. For data pre-processing, SMOTE and standard scalar methods are in use. | The hybrid system, as a well advanced preprocessing method, enhances the model performance. | While compared to other methods, this approach has a poorer accuracy score. | This method has an accuracy of 86.6%. |

| 9 | Liu et al. | 2022 | Liu et al. [33] used a novel multimodal learning method to predict cardiovascular diseases. Electrocardiograms and phonocardiograms have been encoded in this technique by building a CNN model. The features have been optimized by GA for feature selection. SVM is in use for classification. The outcomes are evaluated using a hidden Markov model. | The use of the hidden Markov model helps the model in terms of evaluation of the outcome, and the CNN model enhances the accuracy. | The model is complex in structure, and while used practically, it is not possible to implement it properly. | The receiver operating characteristics curve value achieved was 0.936. |
| 10 | Obasi et al. | 2022 | Obasi et al. in [34] have proposed a method using Random Forest, Bayesian Classification and Logistic Regression to predict heart disease and the risk factor of heart disease. The dataset contains 18 risk factors. | An efficient way to build a heart disease prediction model. | While compared to other techniques, this method has a considerable performance degradation. | The accuracy of using Random Forest, Bayesian Classifier and Logistic Regression is 92.44%, 61.96% and 59.7%, respectively. |

TABLE 11.2   Dataset Description

| Serial Number | Attribute Name | Attribute Description |
|---|---|---|
| 1 | Age | Age of the person in years |
| 2 | Sex | Gender of the mentioned person [1: Male; 0: Female] |
| 3 | Cp | Chest pain type [1: Typical type; 2: Atypical type angina; 3: Non-angina pain; 4: Asymptomatic] |
| 4 | Trestbps | Resting blood pressure in mm Hg |
| 5 | Chol | Serum cholesterol in mg/dl |
| 6 | FBS | Fasting blood sugar in mg/dl |
| 7 | Restecg | Resting electrocardiographic results |
| 8 | Thalach | Maximum heart rate received |
| 9 | Exang | Exercise induced angina |
| 10 | OldPeak | ST depression-induced by exercise relative to rest |
| 11 | Slope | Slope of the peak exercise ST segment |
| 12 | Ca | Number of major vessels colored by fluoroscopy |
| 13 | Thal | [3-Normal; 6-Fixed Defect; 7- Reversible defect] |
| 14 | Condition | Class attribute |

is restricted. Type 1 angina is a type of chest discomfort that develops because of mental or emotional stress. Non-angina chest discomfort can be caused by a variety of factors. It is not always attributable to genuine heart disease. The fourth category, asymptomatic, may not be a symptom of heart disease. The reading of resting blood pressure value is measured by the attribute TRESTBPS. The cholesterol level is measured in CHOL. FBS stands for fasting blood sugar level; it is assigned a value of 1 if it is less than 120 mg/dl and 0 if it is more. The resting electrocardiographic result is denoted as RESTECG, and the highest heart rate is measured by the attribute THALACH, and EXANG is exercise-induced angina, which is reported as 0 in the absence of pain and 1 in the presence of pain. The exercise-induced ST depression is known as OLDPEAK, whereas SLOPE is the peak exercise ST segment slope, and CA is the number of main vessels colored by fluoroscopy, whereas THAL is the exercise test duration in minutes, and CONDITION is the target attribute. The class attribute has a score of 0 for healthy patients and 1 for heart disease patients [23].

### 11.3.2  Dataset Visualization

The preceding dataset is visualized in the following ways to interpret the dataset efficiently.

- Figure 11.2 displays the count of persons having a heart disease vs. the same of persons not having a heart disease.

- In Figure 11.3, the bar plot represents the features along with their importance values, where the importance value is the probability that the feature is used mostly.

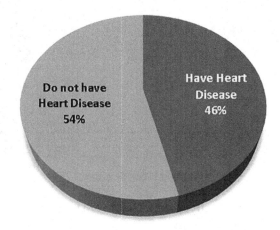

FIGURE 11.2    Data set description.

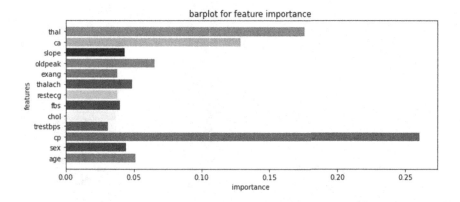

FIGURE 11.3    Bar plot representing important features of the dataset.

- A comparison of different attribute values of each feature is shown using the bar graphs in Figures 11.4–11.8.

- The statistical description of the Cleveland dataset is also displayed in Figure 11.9 to interpret the pattern of each attribute.

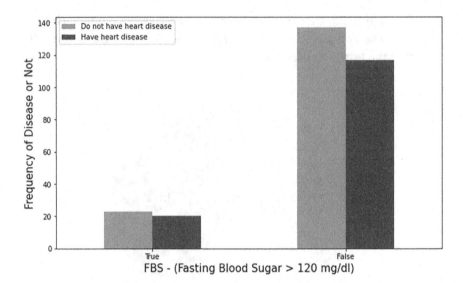

FIGURE 11.4   Heart disease frequency according to FBS.

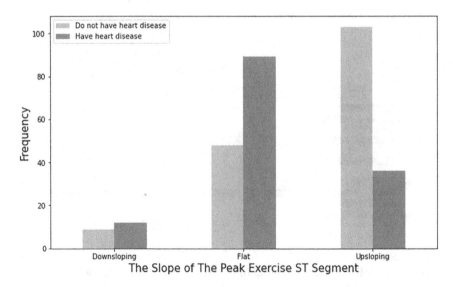

FIGURE 11.5   Heart disease frequency for slope.

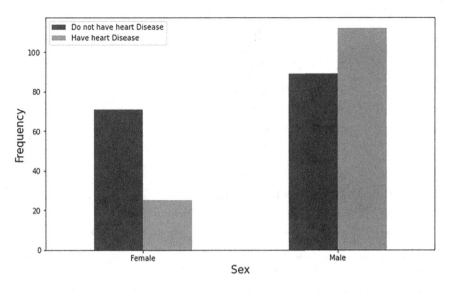

FIGURE 11.6   Heart disease vs. sex.

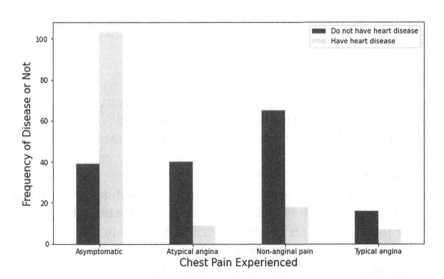

FIGURE 11.7   Heart disease frequency according to chest pain experience.

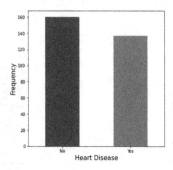

FIGURE 11.8  Distribution of target variable.

| | age | sex | cp | trestbps | chol | fbs | restecg | thalach | exang | oldpeak | slope |
|---|---|---|---|---|---|---|---|---|---|---|---|
| count | 297.000000 | 297.000000 | 297.000000 | 297.000000 | 297.000000 | 297.000000 | 297.000000 | 297.000000 | 297.000000 | 297.000000 | 297.000000 |
| mean | 54.542088 | 0.676768 | 2.158249 | 131.693603 | 247.350168 | 0.144781 | 0.996633 | 149.599327 | 0.326599 | 1.055556 | 0.602694 |
| std | 9.049736 | 0.468500 | 0.964859 | 17.762806 | 51.997583 | 0.352474 | 0.994914 | 22.941562 | 0.469761 | 1.166123 | 0.618187 |
| min | 29.000000 | 0.000000 | 0.000000 | 94.000000 | 126.000000 | 0.000000 | 0.000000 | 71.000000 | 0.000000 | 0.000000 | 0.000000 |
| 25% | 48.000000 | 0.000000 | 2.000000 | 120.000000 | 211.000000 | 0.000000 | 0.000000 | 133.000000 | 0.000000 | 0.000000 | 0.000000 |
| 50% | 56.000000 | 1.000000 | 2.000000 | 130.000000 | 243.000000 | 0.000000 | 1.000000 | 153.000000 | 0.000000 | 0.800000 | 1.000000 |
| 75% | 61.000000 | 1.000000 | 3.000000 | 140.000000 | 276.000000 | 0.000000 | 2.000000 | 166.000000 | 1.000000 | 1.600000 | 1.000000 |
| max | 77.000000 | 1.000000 | 3.000000 | 200.000000 | 564.000000 | 1.000000 | 2.000000 | 202.000000 | 1.000000 | 6.200000 | 2.000000 |

FIGURE 11.9  Statistical description of the Cleveland dataset.

## 11.3.3 Implemented Algorithms

There are many open repository datasets [35, 36] on heart disease prediction; however, the Cleveland dataset is considered for this study. The proposed framework incorporates an ensemble machine-learning method.

### 11.3.3.1 Ensemble Learning Techniques

Ensemble learning is a broad meta-approach to machine learning that combines predictions from different models to improve predictive performance [14, 15]. There are several ensemble techniques in machine learning, such Max-Voting, Averaging, Weighted Average, Stacking, Bagging, Blending and Boosting [37]. An ensemble model can infer a better decision with higher accuracy as compared to individuals [38].

In this chapter, the ensemble model for Naïve Bayes [16], Decision Tree [17], Support Vector Machine [18] and Random Forest [19] is considered using a Max-Voting classifier to improve the accuracy and performance of the proposed model.

### 11.3.3.2 Naïve Bayes Classifier

Bayes' theorem (also known as Bayes's rule after Thomas Bayes) links the conditional and marginal probabilities of two random occurrences in probability theory. It's frequently used to calculate posterior probabilities based on data. The term "Naïve Bayes classifier" refers to a rudimentary probabilistic classification based on Bayes's theorem [39, 40].

11.3.3.2.1 Bayes's Theorem:

$$P(A/B) = \frac{P(B|A) \times P(A)}{P(B)}, \text{ where } A, B = \text{events}$$

$P(A|B)$ = probability of occurrence of $A$ given $B$ is true.

$P(B|A)$ = probability of occurrence of $B$ given $A$ is true.

$P(A), P(B)$ = the independent probabilities of $A$ and $B$.

A Naïve Bayes classifier assumes that the presence (or absence) of a particular characteristic of a class has no effect on the presence (or absence) of any other feature. The Naïve Bayes classifier has the benefit of only having a small quantity of training data to estimate the parameters (variable means and variances) required for classification [41, 42].

In this research, the addition of the probabilistic approach of Naïve Bayes in the model enhances the chances of getting predicted data more accurately.

### 11.3.3.3 Decision Tree

A Decision Tree is a graph that illustrates every feasible outcome of a decision using a branching strategy. To resolve those categorization issues, the Decision Tree technique is more powerful. This approach has two steps: creating a tree and applying the tree to the dataset [43, 44].

Here, the Gini Index algorithm [45] among all Decision Tree methods is chosen for this chapter. The Gini Index is a crucial criterion for building decision trees. It is a function that measures how well a decision tree is split. Essentially, it assists us in determining which splitter is optimal so that we can construct a pure decision tree. This measure has a value between 0 and 0.5. The purpose of using Gini impurity is to optimize the split and to develop a better ensemble algorithm using a pure decision tree [46].

### 11.3.3.4 Support Vector Machine

Support Vector Machine is supervised learning used for regression [47] or classification [48]. The Support Vector Machine model is an appropriate model to separate or classify the collected data points linearly through a hyperplane support vector. The mapping of the data points is the main purpose of that classifier [49]. Basically, the mapping technique is performed by support vector or kernel estimation. The mapping incorporates both linear and nonlinear data information [50, 51].

In this chapter, the radial basis kernel function [52] is utilized. A radial basis kernel is a good classifier in case the data is not linearly separable.

### 11.3.3.5 Random Forest

Random Forest is an ensemble learning technique for classification that is powered by decision trees and the majority voting mechanism [53]. This method adds some additional randomness to the process of developing trees. Instead of looking for an essential feature when dividing a node, it looks for the best feature among a random group of features [54]. As a result, it lowers overfitting in decision trees and decreases variance, enhancing accuracy [55–57].

In this proposed model, the number of estimators is 1000. Such a maximum number of estimators improves the performance of the model as well as reducing the overfitting in decision trees [58].

### 11.3.3.6 Max-Voting Classifier

The Max-Voting classifier is a meta-classifier that employs majority voting to merge any classifier [59]. The class label that a large percentage of the classifiers predicted would be the final class label. The following term defines the final class label $d_j$:

$$d_j = mode\{C_1, C_2, \ldots, C_n\}$$

where $\{C_1, C_2, \ldots, C_n\}$ indicates the individual classifiers that participate in the voting technique [60]. The Max-Voting algorithm is shown here:

#### 11.3.3.6.1 Max-Voting Algorithm

Let $c_{i,j}$ be the predicted score on a class of $j$ labels of the $i$th classifier:

$$\sum_{i=1}^{n} c_{i,j} = \max_{j=1,\ldots,m} = \sum_{t=1}^{n} c_{i,j}$$

The likelihood of the ensemble classifier for the decision to be better is:

$$P_{ensemble} = \sum_{k=\left(\frac{n}{2}\right)+1}^{n} {}^{n}C_{k} \, p^{k} \left(1-p\right)^{n-k}$$

where $n$ is the number of observations and $p$ the probability for each observation.

To predict cardiac disease, learning techniques are used. First, the data is split into train data and test data and used to train the proposed method in the view of the Ensemble of Support Vector Machine, Naïve Bayes, Decision Tree classifiers, and Random Forest method. Then the model is tested with test data for prediction to get the best accuracy and to find the model's behavior. The algorithm results in a category of 1 and 0 for the presence and absence of cardiac disease [61].

In this chapter, a comparative analysis of the proposed ensemble method with other individuals supervised algorithms (Logistic Regression, Support Vector Machines, Decision Tree classifier, Naïve Bayes classifier, and k-Nearest Neighbor classifier) has also been performed to determine the appropriate model for heart disease prediction in the view of Cleveland dataset.

### 11.3.4 Proposed Model Architecture

Classification is a supervised learning process for predicting outcomes from the extraction of information [62]. This research suggests utilizing classification algorithms to diagnose cardiac illness and employing an ensemble of algorithms to increase classification accuracy. The classification of this data is conducted using a medical dataset called the Cleveland dataset. The dataset has been separated into a training set and a test set (70:30), and, using the training data, all the individual classifiers are trained. Using the test dataset, the classifiers' efficiency is assessed. In this chapter, the operation of each classifier is thoroughly illustrated.

The system architecture provides an overview of how the system works for ensemble learning in the context of the Cleveland dataset.

The proposed system's procedure begins with gathering information, and important features of attributes are extracted in order to choose which attributes to employ in the proposed model. The relevant data is then preprocessed and converted to a suitable format [63]. The data is then separated into two categories: training and testing. The ensemble learning algorithms are used to train the model using the training data. The system's accuracy and outcomes of the model are determined by analyzing it using the testing data. In this research, the system is implemented using the following steps:

1. Dataset collection

2. Data preprocessing

3. Attributes selection

4. Prediction of outcome (disease)

### 11.3.4.1 Dataset Collection

Initially, the Cleveland dataset [23] is collected from Kaggle. The dataset consists of 298 instances and 14 attributes. The dataset is separated into training data and testing data once it is collected. The training dataset is used to learn the prediction model, while the testing dataset is used to evaluate the model. Seventy percent of the entire data is utilized for training the model, whereas 30% of the data is used for testing.

### 11.3.4.2 Data Preprocessing

The method of transforming raw data into a comprehensible format is known as data preprocessing [64]. Importing datasets, dividing datasets, attribute scaling and other actions are all part of data preprocessing. Data preprocessing is essential to improve the model's accuracy.

### 11.3.4.3 Attributes Selection

Attribute or feature selection includes the selection of appropriate attributes for the heart disease prediction system [65]. This is used to improve the efficiency of the proposed system. The patient record is uniquely identified by two dataset features—sex and age—from the given 14 features in the dataset. The rest of the attributes consist of medical information. Medical information is an important attribute for predicting heart disease. The model's attribute selection is based on a correlation matrix (Figure 11.10) that is applied to all 13 attributes with the target value in order to choose the features with the highest and most positive correlation [66, 67].

### 11.3.4.4 Prediction of Outcome (Disease)

An ensemble of Naïve Bayes, Support Vector Machine, Decision Tree classifier and Random Forest is accomplished to perform the prediction of heart disease. A comparative study of the proposed method and other individual algorithms is carried out in order to find an effective method for disease prediction in the healthcare field. It is observed that the ensemble technique results in superior accuracy than other existing individual algorithms in the context of the Cleveland dataset [16–19, 68].

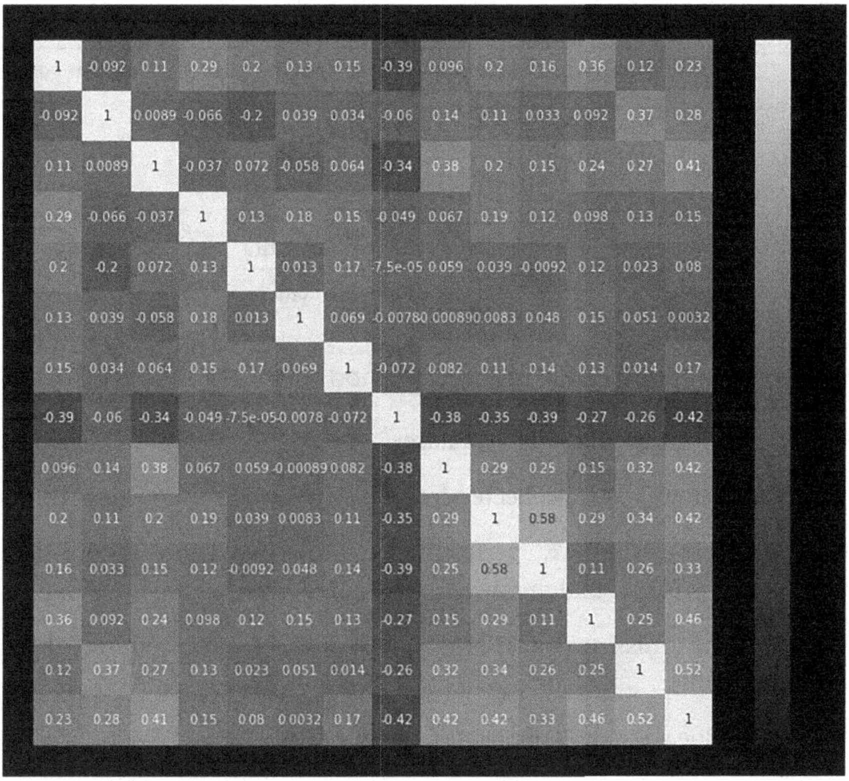

FIGURE 11.10   Correlation matrix.

## 11.3.5 Performance Evaluation Criteria

The performance of the proposed method is determined by using four metrics: precision, accuracy, recall, and $F1$ score [69]. These four metrics are analyzed using the number of true positives, true negatives, false positives, and false negatives in binary classifier predictions.

The percentage of true predictions is termed "accuracy." The capacity of the classifier to discover all the positive samples is measured by recall. Precision refers to the classifier's ability to avoid labeling a negative sample as positive. The $F1$ score evaluates values in the range [0,1], which is the harmonic mean of precision and recall [70].

The metrics are computed using the following formulae:

$$\text{Precision: } \frac{\text{True positives}}{\text{True positives} + \text{False positives}}$$

$$\text{Accuracy:} \frac{\text{True positives} + \text{True negatives}}{\text{True positives} + \text{False positives} + \text{True negatives} + \text{False negatives}}$$

$$\text{Recall:} \frac{\text{True positives}}{\text{True positives} + \text{False negatives}}$$

$$\text{F1 score:} \frac{2 \times (\text{Precision} \times \text{Recall})}{(\text{Precision} + \text{Recall})}$$

### 11.3.6 Algorithm for the Proposed Method

1. Choosing the best suitable dataset

2. Importing the data collected from the survey (Cleveland dataset)

3. Data processing, i.e., performing cleaning, data integration, data transformation and finally, dimension reduction

   Perform missing value/NA value analysis and remove those anomalies.

   Combine the data if duplicates are found.

   Standardization of data is performed to accelerate the performance of the method.

4. Feature or attribute selection based on the probability values

   If the probability value is greater:

   Then consider that feature for further use.

   Else:

   Remove that column.

5. Training-testing the split of the data (70:30)

   If train data:

   Use the data for model training.

   Else:

   Use to test the model efficiency.

6. Ensemble model building using Naïve Bayes, Support Vector Machine, Decision Trees and Random Forest classifier.

Ensemble model = Naïve Bayes + Support Vector Machine + Decision Tree + Random Forest

7. Train the split dataset using the constructed model.

8. Hyperparameter tuning, and repeat step 7 until the model is the best fit.

9. Model the evaluation in terms of accuracy, precision, recall, and $F1$ score.

10. Conclude the best-fitted trained model.

11. Apply the trained model to the test dataset.

12. Perform classification techniques to determine the presence or absence of heart disease.

13. Getting the binary outcome as the result of the entire procedure: 1, the presence of heart disease; 0, absence of heart disease.

If outcome is 0:

Print(" the person does not have heart disease")

Else (outcome is 1):

Print(" the person has heart disease")

## 11.4  EXPERIMENTS AND RESULTS

The findings of ensemble learning algorithms are examined in this section. The medical dataset, named Cleveland dataset, which consists of 13 different parameters (except the target value), is used to categorize the presence or absence of heart disease. The trained model is implemented on the test data after the data is trained using the ensemble approach, yielding 92% accuracy, indicating that this method is most promising for heart disease prediction. The four performance metric scores for the proposed method are shown in Table 11.3.

Accuracy, $F1$ score, precision and recall measures of different supervised algorithms are plotted in Figures 11.11 and 11.12 to compare with the proposed method's measure.

The model's performance is enumerated by using the confusion matrix (Figure 11.13). It can be concluded that the suggested approach

TABLE 11.3  Performance Measures of the Proposed Method

| Performance Metrics | Measurement |
| --- | --- |
| Accuracy | 95.51 |
| Precision | 92.34 |
| Recall | 90.81 |
| *F*1 score | 96.78 |

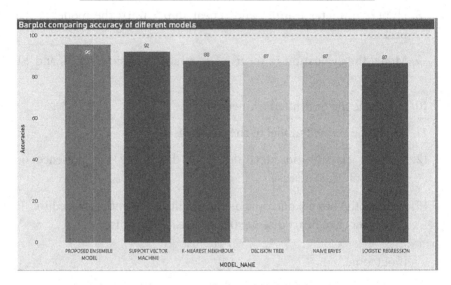

FIGURE 11.11  Comparison of accuracy measures of the proposed method with other supervised algorithms such as Logistic Regression, Naïve Bayes classifier, k-Nearest Neighbor, Support Vector Machine, and Decision Tree.

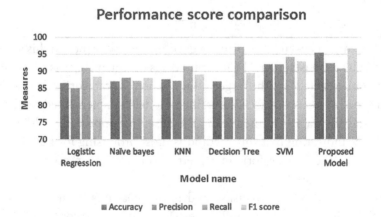

FIGURE 11.12  Comparison of four performance metrics (accuracy, precision, recall and *F*1 score) of the proposed method with other supervised algorithms such as Logistic Regression, Naïve Bayes classifier, k-Nearest Neighbor, Support Vector Machine and Decision Tree.

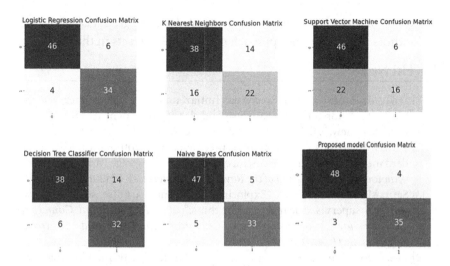

FIGURE 11.13   Confusion matrix results of the algorithms: Logistic Regression, Naïve Bayes classifier, k-Nearest Neighbor's classifier, Support Vector Machine, Decision Tree, and the proposed ensemble method.

has relatively low error values compared to other existing methods and a higher measure of correct predictions.

It is also observed that the computational time of the trained model is 1.73 s, which is much less as compared to others' computational time.

Thus, it is proved that the proposed method is more appropriate in terms of the performance measure as well as the based on the computational time.

## 11.5 CONCLUSION

One of the most significant fields in the healthcare domain is the prediction of heart disease, which utilizes the patient's available data to forecast the existence or absence of cardiac illness. For heart disease prediction, multiple tools and strategies are available. In this research, an ensemble of a few supervised algorithms (Naïve Bayes classifier, Support Vector Machine, Decision Tree and Random Forest) are used to classify heart disease. Preprocessing of the raw data, such as cleaning and detecting missing values, is done to enhance performance. The crucial aspect of this research is feature selection, which improves algorithm accuracy and even focuses on algorithm behavior. The ensemble method is trained to the data, resulting in 95.51% accuracy while applied to the test data. The results outcomes are much improved while compared with the existing research works. The limitation of this study is that it only employed the Kaggle dataset; however, the authors plan to use the approach on different datasets in the future.

## REFERENCES

[1] Dwivedi, Amit Krishna, Syed Anas Imtiaz, and Esther Rodriguez-Villegas. "Algorithms for automated analysis and classification of heart sounds, a systematic review." *IEEE Access* 7 (2018): 8316–8345.

[2] Tsanas, Athanasios, et al. "Nonlinear speech analysis algorithms mapped to a standard metric achieve clinically useful quantification of average Parkinson's disease symptom severity." *Journal of the Royal Society Interface* 8.59 (2011): 842–855.

[3] Satu, Md Shahriare, et al. "Exploring significant heart disease factors based on semi supervised learning algorithms." *2018 International Conference on Computer, Communication, Chemical, Material and Electronic-Engineering (IC4ME2)*. IEEE, 2018.

[4] Lee, Heon Gyu, Ki Yong Noh, and Keun Ho Ryu. "Mining biosignal data: Coronary artery disease diagnosis using linear and nonlinear features of HRV." *Pacific-Asia Conference on Knowledge Discovery and Data Mining*. Springer, Berlin, Heidelberg, 2007.

[5] Budholiya, Kartik, Shailendra Kumar Shrivastava, and Vivek Sharma. "An optimized XGBoost based diagnostic system for effective prediction of heart disease." *Journal of King Saud University-Computer and Information Sciences* 34.7 (2022): 4514–4523.

[6] Johri, Amer M., et al. "Deep learning artificial intelligence framework for multiclass coronary artery disease prediction using combination of conventional risk factors, carotid ultrasound, and intraplaque neovascularization." *Computers in Biology and Medicine* 150 (2022): 106018.

[7] Thomas, J., and R. Theresa Princy. "Human heart-disease prediction system using data mining techniques." *2016 International Conference on Circuit, Power and Computing Technologies (ICCPCT)*. IEEE, 2016.

[8] Nahar, Jesmin, et al. "Computational intelligence for heart disease diagnosis: A medical knowledge driven approach." *Expert Systems with Applications* 40.1 (2013): 96–104.

[9] Khazaee, Ali. "Heart beat classification using particle swarm optimization." *International Journal of Intelligent Systems and Applications* 5 (2013): 25–33. http://dx.doi.org/10.5815/ijisa.2013.06.03.

[10] Amin, Mohammad Shafenoor, Yin Kia Chiam, and Kasturi Dewi Varathan. "Identification of significant features and data mining techniques in predicting heart-disease." *Telematics and Informatics* 36 (2019): 82–93.

[11] Ayon, Safial Islam, Md Milon Islam, and Md Rahat Hossain. "Coronary artery heart disease prediction: A comparative study of computational intelligence techniques." *IETE Journal of Research* 68.4 (2022): 2488–2507.

[12] Riyaz, Lubna, et al. "Heart disease prediction using machine learning techniques: A quantitative review." *International Conference on Innovative Computing and Communications: Proceedings of ICICC 2021, Volume 3*. Springer, Singapore, 2022.

[13] El-Hasnony, Ibrahim M., et al. "Multi-label active learning-based machine learning model for heart disease prediction." *Sensors* 22.3 (2022): 1184.

[14] Mishra, Nilamadhab, et al. "Visual analysis of cardiac arrest prediction using Machine learning algorithms: A health education awareness initiative." *Handbook of Research on Instructional Technologies in Health Education and Allied Disciplines*. IGI Global, 2023: 331–363.

[15] Mohapatra, Debasis, et al. "Distribution preserving train-test split directed ensemble classifier for heart disease prediction." *International Journal of Information Technology* 14.4 (2022): 1763–1769.

[16] Balakrishnan, Baranidharan. "A comprehensive performance analysis of various classifier models for coronary artery disease prediction." *International Journal of Cognitive Informatics and Natural Intelligence (IJCINI)* 15.4 (2021): 1–14.

[17] Reddy, V. Sai Krishna, et al. "Prediction on cardiovascular disease using decision tree and Naïve Bayes classifiers." *Journal of Physics: Conference Series* 2161.1 (2022). IOP Publishing.

[18] Behera, Mandakini Priyadarshani, et al. "A hybrid machine learning algorithm for heart and liver disease prediction using modified particle swarm optimization with support vector machine." *Procedia Computer Science* 218 (2023): 818–827.

[19] Wang, Jing, et al. "Risk assessment of coronary heart disease based on cloud-random forest." *Artificial Intelligence Review* 56.1 (2023): 203–232.

[20] Mishra, Nilamadhab, et al. "Visual analysis of cardiac arrest prediction using machine learning algorithms: A health education awareness initiative." *Handbook of Research on Instructional Technologies in Health Education and Allied Disciplines*. IGI Global, 2023: 331–363.

[21] Shah, Devansh, Samir Patel, and Santosh Kumar Bharti. "Heart disease prediction using machine learning techniques." *SN Computer Science* 1.6 (2020): 1–6.

[22] Gaidai, O., Y. Xing, R. Balakrishna, et al. "Prediction of death rates for cardiovascular diseases and cancers." *Cancer Innovation* 2.2 (2023): 140–147.

[23] Dataset link. https://www.kaggle.com/datasets/johnsmith88/heart-disease-dataset.

[24] Dileep, P., et al. "An automatic heart disease prediction using cluster-based bi-directional LSTM (C-BiLSTM) algorithm." *Neural Computing and Applications* (2022): 1–14.

[25] Saxena, Kanak, and Richa Sharma. "Efficient heart disease prediction system." *Procedia Computer Science* 85 (2016): 962–969.

[26] Kannan, R., and V. Vasanthi. "Machine learning algorithms with ROC curve for predicting and diagnosing the heart disease." *Soft Computing and Medical Bioinformatics*. Springer, 2019: 63–72.

[27] Mohan, Senthilkumar, Chandrasegar Thirumalai, and Gautam Srivastava. "Effective heart-disease prediction using hybrid machine learning techniques." *IEEE Access* 7 (2019): 81542–81554.

[28] Chaurasia, Vikas, and Saurabh Pal. "Early prediction of heart diseases using data mining techniques." *Caribbean Journal of Science and Technology* 1 (2013): 208–217.

[29] Latifah, Firda Anindita, Isnandar Slamet, and Sugiyanto. "Comparison of heart disease classification with logistic regression algorithm and random forest algorithm." *AIP Conference Proceedings* 2296.1: (2020). AIP Publishing LLC.

[30] Khan, Zameer, et al. "Empirical study of various classification techniques for heart disease prediction." *2020 IEEE 5th-International Conference on Computing Communication and Automation (ICCCA).* IEEE, 2020.

[31] Chen, Joy Iong Zong, and P. Hengjinda. "Early prediction of coronary artery disease by machine learning method-a comparative study." *Journal of Artificial Intelligence* 3.01 (2021): 17–33.

[32] Thomas, Frank Mathews, and Anit James. "Heart stroke prediction using machine learning: A comparative analysis and implementation." *Proceedings of the National Conference on Emerging Computer Applications (NCECA)* 4.1: (2022).

[33] Li, Pengpai, Yongmei Hu, and Zhi-Ping Liu. "Prediction of cardiovascular diseases by integrating multi-modal features with machine learning methods." *Biomedical Signal Processing and Control* 66 (2021): 102474.

[34] Obasi, Thankgod, and M. Omair Shafiq. "Towards comparing and using Machine Learning techniques for detecting and predicting Heart Attack and Diseases." *2019 IEEE International Conference on Big Data (Big Data).* IEEE, 2019.

[35] Gupta, Chiradeep, et al. "Cardiac disease prediction using supervised machine learning techniques." *Journal of Physics: Conference Series* 2161.1 (2022). IOP Publishing.

[36] Magesh, G., and P. Swarnalatha. "Optimal feature selection through a cluster-based DT learning (CDTL) in heart disease prediction." *Evolutionary Intelligence* 14 (2021): 583–593.

[37] Thenmozhi, K., and P. Deepika. "Heart disease prediction using classification with different decision tree techniques." *International Journal of Engineering Research and General Science* 2.6 (2014): 6–11.

[38] Gupta, Aditya, Vibha Jain, and Amritpal Singh. "Stacking ensemble-based intelligent machine learning model for predicting post-COVID-19 complications." *New Generation Computing* 40.4 (2022): 987–1007.

[39] Khan, Arsalan, et al. "A novel study on machine learning algorithm-based cardiovascular disease prediction." *Health & Social Care in the Community* 2023 (2023).

[40] Chandrasekhar, Nadikatla, and Samineni Peddakrishna. "Enhancing heart disease prediction accuracy through machine learning techniques and optimization." *Processes* 11.4 (2023): 1210.

[41] Mienye, Ibomoiye Domor, Yanxia Sun, and Zenghui Wang. "An improved ensemble-learning approach for the prediction of heart disease risk." *Informatics in Medicine Unlocked* 20 (2020): 100402.

[42] Karuppiah, Kalaivani, N. Balamurugan, and R. Venkatesh. "Diagnosis of heart disease using improved genetic algorithm-based Naive Bayes classifier." *Using Multimedia Systems, Tools, and Technologies for Smart Healthcare Services.* IGI Global, 2023: 117–140.

[43] Chen, Austin H., et al. "HDPS: Heart disease prediction system." *2011 Computing in Cardiology*. IEEE, 2011.

[44] Hambali, Moshood Abiola, Morufat Damola Gbolagade, and Yinusa Ademola Olasupo. "Heart disease prediction using principal component analysis and decision tree algorithm." *Journal of Computer Science and Engineering (JCSE)* 4.1 (2023): 1–14.

[45] Boadh, Rahul, et al. "Diagnosis of skin cancer by using fuzzy-ANN expert system with unification of improved Gini index random forest-based feature." ResearchGate 14 (2023): 1445–1451.

[46] Fathima, M. Dhilsath, et al. "Lifestyle disease influencing attribute prediction using novel majority voting feature selection." *Advanced Network Technologies and Intelligent Computing: Second International Conference, ANTIC 2022, Varanasi, India, December 22–24, 2022, Proceedings, Part II.* Cham: Springer Nature Switzerland, 2023.

[47] Yaseliani, Mohammad, and Majid Khedmati. "Prediction of heart diseases using logistic regression and likelihood ratios." *International Journal of Industrial Engineering & Production Research* 34.1 (2023): 1–15.

[48] Kumar, Parvathaneni Rajendra, Suban Ravichandran, and Satyala Narayana. "Ensemble classification technique for heart disease prediction with meta-heuristic-enabled training system." *Bio-Algorithms and Med-Systems* 17.2 (2020): 119–136.

[49] Yaseliani, Mohammad, and Majid Khedmati. "Prediction of heart diseases using logistic regression and likelihood ratios." *International Journal of Industrial Engineering & Production Research* 34.1 (2023): 1–15.

[50] Gupta, Akansh, et al. "Heart disease prediction using classification (Naive Bayes)." *Proceedings of First-International Conference on Computing, Communications, and CyberSecurity (IC4S 2019)*. Springer, Singapore, 2020.

[51] Snigdha, Asif Rahman, et al. "Early prediction of heart attack using machine learning algorithms." *Proceedings of the 2nd-International Conference on Computing Advancements*, 2022.

[52] Yaqoob, Muhammad Mateen, et al. "Hybrid classifier-based federated learning in health service providers for cardiovascular disease prediction." *Applied Sciences* 13.3 (2023): 1911.

[53] Barry, Khalidou Abdoulaye, et al. "Exploring the use of association rules in random forest for predicting heart disease." *Computer Methods in Biomechanics and Biomedical Engineering* (2023): 1–9.

[54] Saeedbakhsh, Saeed, et al. "Diagnosis of coronary artery disease based on machine learning algorithms support vector machine, artificial neural network, and random forest." *Advanced Biomedical Research* 12.1 (2023): 51.

[55] Latha, C. Beulah Christalin, and S. Carolin Jeeva. "Improving the accuracy of prediction of heart-disease risk based on ensemble-classification techniques." *Informatics in Medicine Unlocked* 16 (2019): 100203.

[56] Hassan, Noor Salah, et al. "A compassion of three data miming algorithms for heart disease prediction." *2021 IEEE Symposium on Industrial Electronics & Applications (ISIEA)*. IEEE, 2021.

[57] Rajendrakumar, S., and V.K. Parvati. "Automation of irrigation system through embedded computing technology proceed." *3rd International Conference Cryptography, Security Privacy*, 2019: 289–293.

[58] Shobana, G., and Nalini Subramanian. "A pipelined framework for the prediction of cardiac disease with dimensionality reduction." *Advanced Network Technologies and Intelligent Computing: Second International Conference, ANTIC 2022*, Varanasi, India, December 22–24, 2022, Proceedings, Part II. Cham: Springer Nature Switzerland, 2023.

[59] Trigka, Maria, and Elias Dritsas. "Long-Term Coronary Artery Disease Risk Prediction with Machine Learning Models." *Sensors* 23.3 (2023): 1193.

[60] Rashme, Tamanna Yesmin, et al. "Early prediction of cardio-vascular diseases using feature selection and machine learning techniques." *2021 6th International Conference on Communication and Electronics Systems (ICCES)*. IEEE, 2021.

[61] Nayak, Omprakash, Tejaswini Pallapothala, and Govind P. Gupta. "Heart disease prediction framework using soft voting-based ensemble learning techniques." *Convergence of Big Data Technologies and Computational Intelligent Techniques*. IGI Global, 2023: 147–165.

[62] Ganesan, M., and N. Sivakumar. "IoT-based heart disease prediction and diagnosis model for healthcare using machine learning models." *2019 IEEE International Conference on System, Computation- Automation and Networking (ICSCAN)*. IEEE, 2019.

[63] Li, Jian Ping, et al. "Heart disease identification method using machine learning classification in e-healthcare." *IEEE Access* 8 (2020): 107562–107582.

[64] Kavitha, S. S., and Narasimha Kaulgud. "Quantum K-means clustering method for detecting heart disease using quantum circuit approach." *Soft Computing* (2022): 1–14.

[65] Gupta, Aditya, and Amritpal Singh. "EDL-NSGA-II: Ensemble deep learning framework with NSGA-II feature selection for heart disease prediction." *Expert Systems* (2023): e13254.

[66] Sanni, Rachana R., and H. S. Guruprasad. "Analysis of performance metrics of heart failured patients using python and machine learning algorithms." *Global Transitions Proceedings* 2.2 (2021): 233–237.

[67] Yuan, Xiaoming, et al. "A stable ai-based binary and multiple class heart disease prediction model for IoMT." *IEEE Transactions on Industrial Informatics* 18.3 (2021): 2032–2040.

[68] Yaqoob, Muhammad Mateen, et al. "Hybrid classifier-based federated learning in health service providers for cardiovascular disease prediction." *Applied Sciences* 13.3 (2023): 1911.

[69] Krishnani, Divya, et al. "Prediction of coronary heart disease using supervised machine learning algorithms." *TENCON 2019–2019 IEEE Region 10 Conference (TENCON)*. IEEE, 2019.

[70] Yang, Huazhong, et al. "Predicting coronary heart disease using an improved LightGBM model: Performance analysis and comparison." *IEEE Access* 11 (2023): 23366–23380.

# Index

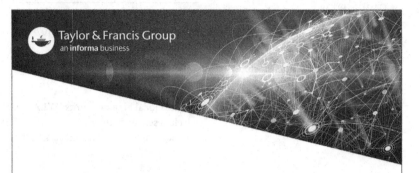